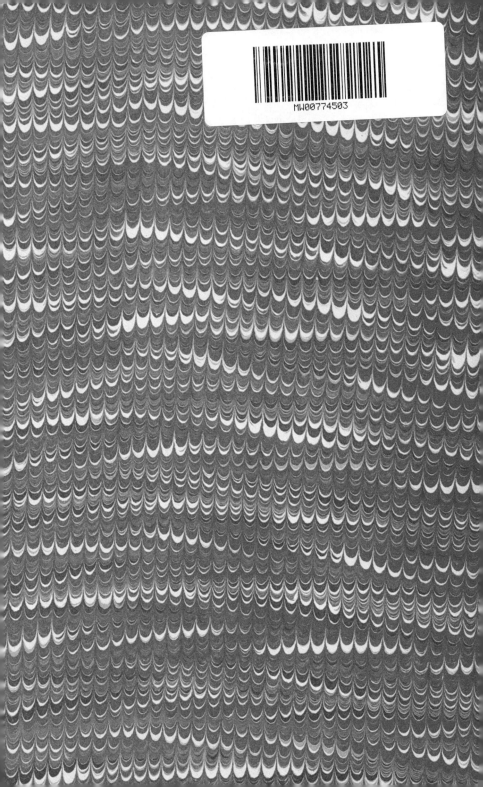

MW00774503

Reprinted 1984 from the 1894 edition.
Cover design © 1981 Time-Life Books Inc.
Library of Congress CIP data following page 233.

This volume is bound in leather.

Lucius W Barber

ARMY MEMOIRS

OF

LUCIUS W. BARBER,

COMPANY "D,"

15TH ILLINOIS VOLUNTEER INFANTRY.

MAY 24, 1861, TO SEPT. 30, 1865.

CHICAGO:

THE J. M. W. JONES STATIONERY AND PRINTING CO.

76 TO 82 SHERMAN STREET.

1894.

COLLECTOR'S
LIBRARY OF THE
CIVIL WAR

Lucius "Lute" Barber seemed to fit the popular image of a Civil War soldier. He was a Midwestern farmboy who eagerly joined the Union Army during the War's first weeks, moved around a lot, fought in several battles, got a taste of prison and returned home safe at War's end. Yet several distinctions set Barber apart from the rank and file: He served in all three major theaters of the War—East, West and Trans-Mississippi; he kept a detailed written record of where he went and what he saw; and he was a man of many strong opinions, which he did not hesitate to air. The *Army Memoirs of Lucius W. Barber* is a lively, highly personal account of his experience during "the four years, five months and 27 days" that he wore "the livery of Uncle Sam."

Barber was born in 1839 in Wyoming County in western New York, the fourth of nine children of Humphrey and Marie Barber. When the boy was 11 years old, the family moved to an 80-acre farm in McHenry County on Illinois's northern border. There young Barber worked on his father's farm until the War began. On April 27, 1861, he enlisted in a local outfit, later designated as Company D of the 15th Illinois Volunteer Infantry Regiment.

The regiment served in Missouri during 1861, and Barber provides rare glimpses of the war in that remote area, "out of reach of assistance if overpowered in an enemy's country, with spies lurking all around us." He fought in the Battle of Shiloh, where with every fresh assault "giant trees would writhe and twist before the iron hail and come crashing to the ground." Next came action at Corinth, Mississippi, and occupation duty in Memphis, Tennessee. The 15th Illinois then moved back into Mississippi. Barber was at the siege of Vicksburg and took part in the fighting around Jackson. He was promoted to corporal and stationed for a time in northern Alabama. Later came the grueling Atlanta Campaign.

On October 4, 1864, Barber was captured in battle at Ackworth, Georgia, and his diary-like narrative tells of short but miserable stays at Andersonville and Millen. Exchanged seven weeks later, Barber rejoined his regiment for General Sherman's offensive through the Carolinas. He proudly

TIME-LIFE BOOKS INC., ALEXANDRIA, VIRGINIA 22314

participated in the May 1865 Grand Review in Washington, D.C. On September 30, 1865, Sergeant Barber received his discharge from the Army, thankful, as he put it, to "lay aside the honorable title of *Soldier* and once more enjoy the proud title of an *American Citizen*."

Barber's memoirs reveal him as a close and sensitive observer. After the fight to capture Fort Donelson, he noted that "the dead lay as they had fallen. Some of the countenances wore a peaceful, glad smile, while on others rested a fiendish look of hate." He wrote with humor about daily life: "Our bacon was so maggoty that it could almost walk; some of the boys positively asserted that it had followed us for about 200 miles." He recorded the men's pranks and outrageous acts of vandalism with candor, and deplored the sale of "ardent spirits," which grew to be a problem in camp.

Predictably, Barber saved some of his sharpest remarks for the Federal generals: Henry W. Halleck "was one of those old fogy commanders with more caution than spirit," he observed when Halleck took almost a month to advance 20 miles on Corinth. In contrast, when Ulysses S. Grant, ignoring orders, rushed to attack Vicksburg, Barber noted admiringly that "it was a perilous move—a move few military men would have dared undertake, but Grant was of that bold, sanguine nature, ever confident of success."

It is hardly unexpected, too, that Barber's narrative, which he wrote soon after the War, would contain exaggerations and prejudices. Like many another former prisoner, he characterized Andersonville commandant Henry Wirz as a "devil in human shape." And he repeated as gospel the old soldier's tale—of North and South alike—that the enemy drank whiskey mixed with gunpowder before every battle to madden themselves.

Young Barber's postwar years were few. On March 12, 1872, at the age of 32, he died of consumption—triggered, his family reported, by the effects of "exposure and maltreatment" while a prisoner. Barber's sister, Rose, published his memoirs in 1894.

—THE EDITORS

TABLE OF CONTENTS.

CHAPTER XIV.

CHAPTER XV.

PREFACE.

In the War for the Preservation of the American Union, the principles which were involved in the struggle met with a glorious triumph in maintaining the integrity of the Union and the supremacy of constitutional law. Striking the shackles from four millions of human beings, it has purged our land from the foul stain of human slavery, thus placing it upon a secure foundation for the preservation of freedom by granting to all who come under its protection "life, liberty and the pursuit of happiness." All the leading incidents connected with the Rebellion are now before the people, and each can trace, if they will, the perilous track through which our noble "Ship of State" so triumphantly breasted the tide of treason and rebellion and rolled back the waves of secession which threatened to engulf us all in one common ruin, and the twenty-five hundred thousand men who shouldered the musket and fought for the cause, are each partakers of the glory of the achievement. And while the historian will faithfully record our united action, as a whole, for the millions to read, yet each has a private record which will more particularly interest his friends. It is my purpose in the following pages to represent in part my record during the terrible struggle of our Nation for existence.

CHAPTER I.

Honest men of every political creed will unite in saying that the institution of slavery and the persistent advocacy of its abolishment by the Abolitionists of the North, the triumph of the Republican Party opposed to its extension, and the ambition of the southern demagogues, were the main causes which brought about the rebellion. The South was continually demanding concessions and new guarantees for the spread and protection of the institution of slavery, and our Government, backed by a Democratic Congress, had yielded to their demands until yielding ceased to be a virtue, and when they saw the tide setting against them, they, with blind, unholy ambition and a fiendish hate, attempted to tear down the framework of our Government and plant upon its ruins a nation founded upon the principle of slavery. The loyal heart of the Nation looked on with apathy while the South was making its final preparations to secede. Our Government had so successfully buffeted the tide of treason in 1832 that the people thought we would safely outride this storm, but no Jackson was at the helm. We could not believe that our southern brethren were in earnest regarding their threats. It was a vain hope, and it was not until our forts had been seized and our flag fired upon that the people were aroused from their stupor. Then as the lightning's flash, the loyal heart of the Nation was aroused. The fire of patriotism and fidelity to our country lit up the altar of freedom from the rock-bound coast of Maine to the far-spreading prairies of the West, illumining every valley, hill-top and plain. Countless thousands thronged to the altar of our country, eager to wipe out the stain upon our flag and to keep its bright stars from paling before the lurid light of secession. In this countless throng I took my stand. Duty pointed with unswerving finger toward our insulted banner. To follow its lead, I freely leave the comforts of home, the society of friends, and haste to the rescue of imperiled freedom.

CHAPTER II.

April 27th, 1861.

On the 27th day of April, A.D. 1861, I enlisted in a military company being formed at Marengo, Illinois, from the towns of Coral, Genoa, Hampshire, Seneca, Dunham, Marengo and Riley. At that time we had little hopes of being accepted under the seventy-five thousand call, so great was the rush of troops. Harley Wayne, one of the leading spirits in getting up the Company, was at that time Clerk of the Assembly of our State Legislature, and through his influence mainly, we were accepted as a military company for the State defense, with the understanding that we should be transferred to the United States' service if the President called for more troops. So we at once proceeded to elect our Company Officers, with the following result:

May 1st.

HARLEY WAYNE, of Union.................Captain.
FRANK S. CURTISS, of Marengo...............1st Lieutenant.
FRED A. SMITH, of Genoa................ 2d Lieutenant.
P. I. LABAGH, of Marengo...................1st Sergeant.
JOHN WALDOCK, of Marengo................2d Sergeant.
MIKE SCHOONMAKER, of Riley...............3d Sergeant.
AARON C. PERRY, of Union ....4th Sergeant.
HARLOW SHAPLEY, of Harmony..............1st Corporal.
ALONZO HOWE, of Harmony ....2d Corporal.
RICHARD D. LANSING, of Marengo......... ...3d Corporal.
GEORGE C. OAKES. of Genoa.................4th Corporal.
GEORGE A. CLARK, of Marengo...............Fifer.
NAT ANDREWS, of Union.....................Drummer.

May 7th.

After the organization of the Company, we held ourselves subject to orders and in readiness to march when called upon. In the meantime, some of the boys returned to their homes and pursued their usual avocations, while some stayed in town and were boarded and lodged by the generosity of the people of Marengo; but soon an order came from Governor Yates ordering us to report at Freeport, Illinois, on the 11th of May and go into Camp of Instruction.

May 11th.

The 11th of May soon came around and the usually quiet streets of Marengo were thronged with spectators, friends and relatives of the soldiers who had come to witness their departure. A few hours before leaving, the ladies of Marengo presented the Company with a fine flag and 'neath its folds we took a solemn vow never to disgrace it or bring it back until our flag could wave in triumph over all our land. The shrill snort of the iron horse now told us that the hour had come to sever home associations and take the tented field. Amidst the tears and benedictions of our friends, the train moved on. Smothering the pent-up emotions which were surging in my soul, I looked forward to the time when I could greet them all again, when peace had folded her mantle over a rescued country. We arrived at Freeport at 11 A. M. and went into camp on the fair grounds, south of the city. We immediately went to work fitting up our quarters to make them so that we could use them for the night. Rows of sheds were built on the outer edge, straw thrown in and on this we made our first bed in camp, each soldier having brought a quilt with him. We found several other companies here from different counties and by Monday night ten full companies had arrived, the complement of a regiment of infantry. We were designated as the 15th Illinois Volunteer Infantry, and were formed from the 1st Congressional District under what was called the "Ten Regiment Bill" which provided for the raising of one regiment in each Congressional District, and one from the State at large. Our regiment was formed from the following counties:

Lake,	One Company (I),	Captain JONES.
McHenry,	One Company (A),	Captain KELLY.
McHenry,	One Company (F),	Captain HENRY.
McHenry,	One Company (D),	Captain WAYNE.
Boone,	One Company (B),	Captain HURLBUT.
Winnebago,	One Company (C),	Captain ELLIS.
Stephenson,	One Company (H),	Captain SWIFT.
Stephenson,	One Company (E),	Captain BURNSIDE.
Jo Daviess,	One Company (G),	Captain GODDARD.
Carroll,	One Company (K),	Captain NASE.

May 13th.

We went into camp with no provision made for rations and cooking utensils. Our supper the first night consisted of raw beef which we cooked by holding on a sharp stick over a poor fire; but nevertheless we enjoyed our supper well and bore our privations in good humor, considering it a good initiation into the beauties of camp life. Many a time since then we would have considered such a meal a rich feast. Monday the camp was put under strict military rules, no one being allowed to pass in or out without a pass from a commanding officer. Company B came provided with muskets and they were used for guard duty. Happy indeed was the fellow who was lucky enough to get on guard, and one would imagine, to see him strutting back and forth, that the "fate of an empire" depended upon his vigilance; but time and service took the "primp" out of us. Soon the guard duty ceased to be a novelty and some of the boys became as anxious to evade duty as they had been to perform it. Their main energies were devoted now to see how they could evade the guard and get down town and have a time. Many stratagems were employed and many tricks were played to accomplish what they wanted, but a large majority of the soldiers lived up to the rules and conducted themselves as properly as they would were they at their own firesides. Drilling soon became the order of the day. We were up and taking the double-quick before breakfast, trotting around camp until sheer exhaustion would compel us to stop; but this practice was soon discontinued as it began to tell on the health of the men. Moderate exercise before breakfast promotes health, but undue exercise destroys it. We had company drill two hours in the morning, then rested one hour and then had battalion drill until dinner. The same order was observed in the afternoon. Prescott was our drill master's name. The roll was called at sunrise and all lights out by ten P. M.

CHAPTER III.

May 15th.

During the week we elected our field officers, which resulted in the selection of—

THOS. J. TURNER, of Freeport, for Colonel.
E. F. W. ELLIS, of Rockford, for Lieut.-Colonel.
WILLIAM R. GODDARD, of Lena, for Major.
LIEUT. BAKER, of Belvidere, appointed Adjutant.
CHAS. F. BARBER, of Polo, appointed Sergt.-Major.
L. WHITE, appointed Drum Major.

The election of field officers was close. The Hon. S. A. Hurlbut ran for Colonel and was beaten by a few votes, but he was soon made a Brigadier-General, which reconciled him to his defeat.

May 18th.

' On the 18th we were sworn into the State service. Here some were rejected on account of height and physical disability, five feet and six inches being the shortest to insure acceptance. So eager were some of the boys to be accepted they would attempt to conceal their deformities and would appear as tall as possible when passing before the mustering officer. Some felt so bad as to shed tears at their rejection; but the increasing demand of the Government for troops necessitated a modification of these rules.

May 24th.

On the 24th of May we were transferred and sworn into the U. S. service for three years, or during the war, by Captain Pope, afterwards Major-General. Our oath simply consisted in swearing allegiance to our Government and obeying all legal orders of our superior officers. On the same day we were sworn in, William and Rollin Mallory, of Riley, and James Barber, of Java, New York, joined the Company. James came for the sole purpose of enlisting and being in the same Company with his brother and myself. James was a noble boy. Too soon he fell a martyr to the Cause. We also on this day received a visit from a load of Riley friends who stayed with us all night. On the next day Joseph Barber and Joe Taylor made me a visit.

June 1st.

June 1st, Elon, James, Rollin, William, Harvey Huntington and myself received three days' leave of absence to go home and make our final adieux. It was the last time I saw home for nearly three years. Ere that time had elapsed the fire blaze of battle had swept over me. Toil, hunger and sickness had left their marks upon me. Death, too, had made its mark in the family circle and took a loved sister to her spirit home. Alzina, how well I remember your last sad goodbye, with your arms thrown around my neck and warm kisses imprinted upon my cheek! Years have elapsed since then, still that last goodbye is as fresh in my memory as though it were yesterday. Even now, I can almost feel your breath upon my cheek, the clasp of your arms about my neck. I know that you are with me. What we call death cannot bar loved ones from our presence. In spirit, they are ever near to comfort and to cheer.

June 3d.

When we got back to camp, we found it dressed in habiliments of mourning in memory of the lamented Douglas. His funeral obsequies were observed in Freeport and the regiment attended en masse.

June 10th.

Each company now drew twenty-five muskets with accoutrements, and army blankets one to two men.

June 18th.

On the 18th of June we were ordered to remove camp to Alton, Illinois. At this time we had more baggage in one company than would be allowed in a whole brigade in one of Sherman's campaigns. It took two heavy trains to remove the regiment. We were vociferously cheered all along the route, the fair sex singing patriotic songs wherever we stopped and expressing their sympathy in various other ways. We arrived at Alton the next day and went into camp one mile north of the city. The Seventeenth, Twentieth and Hecker's German Regiment, Twenty-fourth, were camped with us, forming a brigade commanded by Brigadier-General John Pope, late Captain Pope. Colonel Turner assumed command of the camp and it was soon placed in a state of rigid discipline. The same order was observed here as at Freeport in regard to drilling, etc. We now had a reorganization in our culinary department. Heretofore the men formed in messes to suit their convenience; now the whole company was put into one mess. A company cook was detailed (John Bliss) and five more were detailed daily to assist him. We bought a large coffee boiler, holding ten gallons, and camp kettles to match. This arrangement gave general dissatisfaction, but the captain was inexorable and would not change.

July 4th.

The Fourth of July was duly observed and celebrated in an appropriate manner. The boys were all allowed a day of freedom and were put upon their honor as men and soldiers to conduct themselves properly, and with a few exceptions, their behavior was good, which is saying a great deal for so large a body of men where it is expected there will be many "bad cases." The jokes and stratagems used by the boys were endless, to elude the guard and get down town. A novel mode of punishment was now inaugurated for very fractious soldiers, which consisted in drumming them out of camp, by two men walking behind the offender with fixed bayonets pressing pretty close to his rear, and two musicians in front playing the rogues' march, passing between two lines of soldiers drawn up for the occasion, his head shaved clean on one side, his clothes turned wrong side out, hooted and jeered at by his companions as he passed along, until he was out of camp. Such cases received very little sympathy from good soldiers, as they were always bringing trouble. Degrading as this kind of punishment was, its moral had very little effect. There is no doubt but that, if it had continued, we would have got rid of all of our hard cases, but it would have wofully decimated our ranks. Too many were too anxious to get out of the army to care in what manner they effected their designs. Another mode of punishment was setting the offender to digging stumps and cleaning camp with a guard stationed over him to see that he kept at work. In this manner our camp was cleared of stumps which thickly covered one hundred acres.

July 10th.

Sickness now began to prevail to a considerable extent, over two hundred being on the sick list at one time. Several deaths occurred while we were camped here. A considerable number were being discharged. Surgeons at this time would make out discharges for slight causes, and, if an order from the War Department had not put a stop to it, our army would soon have become

16

badly decimated. The U. S. inspecting officer visited us here and he paid the regiment a high compliment for its appearance and the military spirit it displayed. I will now give a detailed account of some of the military manœuvers which were a part of our daily routine of duty, such as guard mounting and dress parade. Reveille was sounded at day-break, which was a signal for the camp to arouse and, at the call of the bugle, for roll call, the different companies fell into line to answer to their names. If any failed to appear, unless a reasonable excuse was given, they were sent to the guard-house. Next came the breakfast call ; then the sick call, and all who were sick or felt as though they were going to be sick, were marched up to receive their regular rations of quinine and get excused from duty if they could. After the sick call, came guard mounting for which two calls were sounded, the first to get ready. Everyone was required to have a clean gun, clean clothes, boots blacked—in short, they were expected to look tidy and neat. Anyone failing to comply with these regulations was sent back to his quarters or to the guard-house. At the sound of the second bugle, the orderlies from each company formed their guard and marched to the place of guard mounting, which is generally near headquarters. They form in line as they arrive at open ranks, standing at parade rest. The last movement is performed from an order arms by placing the hollow of the right foot two inches in the rear, and at a right angle with the left heel, at the same time turning your gun partly around, lock plate in; carry the muzzle of your gun in front of you, seizing the stock just below the first band with your right hand and just above it with your left, throwing your weight upon your left leg. After the guard is all in line, properly covered, counted off and the detail verified by the sergeant-major, the adjutant takes his position on the right of the detail next to the officer of the guard. The sergeant-major takes his position on the left and the non-commissioned officers in the rear, then the adjutant steps two paces to the front and comes to a left face and commands "Guard, attention. Shoulder arms. Right dress. Front. Present arms. Order arms. Parade rest." Then turning to the music on his right commands, "Troops lead off." The roll is sounded and then the band marches five paces to the front, file left and play slow time along the length of the detail. They then counter-march, playing quick time, and resume their original position. The adjutant then commands "Shoulder arms.

Rear rank. Right dress. Front.'' At the latter command, the officers and non-commissioned officers take their position in front of the detail, the officer of the guard in advance, the sergeant in rear of the officer of the guard, single file, and the corporals in rear of the sergeant. The adjutant then salutes the officer of the day and brings the guard to a "present arms," then to " shoulder arms " and commands, "Officers and non-commissioned officers to your posts. March.'' The officer of the guard remaining in the same position at an about face, the non-commissioned officers going back to their original position. Officer of the guard then commands "Inspection arms.'' At the latter command, the guard bring their pieces to the front, placing the butt between the feet with the barrel outward, draw the rammer and insert it in the barrel. When the inspecting officer comes to him, he seizes the gun at the lower band, tosses it up to his left hip, catching it in his left hand at the lower band, the breech resting just above the hip, bringing the middle band about on the level with the eye, lock plate out, muzzle thrown forward at an angle of about forty-five degrees, in which position the inspecting officer receives the gun. The officer of the guard, if he outranks the adjutant, inspects the front rank and the adjutant the rear. The band plays during inspection. After inspection, the adjutant brings the guard to a "shoulder arms," "right wheel," or "right face," pass in review before the officer of the day and then march to the guard-house where they are divided off into the first, second and third relief.

Dress Parade. At the call of the first bugle the men get ready by dressing in uniform, putting on their accoutrements. At the second call, the different orderlies form their companies, call the roll, mark all the absentees. The captain then marches his company to its proper position in the regiment on the parade ground. On coming into line, he throws out his right guide if dressing on the left, left guide if dressing on the right. (It is customary to dress on the center or flag company.) The adjutant arranges the guides and forms the line, after which he steps two paces to the front, comes to a left face and commands "Guide posts.'' The captain then brings his company to a "support arms" and takes his position on the right of his company; then commencing at the right of the regiment each company comes in succession to a "shoulder and order arms; parade rest.'' . The adjutant then commands "Troops lead off.'' The band then plays as in guard mounting, after which the adjutant gives the command "Attention Battallion. Shoulder arms. Prepare to open ranks," when the guides step back three paces and align themselves. Then comes the rest of the order, "To the rear; open order; march." Rear rank then steps back and dresses on the guides; then comes the order, "Rear rank; right dress; front." At the latter command, the line officers step two paces to the front of the regiment, the orderly to the right of the company, the lieutenant-colonel on the left in front of the line officers, and the major on the right of the regiment, four paces in front of the line officers. The colonel takes his position fifty paces in front and center of the battalion.

The adjutant now marches down in front of the regiment and in rear of the line officers to the center; then comes to a "right face" and marches twenty-five paces to the front; about faces and commands "Present arms." (Officers salute.) He then about faces again, salutes the colonel and marches around his right and takes position three paces to the rear and left of colonel. The colonel then draws sword and puts the battalion through the manual of arms, after which the adjutant marches back to within twenty-five paces of the regiment and commands, "First sergeants to the front and center; march." After they have closed on the center they are commanded to "Front face. Report." Then commencing on the right, each sergeant reports those present, accounted for and absent without leave. After which comes the command "First sergeants outward face. To your posts. March." After which the adjutant again about faces, salutes, about face again and if there are any orders, proceeds to read them, if not, commands "Parade, dismiss." The music then strikes up; the line officers close on the center, front face, and marching to within ten paces of the colonel, salute. The colonel if he sees fit, makes some remarks, after which the orderlies march their companies back to their quarters.

Our camp life at Alton was nothing but a severe routine of military duty; occasionally some little incident would transpire to vary the monotony. The sale of ardent spirits soon got to be a growing evil in our camp, and Colonel Turner took measures to suppress it, but one man more bold than the others defied him. He moved his shop outside the camp, supposing that he was out of reach of the Colonel's authority, and continued to sell his hellish fires. Whereupon Colonel Turner gave permission for a squad of

soldiers to go and arrest him and spill his whisky. These proceedings completely broke up the whisky ring. The camp was
alarmed one night by a report that our guard stationed over a
spring of water had been fired upon and an effort was being made
to poison the water, but I believe the alarm was groundless. I
think some scamp fired a gun merely to frighten the guard. It
did not take much to alarm us at that time.

July 18th.

On the 18th of July, we were ordered to move camp again,
where, we knew not. I was again detailed to look for the baggage and it was ten o'clock P. M. before everything was down to
the levee. The regiment took up their quarters for the night in
the old State Prison. I stayed with the baggage.

July 19th.

Early the next morning the steamer "Alton" arrived and we
embarked and proceeded down to the mouth of the Missouri
river. We then turned our course up that stream. Just as we
turned our course, a soldier from Company H fell overboard, and
just as assistance was within reach, he sank to rise no more. We
proceeded up the river as far as St. Charles, Missouri, where we
arrived the next evening at nine o'clock (July 20th), and we immediately disembarked and went into camp one mile above the
city. We apprehended some trouble on landing, as the rebels
were rampant, but no serious difficulty occurred. We were now
for the first time in what we considered an enemy's country.

CHAPTER IV.

July 22d.

We could say now that our actual military life had just begun. I was placed on picket the first night at St. Charles, and well I remember my feelings on that occasion. Word was sent round to us that an attack was expected. You may imagine that I did not sleep any. Every noise was noticed and every dark object turned into imaginary rebels. I could plainly hear the pulsations of my own heart. I was not what would be termed "scared," but when I considered that the safety of the camp depended upon my watchfulness, I was afraid I could not do my duty. The fellow that was with me was completely demoralized, hence it required greater vigilance on my part. He deserted the same night and nothing have I heard of him since. Here we heard of the terrible and disastrous battle of Bull Run, and a deep, burning shame crimsoned our cheeks at the defeat and disgrace of our arms. The first reports were favorable, but the sad sequel soon came and our Government learned a lesson which they did not soon forget. The clamor and impatience of the North urged on that battle before it should have been fought, but the people soon found out that the Rebellion was a monster which was not to be crushed in a few days with a few thousand men. General Pope moved his headquarters here for the present.

July 30th.

We now practiced target-shooting daily. We had drawn our full complement of guns, tents and other equipments before we left Alton. We now began to get a foretaste of army fare. Our bacon was so maggoty that it could almost walk, and our hard-tack so hard we could hardly break it. We were not sorry when the order came for us to move camp to Mexico, Missouri, which was about two hundred miles from St. Charles. The road was infested with guerrillas and bushwhackers. A detachment of the 21st Illinois came from Mexico and guarded a railroad train which was to move us. They had a skirmish on the way down, without anything very serious occurring except two or three breakdowns and smashups on the road. We passed through some splendid looking country on the route, the surface of the country being even and mostly prairie. The country about Mexico is very level, soil sandy, with a great scarcity of water and timber.

August 1st.

We found the 21st Illinois Regiment Volunteer Infantry here, commanded by Colonel Ulysses S. Grant, afterward the great hero of the War. There was a sharp strife between Colonels Turner and Grant as to which outranked. Turner claimed superiority on account of the date of commission. Grant claimed it on account of having belonged to the regular army, and with his usual pertinacity and Pope's order, gained his point and assumed command of the camp. The first order he issued was for a detail from the 15th to clean up his regiment's quarters. It was needed bad enough, but the order did not set well on our stomachs. We had just put our own camp in splendid order and we did not feel like doing the dirty work of his regiment. Luckily for us, Col. Turner was away when the order came and Lieut.-Col. Ellis was in command. He took the order, read it, his face burning with anger, and sent word to Col. Ulysses S. Grant that his regiment did not enlist as "niggers" to do the dirty work of his or any other regiment. This emphatic protest brought Col. Grant over at once. High words ensued, which resulted in Lieut.-Col. Ellis tendering Col. Grant his sword, but as for obeying that order, he should never do it. I think Grant must have admired his spirit, as he refused to receive his sword and did not enforce the order. As a natural consequence, the 15th Regiment Illinois Volunteer Infantry did not fall in love with Grant then, but we surely did with Lieut.-Col. Ellis. We saw the stuff he was made of and the bold stand he took for his own and our rights and we would have followed him to the death if he had so ordered. It was not until Grant had showed great courage, indomitable perseverance and lofty patriotism that we could regard him with any degree of favor.

August 5th.

Gen. Pope established his headquarters near us in a farm house. Some of the boys began to get sick here on account of the poor water we had to use, and our rations grew no better very fast. Some of the boys positively asserted that our bacon had followed us from St. Charles, and our hard-tack was harder still, and it was not surprising that we hailed the advent of a barrel of flour with great joy, although we had no conveniences for cooking it. But "necessity is the mother of invention," so we hatched up a plan whereby we could have pancakes for supper, though "Biddy," the cook, would have been horrified at the idea of calling them pancakes; but in the absence of anything better, we voted them excellent, but the stomachs refused to sanction our decision. We now concocted a plan to get rid of our old defunct rations. The boys gathered all of the hard-tack together, placed it upon the back of the bacon and proceeded to "drum them out of camp," the bacon carrying the hard-tack; but what was our surprise, the next morning, to find that the bacon had come back during the night and was highly indignant at the treatment it had received; but our hardened hearts had no sympathy for it and it was again expelled, and the last we heard from it was from a fellow who said he saw it wandering about the country inquiring for the 15th. (Of course my readers can believe as much as they choose about the bacon, but it is as true as most of the camp yarns.)

August 8th.

Elon and Harvey, two of my tent mates, were taken sick here, Harvey with very sore eyes. The dull monotony of camp life was now broken by an order to march, the left to Hannibal, Missouri, and the right to Fulton, Missouri. The march was to be performed afoot, consequently all the sick had to be left, Elon and Harvey among the number. The weather was extremely hot and I came very near "bushing" the first day, but being too proud to show symptoms of distress, I struggled on, although I could scarcely put one foot before the other. It was ten o'clock that night before we went into camp, and I was about used up and immediately retired, supperless and sick. We had marched twenty miles since noon. Our camp was situated near where was fought one of the first battles in Missouri for the Union, and there was great danger of being attacked during the night, and here the noble qualities of Major Goddard, who was in command, were shown. He kept a tireless viligance over the camp all night and allowed his tired soldiers rest, and from that time forward Major Goddard had a firm hold of the affections on the men under his command. We slept on our arms that night. Armed traitors were lurking around us, ready to take the least advantage. We were on the move before daylight the next morning. I was feeling some better but I had no appetite for breakfast. We had fifteen miles to march and we made it before ten o'clock. The different companies got on a strife to see which could out-march. Some of the time we made four miles per hour. We halted at one of the churches in Fulton and rested. A collection was taken up to procure a dinner, and we had the satisfaction of soon sitting down to a nice, warm meal. My appetite had now returned and I ate heartily and felt much refreshed. On our march we passed a splendid plantation owned by one Dr. Rodman. Our flag was floating from every window. He was very demonstrative in his patriotism. We halted here a few moments to rest. He said he had converted his plantation into a fortress and put arms into the hands of his negroes, being resolved to defend himself to the last if attacked by guerrillas or rebels. He stated that his life and preperty had been threatened by rebels and he counted on the fidelity of his slaves, of whom he had over two hundred, to defend him. I thought that his profession of Union sentiments were too profuse to be believed. I believe he was a rank rebel and adopted this ruse to protect his property. He had a large peach orchard loaded with delicious fruit and he asked for a safeguard to protect it. Toward evening we went into camp one-half mile west of the city on the fair grounds. Fulton is a splendid looking village containing several thousand inhabitants. Some of the finest buildings in the State are located here. Among them were the State Lunatic Asylum and several colleges. The president of the asylum sent an invitation for the battalion to visit the institution —an invitation which we gladly accepted. We were conducted all through the institution and the principles upon which it was conducted explained. There were about two hundred patients in it at the time. The grounds around the institution were beautifully laid out and the patients, under careful survelliance, were allowed to walk around them in pleasant weather. Our situation here was a dangerous one. We had only four hundred men and were isolated from any other command, and out of reach of assistance if overpowered, in an enemy's country, with spies lurking all around us. There was nothing to prevent a large force from defeating us except the indomitable vigilance of our commander, Major Goddard. We were always on the alert and always prepared for emergencies and our pickets were well posted and positions changed every night, and spies and scouts sent out to give us notice of approaching danger. Our position was admirably situated for defensive operations. A river encircled us on two sides, a swamp on a third, and a high and tight board fence surrounded the camp, affording us protection from bullets.

August 12th.

We were alarmed one night by a report that a party of rebels were tearing down our flag on the court house. Company D was called upon to go up and see what the matter was. This was about ten o'clock P. M., after we had all retired. It was amusing to witness the effect of the announcement upon some of the men. We were ordered to arm and fall in line as quickly as possible. Some were taken suddenly ill—one boy was chilly, another was lame, and one great over-grown booby wanted to be excused on account of having the "belly-ache." We could hear the chattering of teeth very audibly. We expected a fight. It was our first call. It is not to be wondered at that some should feel a little shaky. The inmates of tent No. 6 were on time and in line promptly. James sprung out like a tiger panting for his prey. In the confusion one of our guns was found missing. It happened to be James'. It had slid out of the back of the tent. James stormed around, accusing each one of us of having taken his gun, said we were so excited we did not know what we were about. He finally found it and we all had a good laugh over it. The alarm proved to be a false one. On our way up we met two delinquents of Company D just returning from town where they had been on a spree, and they stated that the alarm was caused by a charivari party which was paying their respects to a newly married couple. With a hearty laugh, we returned to camp stripped of our imaginary laurels, and the delinquents of Company D were put to extra duty for violating orders. The sick, chilly and lame ones suffered unmercifully by being the butt of all jokes cracked in the battalion. Thus our time was passed in continual alarms, but nothing very serious happened. One night one of the best soldiers in the company was found sleeping on his post. He had his trial. The company was very much concerned about it. We knew the penalty was death. He was a general favorite and we could not bear the thoughts of his execution. It being the first offense and the character of the soldier saved him. Had anyone else had the dealing of his case, he would not have escaped as he did. It was our custom every evening to go out on the green near the city and have dress parade. On such occasions the citizens of the town all flocked to see our performance. I believe I never saw so many homely ladies together as I did on these occasions. The darkies were especially delighted at our performances and we could see a broad grin on almost every face. About the 12th of August we received an order to march. A squad of men was sent out to press teams to move our baggage, and early the next morning we were on the march. Our destination was St. Aubert on the Missouri river, forty miles from Fulton. We marched twenty-five miles the first day and I was quite used up when I got into camp. I could not stand the hot weather.

August 13th.

We resumed the march early the next morning. The day was very hot. Before two hours had elapsed, I had a touch of a sunstroke and I had to "wilt." I was placed in a wagon. One of our officers had his wife along and she pillowed my head in her lap. I thought if this was the treatment for sunstroke, I would not object to being struck a little every day, but Dr. Buck soon came around and gave me some brandy and water which revived me a great deal. We arrived at St. Aubert about nine o'clock the next morning, having marched fifteen miles in four hours. Some of the boys were now guilty of great imprudence by going into the river when their blood was so hot. Rollin Mallory and Sidney Babcock swam across the river and poor Sid paid the penalty with his life soon after. He was taken sick and died at Keokuk, Ia. The regiment remained here over night. I recovered sufficiently to be able to go on picket. A band of rebels were hovering around, but finding us well prepared, did not venture to attack us. Just across the river from where we were, the Home Guard had had a brush with the rebels just a few days before.

August 14th.

This morning a steamer hauled up and we embarked on it and we were soon borne on the sluggish current of the Missouri towards St. Louis. The channel of this river is so changeable that it requires a most skillful pilot to run. The sand bars change every few days. We soon ran afoul of one of them, but we soon succeeded in sparring off. Soon after we ran into a snag which detained us for several hours. The navigation of the Missouri river is exceedingly difficult and at times dangerous. The next day we passed St. Louis and landed twelve miles below at Jefferson Barracks, where we found the left wing of the regiment waiting for us. The sick were also here. Elon had nearly got well, but Harvey's eyes were so bad that he was discharged, as were also John Burst and Charlie Pierce. We had not fairly got settled in

2

camp before an order came for us to again take the transport and proceed to St. Louis. Tidings of the bloody battle of Wilson Creek began to reach us and we were hastened forward to reinforce that gallant little army contending against such fearful odds. Soon the news of the death of the brave Lyons reached us and that his shattered little army under Sigel was retreating. On arriving at St. Louis, I was again detailed to help transfer the baggage to the cars and it was midnight before our task was done. In the meantime, the boys had been behaving badly and having lots of fun. They had been deprived of their dinner and supper and as they were passing along Market St. and noticed its richly laden viands, etc., they pitched in and helped themselves, much to the indignation of the proprietors and the amusement of the bystanders. While they were trying to catch one thief, a dozen would steal still more. The police, from some unknown cause, did not interfere; whether they enjoyed the fun or were afraid, still remains a mystery. Most of the boys got their fill. I was kindly remembered. I was too hungry to inquire how they got it. The old adage that "the partaker is equally guilty with the thief" induced me to keep silent, although I must say that their conduct was reprehensible, still they had some excuse for their actions. The train left at one o'clock A. M., and the next morning we arrived in camp at Rolla (August 18th).

CHAPTER V.

August 20th.

Rolla at this time was the terminus of the Pacific Railroad. It contained but two or three hundred inhabitants. The soil is barren, fruit being the chief article of culture. We found in camp here the 13th Illinois Volunteer Infantry (Col. Wyman). My friend, J. M. Eddy, was in this regiment and he soon came over to see me. Maj.-Gen. John C. Fremont was in command of the Western Department and he now advanced out of his own pocket $10.00 to each man on our wages, an act of generosity on his part which we never forgot. We had not been in camp but a few days before Sigel's brave and shattered army came straggling in. It was sorrowful to look at them. Some were sorely wounded and it must have been very painful for them to march, but they seemed to be cheerful, though all looked nearly worn out. Their clothes were in tatters. Footsore and weary, they struggled on. Brave men! they deserved a better fate. The most of these soldiers' time (three months) had expired before the battle, but rather than leave with a foe at their backs without punishing them, they voluntarily went into the fight, and on that bloody field many of them voluntarily gave up their lives. Our country cannot appreciate too highly such noble sacrifice and devotion to our flag. We here became associated with the 14th Illinois Volunteer Infantry and the two regiments remained in the same brigade during the entire war, and a very cordial feeling was engendered between the two regiments, which was never impaired. They regarded each other as brothers. In the field, on the march, in the fight, in victory or defeat, they were ever by our side. We now had another re-organization in our cooking department by being divided off into five messes. A cook was appointed for each mess, who was excused from all camp duties. This arrangement gave general satisfaction and was ever after continued.

August 28th.

We were now set to work building forts and fortifications, and every man not on the sick list was on duty every other day. The men had their choice of duty, that is, fatigue or guard duty. I chose the latter. Those that chose the former were lured by the prospect of the ration of whisky and extra pay. I was philosopher enough to know that Uncle Sam would not pay double for men doing what it was their duty to do. They were all disappointed in receiving extra pay.

Soon several strong forts were built with heavy abattis to each, with rifle pits connecting the forts. As soon as this work was done, we were set to work clearing up a drill and parade ground, after which we had company and battalion drill daily. Every man not on duty, who was not excused, had to be at these drills. Our duty was very heavy. We were made to follow out strictly the army regulations, which were read to us one hour every Sunday so that we might be posted. Sickness now began to prevail to an alarming extent. Our hospitals were overflowing. Over two hundred were on the sick list in our regiment alone at one time and deaths were quite frequent, and we soon became accustomed to the slow and solemn dirge of the soldier's obsequies. Elon began to get worse and was getting quite homesick. It was evident that he would not live long if he remained in the army, so the doctor concluded to discharge him. About one dozen from our company were discharged from this camp, and we also had three or four deaths. Up to the present time my health had been pretty good, but one day a peddler came into camp who had pies and cider for sale, and James and I bought some. Soon after I was taken violently ill, but a thorough purging set me on my feet again. I stayed in the hospital only one night. In the morning, before daylight, I ran away. James soon commenced joking me about the cider and pie—about my not being able to stand much. In a few days he was taken sick, never more to rise until his brave spirit soared to its rest. Soon after James was taken sick, Elon left, but James was not considered dangerous then, and we thought that he was on the gain.

September 10th.

Up to this time, James had remained in our tent, as the hospital was somewhat crowded, but he had gotten so bad that it was necessary to have him removed where he could be more quiet and get more care. I had spoken to Dr. McKim, the surgeon, several times about it, but he kept putting it off. I finally determined that I would not be put off any longer, and I importuned the doctor so much that he got angry and gave me a terrible raking, interspersed with a variety of choice oaths. I waited until he had spent his wrath and then told him that I did not feel guilty of anything wrong in this matter. It was only my intense anxiety for my cousin that induced me to endeavor to procure him better treatment and I supposed that it was his duty as surgeon of the regiment to see that the sick were well cared for. He cooled down and prepared a place for him and had James removed. Ever after Dr. McKim was a friend to me. He did all that he could to save James, but human aid was unavailing. While not on duty, I was by his bedside. He was not content to have me away a moment. I once began to flatter myself that he would get well, but one day while I was on duty, a summons came for me from Dr. McKim to repair immediately to the bedside of James. I was released from duty and thereafter remained with James as long as he lived. I found him suffering a terrible relapse and in the agonies of a congestive chill. He did not know me and was raving terribly. Hope sank within me now. I knew that I must lose one of my nearest and dearest friends. A brother's love could not have been greater than that I bore for James, and I know that that love was reciprocated. The closest confidence existed between us. In his wild delirium he would throw his arms around my neck and call me "brother." All that affection could prompt and skill perform, were done to save him. On the 18th of September, at two o'clock A. M., he breathed his last, under the influence of ether. It was a sad blow to his kindred and friends. I felt desolate indeed when the grave closed over his inanimate form. Missouri's soil covers the form of no nobler man than he. A truer patriot never breathed. He was honest, upright, brave and true. His death left a void in many an aching heart. He was a general favorite with all the company. None knew him but to respect him. Thus three of my relatives and friends had left me, and this last blow was hard to bear. Sleep on, brave boy, in peace! In a better clime I hope to meet you.

September 20th.

Rumors of an attack now became rife in camp. Price and McCulloch were reported to be near with a large army. This just served to keep up excitement enough to destroy the ennui of army life. Maj.-Gen. Hunter was in command of the post now. He received a wound at the battle of Bull Run. We made several forced marches out to meet the enemy, but each time failed to bring them to an engagement; as soon as our backs were turned, they would commence bushwhacking. A great many of the citizens adopted the role of being friends to our face and foes to our back.

September 22d.

A difficulty occurring at this time between Lieut. Curtis and Capt. Wayne, was settled by the former resigning. We now prepared for a long campaign. We were furnished with fifteen six-mule teams, and well supplied with clothing, etc. We were expecting orders to move every day.

September 23d.

On the 23d of September we received twenty-one recruits for Company D. Amongst them were some of my personal friends and acquaintances, namely:—Samuel Cooper, Milton Mackey and Charlie Mitchell. Milton was not eighteen years old yet, but was full of life and spirit, endowed with more than ordinary intellect, and an ardent patriot. He soon became a favorite in the company. Poor boy, he, too, met a sad fate.

September 24th.

The next day after the arrival of the recruits, we were ordered to march and we considered this a good time to break in the recruits, so we started off at a rapid pace, but about one P. M. we received orders to counter-march, and our march back was more rapid than when we started out. Some of the recruits stood it bravely, but some whined most piteously. Sam, Milton and Charlie stood it as well as any of them. As for me, I was about "petered out," but I kept it to myself. In our efforts to "bush" the recruits, we had nearly "bushed" ourselves. We supposed that we had started out for Springfield, Missouri, one hundred and fifty miles from Rolla. We went as far as the Gasconade river and received orders to return. Whether it was a ruse to blind the enemy as to our movements or the enemy was too strong for us, we have never yet learned.

October 1st.

We now enjoyed over a week's repose in camp, but we knew we would have to move soon. It was interesting when the mail hour arrived to witness the eagerness of the boys to receive mail. It was the one great joy of camp life to receive kind and encouraging letters from our friends. They were as dove-winged messengers spreading a halo of light and joy over the hearts and minds of the soldiers. I considered myself blessed above the most of my fellow soldiers by having such true and noble sisters to feed my soul with the light and love of pure and holy affection. Those angel messengers called out and kept bright all that was good and true within me. Their trusting confidence and love were a shield and safeguard from all temptations. To them I owe more than I can ever repay. I could not violate the confidence they reposed in me, and ever meet them again as a perjured wretch. When temptation assailed me, like a flash of heavenly light came the holy tie of confidence and love to protect me. When weary and sick, the ever-gentle, silent, potent and powerful voice of sympathy in those welcome missives cheered and sustained me, and through those four years of dreadful scenes of carnage and battle, the same pure and steadfast devotion was a beacon light to cheer me on and comfort me. Other friends, too, I had, whose sympathy and confidence I felt, a parent's love, a brother's true devotion, but to my sisters will I give the highest honors. In those dark and trying times, when all else seemed to fail me, theirs alone was the hand to lead me on.

October 4th.

On the 4th of October, Zine's birthday, we took the cars at Rolla, bound for Jefferson City, where we arrived the next day.

October 5th.

It rained all night and continued to rain all day. We were in open cars and got thoroughly drenched. When we arrived at Jefferson City, we were ordered to keep on the train in the pelting storm until further orders, but those orders came right speedily. Lieutenant-Colonel Ellis defied the authority of the commander of the post and told his men to seek shelter, which they were not slow in doing. Colonel Ellis was immediately put under arrest, and there was a fair prospect for a general row. The boys were determined to see Ellis all right if they had to fight for him, but he was soon released and marched us up to the State Capitol, within whose walls we took shelter. Our company took up their quarters in the Senate Chamber, where only a few months before the traitor Governor of Missouri, Jackson, and his confederates, were plotting treason and endeavoring to drag Missouri into the whirlpool of secession. On the walls hung life-sized portraits of Benton and Jackson. Though dumb, they seemed to speak to us in burning words of eloquence to drive the traitorous foe from the soil of Missouri. The streets of the city wore a desolate aspect. War's rude finger had left its mark. Traitors and patriots met on the street with set teeth and blazing eyes, brother against brother and father against son. Missouri at this time was in a terrible state of anarchy. Her traitorous governor and the hoary headed Price were desolating her soil with a large army, and the true and faithful were vainly contending with these tyrant monsters.

Back and forth over the beautiful plains of Missouri, the bloody tide of war swept, destroying everything in its path and reddening its soil with the life-blood of the noblest in the land; but the day of her deliverance came and fair Missouri is now a ransomed and regenerated State. The next day an order came for us to continue on as far as Tipton, at which place we arrived the same day and went into camp in the suburbs of the town. Tipton is a nice village, containing one thousand inhabitants, surrounded by as splendid a country as the eye ever looked upon. Here Fremont's grand army was concentrating preparatory to that grand campaign which was to sweep the rebel horde from Missouri, but strange to say, Fremont permitted Price and his army which had been up to Lexington and captured Mulligan and his command, to pass back across his flank without molesting him. While we were camped here, we received a visit from the Secretary of War—Cameron. The weather soon set in very rainy and we were in danger of being flooded. In this emergency, the boys commenced tearing down several old buildings near camp to get lumber to protect us from the wet, but our proceedings were summarily stopped by an order from Colonel Turner, who declared we should pay for every board and stick we had taken; but Colonel Ellis was standing by and he gave the boys one of his peculiar winks and then we knew we had a strong advocate in our behalf. General Fremont soon issued an order for us to go to the lumber yard and get what lumber was necessary to build floors in our tents, but we did not stay long to enjoy it.

October 10th.

We were now paid two months' wages, less the $10.00 received from General Fremont, and moved camp three miles south of town to Camp Hunter. We now commenced preparations to march. The army was divided into three divisions. General Hunter commanded the first, McKinstry the second and General Asboth the third. The 15th was in the first brigade, Grand Army of the West.

Lieut.-Col. Ellis now put us through a very thorough course of drilling and we soon had the name of being one of the best drilled regiments in the army. Col. Turner lacked the necessary qualifications for drill-master, and he made bungling work whenever he attempted to drill the regiment, but he was a strict disciplinarian —so strict that he got the ill-will of most of his men—and he soon became unpopular. He felt it and kept aloof from the regiment a great deal. I came across Mark Whitney here. He belonged to the Douglas brigade, 42d Illinois Volunteers.

October 20th.

The day before marching the company bought an ox-team to carry our knapsacks. It only cost us a dollar and a quarter apiece and it saved us an immense amount of fatigue.

October 21st.

Finally the order came to break up camp. On the 21st the army was put in motion in pursuit of Price and his army. It proved to be a long, exciting and fruitless march. Some days he was reported only a day's march ahead of us and we would press on with renewed vigor in hopes of overtaking him, but Price and his army proved to be like the Dutchman's flea—" When you put your finger where he was, he wasn't there."

October 22d.

The first night we camped near Versailles, having made but fifteen miles. The army was in splendid spirits. The country looked splendid and the weather was delightful. The cool, bracing breezes of October seemed to put life in every limb.

October 23d.

The next morning we were early on the move ; marched twenty miles, and on the 23d we camped on the south side of the Osage opposite the ruined city of Warsaw. We laid over here one day—for what purpose I do not know. Price was reported only twenty-five miles off. We gave him an opportunity to disband that portion of his army who lived in the country through which he passed and rest the remainder. Then we started after him again. We got as far as Mt. Au Revoir and halted again. We were pressing Price too hard. It would never do. We must wait and let him get farther ahead. So we waited a week.

October 30th.

While we were in camp at Mt. Au Revoir, numerous peddlers

frequented our camp, peddling apples, peaches, etc., and we had good reasons for believing that these very peddlers were a portion of the rebel army, and as these came to their homes, they were permitted to remain, attend to their farms, gather in their harvest, etc., and at a call from Price, again take the field. It was a very common sight to see three or four able-bodied young men at the different farm houses along the route, eyeing us with a look of triumph. They all professed to be peaceful citizens and perfectly neutral. I never had a doubt in my own mind but what Price disbanded a large part of his army in this way. He knew perfectly well that he could not cope with us in battle and so he adopted that plan as the most feasible way of saving his army and annoying us. He succeeded but too well.

November 1st.

One day one of these neutral rebs came into camp with a load of apples to sell. He inadvertently betrayed his sentiments and, with the permission of Col. Ellis, the boys relieved him of his apples in less time than it takes me to write it. Rollin and Milton, who were always on hand at such a time, managed to secure two bushels for tent No. 6. The fellow was lucky in getting off as well as he did. We soon resumed our march. We left here all the surplus baggage that could be spared and our sick with a guard to protect them. We then stripped ourselves for a hard march, making from twenty to thirty miles per day. We had a splendid country to march through. It was well watered and timbered. Gen. Hunter was an admirable officer to conduct a march. Everything was as orderly as clockwork. We halted an hour for dinner and always went into camp in time to get our supper before dark, and were on the move by daylight in the morning. The last day but one before reaching Springfield, we had marched twenty-seven miles and had just eaten our supper and were preparing to lie down when an order came for us to reach Springfield by daylight if possible, as a battle was expected the next day.

November 2d.

The other divisions had taken different routes and reached Springfield first. We had twenty-seven miles to go yet, but the roads were so muddy and the country so rough that it was long past daylight before our division came in sight of the city, and then only about one-third of the command came in together. The rest were worn out for want of sleep and rest and stopped on the road. By using extra exertion, I managed to keep my accustomed place in the front file. Indeed, in all that march of three hundred miles, I was not away from my position longer than ten minutes at a time, and then only when necessity required it, but that night I was nearly fagged out. We had marched nearly sixty miles without sleep and very little rest, and to our mortification there was no prospect of a battle at that time. There was no enemy of any considerable force within forty miles of us. We kept receiving orders to hurry up. Rumors came of a battle in progress. The artillery went thundering past us at a killing rate to get to the front, and all for what? Because some blunderhead of an officer had magnified rumors into realities. A few days before, Fremont's body guard, under command of Maj. Zagonyi, had had a severe battle at Springfield. With this small body of men, he charged twenty times his number and drove the enemy from town, but over one-half of his command perished in the fight. This charge is one of the most brilliant and bravest on record, and will ever be sung in song and repeated in story, while chivalry holds its sway over the passions of men. These men had been called "baby soldiers," and smarting under the appellation, they now had a chance to prove their mettle and refute the charge. So with the war cry of "Fremont and the Union" on their lips, they went forth to do and to die. Gen. Fremont was now relieved of his command and Gen. Hunter assumed temporary command. Springfield was a beautiful young city, but like many other places in Missouri, war had left its blighting marks there. The bloody battle field of Wilson's Creek was only twelve miles from here.

After resting for a few days, we were ordered to counter-march, thus leaving all southern Missouri open again to the ravages of the enemy, besides having the miserable consciousness that our campaign had been a miserable failure. Our march back was easy and slow, making from ten to fifteen miles per day. Our ox team proved to be of great good to us. They kept up to the train without any difficulty. The different routes of the three divisions converged to a point near the Osage river, and there was a strife to see which would get the lead. Col. Turner, who now commanded our division, put his men on a double-quick for a mile or more and secured it, but the other divisions had sent teams ahead to block the way and detain us. Our regiment was in the lead. The officer of the train refused to yield. Hard words were passed between Goddard, Ellis and the officers of the train-guard which ended in Ellis ordering his men to fix bayonets and clear the road. This move had the desired effect and we marched triumphantly on. We halted at Warsaw a few days and then went back to our old Camp Hunter.

We had consumed a month's time in this campaign and the result was anything but satisfactory to us or the country, but the march left the army in splendid condition. An army is always more efficient and in better trim on an ordinary march than when lying idle in camp. The cool and invigorating atmosphere of Missouri, combined with the beauty of its natural scenery, had a happy influence upon the soldiers, though at times we suffered for want of food, but, as a general thing, we had plenty to eat. We had a considerable quantity of fruit and vegetables and a good deal of fresh meat. The latter article the boys procured mostly by confiscating such unlucky porkers as happened to come in their way. We had fresh beef issued to us two or three times a week. There was a set of grumblers in camp who were continually writing home how much we suffered for want of food, keeping our friends in a constant state of anxiety. We did not remain in Camp Hunter but a few days, but moved camp one and one-half miles north of Tipton.

November 28th.

We now enjoyed a short season of rest, but winter had now set in and we had to hustle ourselves to make our quarters comfortable. The nutting season had now arrived and we feasted on black walnuts and hickory nuts to our heart's content. Very strict orders were issued by the General against our killing hogs, but Col. Ellis, who was ever ready to humor the boys when he could without implicating himself or violating his honor, managed to elude somewhat this order. He told the boys not to let him see them with fresh pork. The boys understood this hint and when they got fresh pork they kept out of his sight, or, when he was around, he would persistently turn the other way, but he had fresh meat for supper nearly every night; but there was one fellow in the company who "blowed" on the boys while the General was in the tent, and as a reward for his faithfulness he was reduced to the ranks (he was a sergeant), but the general gave him a detail at head-quarters which consoled him for the loss of his position in the company.

CHAPTER VI.

December 3d.

We were now ordered to Syracuse, twelve miles west of Tipton. We camped there a few days and then made another short march. Then we returned to Tipton again. Indeed, we were on the move so much that we did not get an opportunity to wash our clothes. Just before the last march we had gone into camp and supposed that we were to remain for awhile, and so we went to washing our dirty clothes. We had just fairly got at it when an order came for us to march immediately. In ten minutes' time we had our half-washed clothes wrung out, done up in the tent, our knapsacks packed and were in line. Such was the celerity we had acquired in obeying orders. We were now ordered to proceed to Otterville and go into winter quarters. A heavy detail had gone on under charge of Major Goddard, to clear up our quarters, but on arriving at Otterville, the Major found that the commander of the post, Brig.-Gen. Jeff C. Davis, of Indiana, had assigned to us as winter-quarters the low, damp ground on the Lamine river, so he waited until the command came up, two days after, before he did anything. When Ellis saw the ground selected for us, with his usual spirit he bolted outright and refused to take his men into this swamp. Others followed the lead of Ellis, and the consequence was that they carried their point and marched their men on the other side of the river and went into camp on high, dry ground.

December 10th.

There were about twenty thousand troops stationed here. Our brigade consisted of the 24th Indiana, Col. Hovey ; 26th Indiana, Col. Wheatley ; 14th Illinois, Col. John M. Palmer, and the 15th Illinois. We were set to work building forts and fortifications. This place was now used as a depot of supplies. The weather soon became intensely cold, and some of the boys froze their hands and feet. Col. Hovey was in command of the brigade and he kept a heavy guard stationed around the camp. It made no difference what the weather was, the guard had to keep walking his beat. Col. Hovey, being absent for a few days, the command devolved on Ellis, and one bitter cold and stormy night, he took off the guard.

We had pickets out and men up to alarm the regiment in case of danger, so he was perfectly safe in doing so. When Col. Hovey returned, he had him placed under arrest for taking off the guard. Ellis demanded a trial, plead his own cause and was acquitted. This affair created a sort of ill-feeling between the Indiana and Illinois regiments. One day the 15th and 24th got to snow-balling, and the sport soon began to wax pretty warm. Something harder than snow began to fly. The Lieut.-Col. of the 24th came out to stop it and was hit by a chunk of ice and knocked down. A general melee seemed inevitable, but at this moment Col. Ellis appeared, and the 15th boys desisted and returned to their quarters. The 26th Indiana were a very inferior looking set of men, and they were certainly the most filthy looking set of men I ever saw. Some of our boys caught one of the dirtiest of them down at the river one day, and they stripped him and soused him in. He came out looking more like a white man. This affair had a wholesome effect on the whole regiment. We made frequent forays out into the country and confiscated corn, etc., from the rebels ; on such occasions there was usually a scrambling to see who would go. Almost invariably the boys would come in loaded down with the best that the country afforded. The weather became so intensely cold now that we had to adopt some plan to keep from freezing. We pegged our tent as close to the ground as possible, and covered over the lap with dirt. We then built a sort of fireplace at the foot, with the chimney just outside the tent, and got a good bed of twigs and straw to lie on; had the opening of the tent so arranged that we could fasten it tight, and at night, beneath our heavy covering, we nestled together like a litter of young pigs. Though the thermometer was ten below zero, we slept warm and comfortable. My tent mates at this time were Charlie Mitchell, William and Rollin Mallory, Milton Mackey and Samuel Cooper. Every night we would huddle around our little fire-place, our feet to the fire, and tell stories, crack jokes and debate. Sometimes our discussions were loud and warm, but very seldom were any ill feelings manifest. The subjects discussed were usually politics, religion or favorite generals. Every night before the entertainment began, we would buy some apples, crackers or oysters to refresh the inner man, while we listened to the torrents of eloquence which fell from one another's lips, and altogether we passed a pleasant, jolly time, even though stern winter did hold us in his

icy grasp. Citizens came in camp frequently peddling cider. On
such occasions the boys would flock around him. Some would
draw his attention one way, while some rogue would tap his barrel,
and before the joke would be discovered, he would be minus perhaps several gallons of his cider. We were now set to work building winter quarters. I shouldered my ax and went into the woods
and felled nine trees, from eighteen inches to two feet in diameter,
and cut them into the right length for building. I was so lame
the next day I could hardly stir. It was laughable to see some of
the raw hands with an ax try to cut down a tree. Most of them
could wield a pen better than they could an ax. The boys all
worked with energy. The prospect of having comfortable houses
during such cold weather was very comforting, but oh, the fallacy
of human hopes! The very next day we were ordered to march—
start out on a winter campaign. After traveling for ten days
through sleet and snow, we surprised and captured thirteen hundred prisoners. There was scarcely any fighting; then went into
camp at Sedalia. General Pope was in command of the expedition
and he deserves a great deal of credit for the ingenuity and military skill he displayed in capturing these rebels. From that time
he was a marked man. He rapidly rose in position and influence
until he ranked among our best generals. While we were at
Sedalia, a very severe snow storm occurred, after which it turned
very cold, and on one of these cold days we were ordered to
march.

                                    December 31st.
We took the old road back toward Otterville, at which place
we arrived after two days' hard marching. On the second day I
gave out. I had long been suffering with a severe cold, and I had
neuralgia in my hip, and the traveling being very difficult on
account of snow and ice, made it very painful for me to travel
Dr. Buck kindly gave me his horse to ride. About this time I
began the acquaintance of Charles F. Barber, soon after adjutant
of the regiment. I soon discovered that he was a relative of father
—second cousin, I believe. When we got back to our old camp,
we found that some rascals had destroyed our fireplace, and our
situation that night was anything but pleasant, but soldier-like, we
did not despond. We scraped the snow off the ground and put up
our tent. It was nine o'clock before we got our supper. Many
went to bed supperless, with the frozen earth for a couch. The

inmates of tent No. 6 slept close that night, but Roll and Charlie, whose turn came to sleep on the outside, suffered with the cold. As nothing more was said about building winter quarters, the inmates of tent No. 6 went to work and built some of their own. We first built a fire-place. In this we patterned after the southern style. They generally build their chimney first and then match their house to it. So we built our chimney and one door, which occupied the front. Then we laid up small logs, house style, some four feet high, and then fastened our tent on top of it for a roof. We built our beds so that our feet came together, and its sides served as a seat before the fire-place. We had plenty of room and cooked all our grub inside. When the other boys came to see how much more comfortable we were, they went and did likewise.

January 5th, 1862.

We now received another installment of pay. A good many of the boys had acquired the habit of gambling. "Chuck Luck" was their favorite game, and no sooner had the boys received their money than they established banks, and the game commenced and continued until either banker or bettor was strapped.

Many a soldier would venture all his hard earnings on the throw of the dice, and thus lose in a few hours what it had taken him months to earn. This species of gaming was carried on to such an extent that an order was issued prohibiting it. If anyone was caught at it, he was arrested and his money confiscated, but this did not stop the practice. So great had the passion of some become for gaming that they would even risk their lives for the sake of indulging it. Gaming engendered other vices and too many of the boys gave free rein to their passions and indulged in all manner of excesses of the grossest nature.

January 12th.

Tidings of the battle of Belmont now reached us, and General Grant rose one peg in our estimation. My health now became considerably impaired. I had had a severe cold for a long time, and it had finally settled on my lungs and a bad cough ensued. I was rendered totally unfit for duty. I sent home for some cough medicine. After taking that awhile I felt some better. They were granting sick furloughs now and discharging the worst cases.

January 14th.

The doctor examined me and told me that he would make out

my discharge papers. I told him that I did not want a discharge, but would be glad of a furlough, and he put me down for a sixty days' furlough, and I supposed that I would get one without doubt. Great was my astonishment when the furloughs were made out, to learn that I did not get one. There was a certain member of Company D who now played a sharp trick in order to get a furlough. G. H. had felt a little unwell for some time and had tried to get a furlough and failed. He now conceived the idea of using strategy to accomplish his design. He wrote to one of his sisters and requested her to write to him stating that his father was very ill and at the point of death and desired to see him before he died, and request him to get a furlough immediately, if possible. In due course of time, the letter arrived written as requested. G. read it, and with well-assumed grief and with tears rolling down his cheeks, he came to us, tent 6, and told us the cause of his grief and requested me to go with him to the captain's tent and intercede for him. I really pitied the fellow and told him I would do what I could.

The captain was very sorry for him. Although it was past bedtime, he went with him to Major Goddard's tent, but the Major told him he could do nothing for him as he had no power to grant furloughs, but learning that he was unwell, he sent to Dr. McKim to get a sick furlough, and under the circumstances, the doctor gave him one, and the boys in my tent raised the money for him to go home with. Captain Wayne went home about the same time and the captain had not been home but a short time before he met G. H's father in the street and expressed surprise to see him around so soon. Mr. H. wanted to know what he meant. "Have you not been sick? the captain asked. "Why, no," he said. The captain began to smell a large sized rat but did not ask any more questions. When G. H. returned to the army, he was joked a great deal about his sick father. Captain Wayne did not say much, but G. knew better than to go to him for any more favors.

January 24th.

I now received the startling and saddening intelligence that sister Zine had left us—gone to her spirit home. I was so shocked and crushed by the news that for a time it seemed as though I lost all consciousness. Soon a letter came from Lester, written while her lifeless remains were yet warm, breathing that deep sympathy which only a brother can feel for a brother. While their own

3

hearts were bleeding, they did not forget the absent one, and in
letters of which every word breathed love and sympathy did they
try to soften the grief which they knew I would feel. She died
very suddenly, rupturing a blood-vessel and choking to death. It
seemed as though it could not be. Only a few days before I had
received a letter from her, full of life and hope. Could it be that
those lips were mute now! That never those dear hands would pen
those words of affection which so stirred the deep founts of my
soul, and call forth those strong chords of love tuned to her touch.
Could it be that never again I would feel her warm kiss upon my
cheek, the clasp of her loving arms around my neck. In my grief
I forgot that her sainted spirit could still hover around me, until
like a flash of heavenly light, I felt her spirit's presence. Then I
was reconciled. I knew that from henceforth she would hover
around me, my guardian angel, my shield from temptation, my
beacon light in the future.

February 1st.

Orders now came for us to march to Jefferson City. Not being
able to travel, I was sent with the sick by rail. I did not leave
Otterville until the next day after the regiment left. On arriving
at Jefferson City, I took up my quarters at a private boarding
house, and one week later when, the regiment arrived, I reported
for duty. The regiment rested here a few days and then took the
the cars for St. Louis (February 9th). The captain now offered to
assist me in getting a furlough. I rejected his proffered services
and told him I did not want one then as my health was much
improved and I did not care about leaving the regiment then. It
was cold and stormy when we arrived at St. Louis. We halted
on the levee and were ordered to remain there until further orders
by Col. Turner, but it required something more than his order to
keep the men there exposed to the cold, pelting storm.

February 12th.

Though I regret to say it, a good many of the boys took refuge
in beer saloons and got tight, or in other words "dead drunk."
You never saw the boys before or since get on such a spree as
they did here. Col. Turner did not seem to have much control
over them. It was a humiliating sight. To-day I was almost
ashamed to say that I belonged to the 15th regiment. A stain
was cast upon its hitherto fair fame which it took a long time to
wipe out, but what was worse, the sober ones had to help bear the

ignominy. By night everything was on board and we were soon sailing down the Mississippi. The next evening (February 14th) we arrived at Cairo where we halted for orders. We now turned our course up the Ohio. When we arrived at Paducah, we learned that a fierce and bloody battle was in progress at Ft. Donelson on the Cumberland river. We soon came to the mouth of the Cumberland and turned our course up that stream. We had no doubt now of our destination. We were all eager to get to the scene of action in time to participate in the fight, but the captain of the boat was a rank rebel and he refused to run nights, and to the shame of Col. Turner he refused to use his authority and compel him to run. On the morning of the 16th a gunboat passed us which a few moments before left the fort with dispatches. From the officers of the boat we learned that Ft. Donelson, with immense stores of provisions, munitions, ordnance and fifteen thousand troops had just been surrendered to General Grant.

February 16th.

It was a glorious victory, and it was the beginning of those series of brilliant victories which added imperishable lustre to the name and fame of Ulysses S. Grant, the hero of the war. The dark clouds of gloom which had begun to settle like a pall over our country were partially lifted by this great victory. After this fight, the General rose amazingly in the estimation of the 15th. At ten o'clock A. M. on the morning of the 16th, we rounded a curve in the river and the high battlements and frowning batteries of Ft. Donelson, with the stars and stripes floating on the ramparts, met our visions. It was a scene well calculated to thrill the minds of the beholders with enthusiasm. The place had surrendered just one hour before we arrived and had it not been for a secesh captain and an over-prudent colonel, we would have been there in time to have shared in the honors of the victory. Ft. Donelson is situated on the Cumberland river, two hundred miles from its mouth and forty miles below Nashville. Nature had made its natural defenses strong, and with its heavy earthworks the place seemed impregnable. The main fort was situated on a high bluff and its guns commanded the river for a mile or more each way. Below the fort, clear down to the water's edge, were a succession of heavy casemated batteries. Against these formidable barriers our gallant little navy hurled their iron missiles, while the answering shots from the batteries came

tearing through the fleet with terrible precision. But nothing
daunted, it persevered until its work was accomplished. Most of
the infantry had marched from Ft. Henry, which was captured by
Com. Foote a few days before, across to Ft. Donelson, fifteen
miles (Ft. Henry is on the Tennessee), so the place was completely invested with the exception of a small space on the upper
side. The rebels made a stubborn resistance and repeatedly
charged our lines in hopes of forcing their way through, but they
met with a bloody repulse. In talking 'with an eye-witness of the
battle, he said the fight was terrific. Charge met charge. Steel
clashed against steel. Generals Logan, McClernand, Wallace and
Smith from Illinois, and Lew Wallace from Indiana, were every-
where on the field, cheering on the men and directing the fight.
Our troops had to lie two nights on the frozen earth, covered
with snow, without fire or shelter. The double-dyed traitor Floyd
succeeded in escaping with a portion of his brigade, leaving his
subordinate, Gen. Buckner, to his fate. When we arrived at the
fort we found everything in a state of confusion. The spoils of
war were being gathered. Guns, accoutrements, clothing,
ammunition, etc., were scattered around in promiscuous profusion.
Some had thrown their arms into the river. The prisoners were
busily embarking on transports, preparatory to going North. As
a general thing the prisoners were a hard looking set of men.
Some were quite communicative and disposed to be cheerful.
Some were very sullen and spoke only to hail vituperations and
abuse on the detested Yankees.

February 18th.

Toward evening we disembarked and went into camp. Volunteers were called for to help attend to the wounded and place them
on transports. In company with several others from Company D,
I offered my services which were accepted. It was nearly midnight before our task was done. It was a pitiful and sickening
sight to see such a mass of mangled limbs and mutilated bodies,
but the patience with which they bore their injuries excited our
admiration. Out of the twenty which I helped carry on the boat,
not one uttered a complaint, even though a leg or an arm were missing. The next day we took a stroll over the battle field. We saw
sights that fairly froze the blood in our veins. The dead lay as
they had fallen, in every conceivable shape, some grasping their
guns as though they were in the act of firing, while others, with a

cartridge in their icy grasp, were in the act of loading. Some of the countenances wore a peaceful, glad smile, while on others rested a fiendish look of hate. It looked as though each countenance was the exact counterpart of the thoughts that were passing through the mind when the death messenger laid them low. Perhaps that noble looking youth, with his smiling up-turned face, with his glossy ringlets matted with his own life-blood, felt a mother's prayer stealing over his senses as his young life went out. Near him lay the young husband with a prayer for his wife and little one yet lingering on his lips. Youth and age, virtue and evil, were represented on those ghastly countenances. But oh, what is that? Before us lay the charred and blackened remains of some who had been burnt alive. They were wounded too badly to move and the fierce elements consumed them.

We now came to where the rebels made their last desperate effort to break our lines, and in a small cleared field the dead were piled up, friend and foe alike in death struggle. All over the field were strewn the implements of war. Could we have realized then that the battle scene spread out before us was the precursor of a battle so terrible that this would sink into insignificance, we would have shuddered with horror, yet so it was. We had seen a battle field with all its horrors and we were soon to realize it. We went back to camp visibly impressed with what we had seen and not until the surging tide of battle had swept over us again and again, did the memory of this battle field cease to haunt us. The fall of Ft. Donelson necessitated the evacuation of Nashville by the rebels, and the next day our forces took quiet possession of the capital of Tennessee. We remained in camp at Ft. Donelson fourteen days, during which time the army recuperated and re-organized, preparatory to a grand campaign in the spring.

February 22d.

The army had received reinforcements until it numbered at this time eighty thousand men. It was organized into six divisions, commanded by McClernand, Prentiss, Wallace and Hurlbut from Illinois, Sherman of Ohio, and Lew Wallace of Indiana. It was a well-appointed army and well commanded. The 15th regiment was assigned to the fourth division, Brigadier-General S. A. Hurlbut, commander. At this time Hurlbut's reputation was resting under a dark cloud. I mention this to show how completely he changed the current of public opinion and won the confidence of the men. That black stain which sullied his reputation in Missouri had to be wiped out and he set to work in good earnest to do it. He proved to be a brave and efficient officer. We were now mud-bound and unable to move. The river had risen forty feet since we came there, reaching the highest water-mark that the oldest inhabitant had ever known. The small village at this place was named Georgetown. A little farther up the river was a place called Clarkville, where was situated an iron foundry. This the rebels destroyed and evacuated the place immediately after the fall of Donelson. Two new articles of food were added to our rations while here, consisting of desiccated potatoes, ground fine, and a compound of vegetables mixed and pressed into large cakes, called desiccated vegetables. We soon got tired of the potato as we did not know how to cook it. At first we cooked it just as we would make a meal pudding. After we learned the proper way of cooking it we prized it highly. It should soak in warm water until it has swelled all it can and then fried in a very little grease. The vegetables we boiled and made a soup of them. Milton was our cook at this time, and well he performed his duties. He could make as nice biscuits as I ever ate at home. The weather still continued to be disagreeable. Our tents were nearly worn out and leaked badly. The consequence was, some of us took severe colds.

March 1st.

This was an unhealthy place and quite a number were taken sick; amongst them were William and Samuel. We were ordered to march about the 1st of March. The sick and surplus baggage were sent around by water. William and Sam were left, but came up the next day.

March 2d.

Our route lay toward Ft. Henry on the Tennessee river. It was a mountainous, wild and sterile region. I saw the first pine and beach trees on this march that I had seen in the South. We took a circuitous route to avoid mud and mountains as much as possible. It was only fifteen miles between the two rivers at this point, and yet it took two days' hard marching. We traveled twelve miles the first day and camped eight miles from our starting point. The teams did not come up that night, they were fast in the mud two miles back. We went to bed supperless and without shelter. During the night it stormed hard, and we awoke

in the morning and found ourselves covered with snow. It was
so late when the teams came up that we did not move that day—
in fact, Colonel Ellis refused to march an inch until his men got
something to eat. The next day we marched to a landing four
miles above Ft. Henry. Here we found some of our sick and the
Captain just from home. We drew new Sibley tents here, but
did not put them up. Here an immense fleet of transports had
collected, which was to convey the army up to a point near Corinth,
to operate against the rebel army which was concentrating all its
available forces at the latter place. The river was so high that it was
almost impossible to get to the landing, but by building temporary
bridges, walking fallen trees and wading some, we managed to get
there. Our regiment was divided here. Four companies, C, F,
D and I went on board the Hastings, which boat was Gen. Hurlbut's headquarters. The other companies (six), went on board
the City of Memphis. The baggage was put on board the City
of Memphis. I was detailed to help transfer the baggage onto
the boat.

March 4th.

I worked all night. I stepped on shore a few minutes in the
morning and before I returned the fleet had loosed its moorings
and sailed. If I had had my knapsack and gun with me I should
not have cared, but I was in time to get onto the City of Memphis.
It was a grand sight to see that magnificent fleet of fifty steamers
sweep around in line, with colors flying and drums beating. It
seemed as though the grand old forests looked on with awe and
admiration at the sight. The Tennessee never bore on its bosom
so precious a cargo before. The fleet halted at Savannah for a
short time, and I was glad to rejoin my comrades. I found my
things all right. The boys had taken good care of them.

March 5th.

Four divisions of the army now proceeded up the river twenty
miles and disembarked at Pittsburg Landing. A gunboat had
had a fight here a few days before with a land battery on the river
bank. The place was almost a perfect wilderness. A few log
shanties were the only signs of human habitation, but now this
wilderness was to be peopled by a mighty host of freemen, awakening the echoes of its solitude by the reverberating tramp of armed
legions, the shrill notes of the bugle's blast and the martial strains
of the fife and drum. The fourth division was the first to land.

Our camp was situated one and a half miles from the landing and in the center of the military position of the army. On our right were Sherman and Prentiss, on the left, McClernand. Wallace's division landed at Crump Landing, a few miles below. The landing of the army on this side of the river was a bold move in Grant as it placed him between the rebel army and the river, thus cutting off his retreat in case of disaster.

March 9th.

The rebels were concentrating all their available forces at Corinth, only twenty miles from us, and the two armies lay watching each other for several weeks, like ferocious bull dogs eager for a fight.

Grant was waiting for Buell to come to his assistance before he commenced offensive operations, but all the while threatening the rebel army. Our camp was a very pleasant one and had been selected with some care. A difficulty arose between Col. Ellis and the colonel of the 6th Iowa as to who should have the ground.

Our boys had cleaned the camp and had got our new Sibley tents nearly all up when the altercation took place and while the two colonels were jawing each other, Maj. Goddard slipped over to Gen. Hurlbut's headquarters and got an order for the 15th to remain where they were.

We had drawn six new Sibley tents for the company,—one tent would accommodate sixteen men. Our camp was formed in regular order, according to army regulations. After we had gotten fairly established in camp we paid our attention to drilling. Col. Ellis drilled the regiment every day and we soon became nearly perfect. There was not a better drilled regiment in the army than the 15th. We became so efficient in the drill that a large portion of the regiment could drill the battalion without making a mistake. The weather was delightful. Spring had just begun to open and the grand old forest was putting on its leafy covering. Our mail came regularly and we were happy as mortals could be under the circumstances. We all knew that a battle was imminent, but never dreamed that the enemy would open the strife. Our great victory at Ft. Donelson had given us great confidence in ourselves and we supposed that we rested in security for the present.

But we were soon awakened from our repose by a spirited dash of the enemy into our very midst making a reconnoissance. This was the Friday before the battle. The 15th was called upon to repulse this attack from the enemy.

April 4th.

Promptly and quietly they obeyed the order and was the first regiment on hand from the fourth division. We received great credit for our behavior on this occassion. Some regiments would march along hooting and hallooing, but never a word did you hear from the 15th, but in the firm look and steadfast eye you could see men who were resolved to do their duty and they chose to show their courage by deeds, rather than by a counterfeit semblance. We did not attribute these qualities as belonging to ourselves entirely, but in a great measure to the confidence we had in our leader, Col. Ellis. Before Col. Ellis dismissed us that night, he made us a speech. It always seemed to me as though that.speech sounded the knell of his own doom. He went on to state his connection with the regiment, how pleasant it had been, how he loved it and how proud he was of it. He prophesied the coming battle, exhorted us all to do our duty in every emergency. He closed with an affecting appeal which brought tears to many eyes. Did he then have a presentiment of his fate? Brave and good man! Illinois sent no nobler man to the field than Lieut.-Col. Edward F. W. Ellis.

CHAPTER VII.

THE DAY BEFORE THE BATTLE.

April 5th, 1862.

Reader, follow me in imagination back into the past. Let your thoughts wander along the spring-decked shore of the Tennessee, girded by dense forests just blossoming into life, until they rest on Shiloh's field, then pause, and take a sweeping glance at the magnificent scene spread out before you. The day is one of the loveliest of spring-time; the golden rays of the sun are gilding the tree-tops with their last expiring light, and reflecting on the camp of the patriot army whose tents so thickly dot the plain. It is a quiet evening—an almost dread silence prevails—a silence which, ere the morning rays of the sun gild the eastern horizon, will be broken by the flash of arms which will make the earth tremble, and the grand old forests echo and re-echo with the crash of artillery, bowing and shivering the giant monarchs of the forest with the fiery blast; but how quiet the scene now! How unconscious are we that the morrow will be ushered in by a blood-red sun and the echoing notes of the deep-toned artillery, and that thousands who are now all unconscious of danger will, ere another sun sets, be sleeping that last long sleep that knows no waking! Thousands of broken home-circles in our land will gather around the family board this day unconscious that their loved ones had laid their lives upon the altar of their country. Many a soldier now, at this quiet evening hour, is writing messages fraught with love and hope to the dear ones at home, or, perchance, they are gathering around the mail-bag while the names are being called, eager to get those welcome messages from home so cheering to a soldier. Now, pass we farther on and we will come to a group who are whiling away the hour by playing a game of euchre, sledge or whist, while others are preparing their evening meal. Others have already eaten and have retired to the shade of some tree and are spinning camp yarns, or perhaps are talking about home and friends. Some are enjoying a game of ball, while others are showing their dexterity by wrestling or jumping. As you wander around camp, you see men engaged in many kinds of amusements.

The vigilant sentinel only is on the lookout to ward off danger and give the camp timely warning of its approach. Soon the martial music of a hundred bands, playing tattoo, breaks the silence, and when these last echoes have floated away on the evening air, the soldier retires to his couch to be awakened by the clash of arms on the morrow.

THE BATTLE.

April 6th.

April 6th and 7th will be remembered by historians as the date of one of the bloodiest battles of modern times. The camp was alarmed Sunday morning, just as the streaks of red began to tinge the eastern sky, by the rapid firing of the pickets, who soon came in with the report that the enemy was marching on us in overwhelming numbers and were even now in sight, as a shower of bullets which fell around too plainly indicated. There was no time to give orders then. It was life or death. The enemy was in camp before it had time to arouse and form a line. Some were shot in their sleep, never knowing what hurt them. Terrible and complete was the surprise.

Our boys fought as only those can fight who are fighting for the right. Rallying amidst a perfect storm of bullets, shot and shell, they tried to form a new line, and as the infuriated enemy, made mad with whisky and gunpowder, hurled themselves against the line, it gradually fell back step by step, forming new and stronger lines and leaving their track strewn with the dead and dying. The onset of the foe was terrific, but instead of the easy victory that had been promised them, they were met with a valor superior to their own, as the cool aim of our boys which strewed the ground with dead, amply testified. Our camp was situated three miles from where the fighting began, and it was not until after sunrise that the tide of battle surged upon us. I heard the distant rattling of musketry and first thought it was something else. I was writing a letter home at the time. But soon the long roll was sounded and then I knew that there was work for us to do. Throwing my unfinished letter to Milton, who was sick, I told him to finish it and tell where I was, then hastily putting on my accoutrements, gun in hand, took my place in the company. In less than five minutes from the time the bugle was sounded, the regiment was on the march to the scene of conflict. Milton, the brave boy, unable to endure the suspense, though so

weak from the effects of fever that he could hardly stand, with
blood now on fire and with artificial strength, followed us to the
field.   No remonstrance of mine or the captain could make him
stay back.   The regiment marched to the fight with drums beating
and colors flying.   I will venture to say that no prouder regiment
stepped to the time of martial music than did the 15th.   There
was no wavering, hesitating or shrinking, but proudly erect they
went forward and filed into the deadly breach.   We had not proceeded far before we met crowds of stragglers skulking to the
rear.   It was a humiliating sight, and our boys heaped curses,
bitter and cutting, on their cowardly heads.   They tried to excuse
their conduct by innumerable excuses, not one of which would
weigh a farthing in this crisis.   Some had received only a slight
scratch and two or three would be supporting him as though his
life depended upon their care.   Reader, do not judge the whole
army by these few sneaking, cowardly things.   There were
enough, yea, too many horrible mutilations to call forth our com-
miseration without bestowing a glance on these wretches.   Long
trains of ambulances now passed us going to the rear, loaded with
the wounded.   We saw two long lines of troops engaged in terrific
fighting—long sheets of fire and smoke from one end of the line to
the other; shot answering shot; charge meeting charge; and the
wild shouts of the combatants at each successive turn of the battle
presented to us a scene terribly sublime.   We halted here to receive orders and to learn in what position we would be placed in
the line.   My eye wandered eagerly and anxiously along the line
of battle, watching the effect of each discharge.   Then it turned to
the 15th, and noted the effect this battle scene had upon them, and
before me I saw pale, determined faces and compressed lips of men
who were resolved to do their duty.   Calmly we conversed of the
scene before us, while not a few saw fit to crack jokes which, despite the occasion, elicited laughter.   I could not join in their
mirth.   The scene before me was too solemn to admit of levity.
It would be difficult to analyze my feelings on this occasion.   To
say that I was perfectly calm and self-possessed would be presum-
ing too much, although, as I then tried to analyze my feelings, I
was not conscious of a tremor.   They seemed more like a deathly
calm.   I knew that I was equal to the task of doing my whole
duty without flinching, but to me, as well as to every other soldier
just before entering the battle, an involuntary awe and dread crept

over me; but if true and brave, these feelings gradually die away in the excitement of the fight until they become almost extinct, unless a sudden reverse throws everything in confusion, then all is terror and excitement.

We soon had a chance to test both of these conditions, but our unlimited confidence in our commanders, Ellis and Goddard, went a great way toward schooling our nerves for the fiery ordeal through which we were about to pass. The clear tones of Colonel Ellis now recalled our wandering minds, and the word, "Forward" was given. The music fell back to the rear, still playing. We marched forward and took our position in line. Just then there was a short lull in the fight. We took our position a little forward of a rise of ground, while a few rods in front, just beyond the brow of a hill, the rebels were effectually concealed from our sight, gathering their energies for a fresh onset. We had, as our support, the 53d Ohio. We had hardly gotten our line formed before the enemy opened on us with grape and canister. At first it fell short of its mark, but nearer and nearer the death-dealing missiles strike, tearing up the earth and filling our eyes with dust. Soon they come crashing through our ranks. We were commanded to lie down. Thick and fast the iron hail comes. Groans reach us as the soldiers, wounded and mangled, crawl to the rear. The emboldened enemy now advanced in solid column, having ten to our one. The 53d Ohio, appalled at the sight, broke and ran without firing a gun and we were left single-handed to contend against these fearful odds. We were now ordered to rise and commence firing. Rapidly and coolly we poured our deadly fire into the advancing column. Now a rebel sergeant, in front of us, performed a brave act worthy of a better cause. He advanced in front of his command and with his own hands planted the rebel flag on a piece of our artillery that they had captured; but this act sealed his doom. He fell, pierced and riddled with bullets. I shot at him, but I hope that it was not my bullet that sealed his eyes in death. The enemy now opened a fire upon us so terrific that our little band seemed likely to be annihilated. Our brave boys were dropping by scores. A ball struck the stock of my musket, shivering it and nearly knocking it from my grasp. Another ball passed through my canteen, while another cut the straps to my haversack. Thick as hailstones the bullets whistled through my hair and around my cheek, still I remained unhurt. The bushes and trees around would writhe, twist and fall before this blast. Early in the action, as Col. Ellis was standing on a log, watching with eager eyes the motions of the enemy, a ball passed through his wrist. Lieut. Smith tied a handkerchief around it and Col. Ellis continued giving his orders as coolly as though nothing had happened, but soon an unerring shot pierced his noble heart, and from this stormy battle his spirit burst its bonds and joined the martyred hosts of liberty in the light of heaven. Soon I saw Maj. Goddard receive his death wound while standing a few feet from me. He had gone to join his compatriot in the spirit-land, and, perchance from their spirit home, they turned and took one long lingering glance at the bloody field and shed bitter tears over the sad fate of so many of our brave boys. Capt. Wayne now came to me and called my attention to a rebel soldier concealed behind a root. He turned, and immediately received his death wound. Lieut. Fred A. Smith was now in command. He was struck by a ball, while standing by my side, and knocked to the ground. As he was falling, he reached his hands out to me for assistance; almost involuntarily I bore him to the rear over the brow of the hill, took his handkerchief and bound up his wound as well as I could, then gave him in charge of Lieut. Bradley, of Company C, who was then passing. I then hastened back to rejoin my company, but what was my astonishment to find not one living member of the 15th regiment. It seems that as soon as Fred was wounded, our boys, to prevent being surrounded and taken prisoners, broke and retreated in disorder and in the tumult, I had not noticed it, so instead of finding our regiment where I left it, I found the ground swarming with rebels. Something within said to me, "This is not a safe place for Lute Barber," and that if I wanted to live to fight another day, I must retreat out of that, and retreat I did, very rapidly too. I cannot say whether I did it in good order or not. To tell the truth, I became slightly confused.

I tried hard to find where the regiment was. Regiment, did I say, no, not regiment, but the broken, disordered fragments of what was once the 15th. Failing in this, I found an Iowa regiment belonging to our division and fought with them until two o'clock P. M. Here I had the satisfaction of seeing the rebels run. Back and forth the tide surged. I had now expended all of my ammunition, and there being a lull in the fight, I determined to again seek for what was left of the 15th regiment. I went to

Gen. Hurlbut and asked where they were and stated the circumstances which separated me from it. He thought that it was down
at the landing, but did not know. He told me that I had better
fall in there for the present. So I did. Gen. Hurlbut was forming a new line, the strongest that had yet been formed, and all
attempts of the enemy to force it back were fruitless. He had a
large number of siege guns planted, which were protected by
heavy works and it was impossible for the enemy to face the fire
of these monsters. In their last attack, they were handsomely
repulsed. Their line was formed within half a mile of the landing.
The enemy had spent their strength and their best efforts could
not move us now. Our cause began to brighten. Gen. Grant had
made every disposition to take the offensive in the morning and
it is my unshaken belief that if Buell had not arrived during the
night, the result would have been the same. During the afternoon the rebel General, A. Sidney Johnson, was killed, and much
of the life of the rebel army went out with his death. He was a
brave man and an able officer. After his death, it was plainly
seen that the rebel army was not handled as skillfully as before
and the remark that Gen. Beauregard made, that he would water
his horse in the Tennessee or in hell, was not realized. The enemy
occupied our camp that night and the thought was not very con-
soling, as all our things were left lying around in the tent in a very
loose manner, which did not look very well to receive company.
I now started out again to look for the regiment, and this time I
had the unspeakable pleasure of being successful. I found them
down at the landing. I don't believe that I ever experienced a
moment of more heartfelt joy than I did when my eye rested on
the 15th, broken and shattered though it was, but with that joy
came a keen sorrow at the thought that so many had perished in
the fight. In the morning we mustered five hundred and fifty
men. Now scarcely two hundred answered to their names.
Company D had only thirteen men out of the fifty that were
mustered in the morning. My comrades supposed that I had
been wounded or taken prisoner, as the last they saw of me was
on the battlefield. I now learned of the movements of the regiment after I became separated from it. The men had rallied
again in camp and were under direction of Charles F. Barber,
adjutant of the regiment. They again took the field, but were
kept in reserve. All our line officers were killed or wounded

excepting three or four. The regiment was now in command of
Captain Kelly. I now learned that Sam Cooper was wounded
severely in the hip and was then in the hospital boat. Rollin was
in the thickest of the fight but passed through unscathed.
Charlie and William also remained unhurt. My mates were
singularly fortunate. Only Sam was hurt. Our regiment camped
that night on the hill by the landing. The night was dark and
stormy. The rain came down in perfect torrents and we had
neither food nor shelter. Through the long dismal night, our rest
was broken by the deep reverberating tones of the guns from the
gunboat which kept up an incessant roar all night. Our thought
anxiously boded on the morrow and tried to pierce the gloom, but
with unwavering faith we believed that to-morrow's sun would see
the broken and disorganized rebel host flying before our victorious
army. The thought that it might be otherwise was perfectly
maddening, and it nerved the men to herculean deeds of valor.

The fire from the gunboats compelled the enemy to move a
portion of their line back during the night. Thus the close of the
first day's fight witnessed the two armies lying within a few rods
of each other, each confident of victory on the morrow. During
the night General Buell crossed over a portion of his army and
marched it to the front. Our success now seemed almost certain.
No one can adequately describe the terrific fighting during the day.
The enemy were perfectly infuriated at our obstinate resistance.
They would mass their strength against the weakest portion of our
line, and then with demoniac yells would hurl themselves against
it, and then for a time the shock of arms would make the earth
tremble. Giant trees would writhe and twist before the iron hail
and come crashing to the ground. The screeching shells, rending
everything before them, cutting huge limbs from the trees, striking the earth and throwing up clouds of dirt, formed a scene of
terrific grandeur. Anon, there was a short lull in the fight and all
was as quiet as the grave. A new disposition of troops is being
made. Soon, simultaneously along the whole line, one terrible
crash of arms follows. It seemed as though the very earth was
opening to swallow up the combatants. The air was black with
fine shot and shell. For an hour this storm of iron hail would
rage. Then its fury would abate and the enemy would prepare
for a fresh onset. Milton stood the ordeal well. I was afraid
that after the excitement of the day was over, a relapse would

come on, but instead, he gained fresh strength. I will now append a list of killed and wounded in Company D, first days' fight:

KILLED.

Captain Harley Wayne, of Union.
Private Thompson Hardy, of Marengo.
Private John Spicer, of Harmony.

WOUNDED.

Lieutenant Fred. A. Smith.
Sergeant M. Schoonmaker, slightly bruised.
Corporal Alonzo Howe, by falling of limb of tree.
Private Morris H. Allen, severely, leg broken.
Private John D. Bliss, severely, mouth and neck.
Private Alvah M. Clark, slightly, shoulder.
Private Thomas T. Gray, slightly, waist.
Private Sam Cooper, severely, thigh.
Private Alfred Dean, severely, left arm.
Private Edward G. Gould, severely, right arm.
Private Joel B. Parker, severely, left shoulder.
Private Newell F. Shapley, severely, through the body.
Private Marshall F. Stephens, severely.
Private Egbert R. Shearer, severely, hip.
Private Charles E. Hotchkiss, mortally, died in hospital.
Private Charles A. Underwood, slightly, in shoulder.
Corporal Eugene A. Wells, mortally, died in hospital.

DESERTED.

George Crumb.

TOTAL.

Killed, three; wounded, seventeen; deserted, one.

April 7th.

The army was astir early Monday morning. In consideration of our disorganized state, we were held in reserve for the greater portion of the day. Company D could only muster thirteen men this morning. We were commanded by Corporal Handy. Lieutenant-Colonel Cam was assigned to command the regiment. As we filed along to our place in line, Gen. Hurlbut gazed on our decimated ranks with watery eyes. The 15th regiment was a favorite of his and in the death of Col. Ellis, Major Goddard, Captains Wayne and Brownell, he mourned the loss of true and tried friends. Gen. Hurlbut had nobly redeemed his reputation. No general on that bloody field handled his troops with more skill or showed greater personal bravery than he. Now the rattling of musketry, increasing in volume every moment, tell us that the ball has been opened by General Grant. The now discouraged rebels begin to yield before our resistless advance. Soon the action

4

became general, and deafening discharges sweep along the whole
line.   Slowly and surely we press them back, our command keeping in sight to be called on as emergency required.   Occasionally
stray shots fall amongst us, inflicting slight damage.   By noon, we
had passed our camp.   Faster and faster the enemy began to yield.
Harder and harder now press on our victorious troops.   The rattling of small arms, the crash of artillery and the screeching of
shells through the air was deafening, but our ears had become
accustomed to the noise and we heeded it not.   The dropping of a
shell in our midst would hardly be noticed.   Occasionally the line
would halt for a few moments and our tired boys would instantly
fall into a doze.   Despite my best efforts to keep awake, I would
at times get drowsy and fall into a fitful slumber.   A heavy battery of Parrott guns was placed in our rear and fired over our
heads.   Even this would fail to arouse us, but when the shouts of
victory from our boys rent the air as the rebs were once more
hurled back, then we would start up and again advance.   About
three o'clock P. M. we received an order which effectually banished
sleep from our eyelids.   We were ordered to the front to prepare
for a charge.   Illinois soldiers were selected to make it.   Soon the
line was formed.   Before us was an open field, skirted on the
farther side by underbrush.   In this brush the rebels lay concealed.
General Grant was here in person to superintend the charge and
as he rode to the front of the line, he was greeted with tremendous
cheers.   Soon the brave McCook rode to the front, drew his sword,
waved it over his head and shouted: "Now give them a touch of
Illinois!   Forward!   Charge!" and with one wild shout, we
sprang forward, making the earth tremble beneath our feet.   The
rebels shrank back dismayed before this charge.   In wild panic
and confusion they broke and ran.   The defeat had now turned
into a perfect rout.   Through woods and swamps, over hills and
through valleys, we pursued the flying foe until sheer exhaustion
compelled us to stop.   The panic-stricken rebels, taking advantage
of our momentary halt, planted a battery to more effectually cover
their retreat.   After a few discharges, they were again compelled
to fly.   The state of the roads and the exhaustion of the troops
obliged us to abandon the pursuit.   Our poor and insufficient
cavalry followed them a short distance.   If we had had good
cavalry, the rebel army would have been completely destroyed.
Some of our boys, who were prisoners at the time, afterwards said

that nothing could exceed the fright of the rebels. Order and discipline were at an end. Thus ended the memorable battle of Shiloh. We now turned our weary steps toward camp, and just as the evening shades began to fall, we reached it. Our camp showed plainly the marks of war. Our tents was riddled by shot and shell and everything was turned upside down. The rebs had stayed there the night before and the uncivil rascals had helped themselves to what they wanted. I could stand in camp and count two hundred dead rebels. There had been a sharp fight on this very ground. Slowly the shades of evening began to fall around us. An unbroken stillness reigned where a short time before echoed the peals of battle. How changed the scene! Out in the darkness lay thousands sleeping their last long sleep. No bugle blast could wake them now. No more will they heed the war cry. The sound of battle will fall unheeded on their ears. They have gone where there is no war. Their tired spirits are at rest.

CHAPTER VIII.

AFTER THE BATTLE.

April 8th, 1862.

The morning succeeding the battle dawned bright and beautiful, and over that bloody field the sun cast its smiling rays upon the faces of the silent sleepers, reflecting its beams upon the bright-green foliage, kissing the dew-drops from the flowrets and tinging all nature with the golden hue of loveliness. What a contrast from the dark picture of the past two days! We busied ourselves that morning putting things to rights and purifying camp. Scarcely was this accomplished before the sharp rattling of musketry caused every soldier to spring for his arms and take his place in line before there was time for orders to be given. We marched out toward the spot from whence the firing proceeded and threw out skirmishers, but to our chagrin, we found that we had been fooled. The alarm was occasioned by the pickets discharging their guns after being relieved. This event, trivial as it was, produced a panic amongst the teamsters. They came rushing in headlong flight to the rear. The din of battle was yet ringing in our ears, and we were easily startled. We now had a painful task before us in burying the dead. In the first place, I sat down and wrote a letter home apprising them of my safety and giving a brief account of the fight. Then I got permission to go and see Samuel. I found him on the Blackhawk and after much difficulty, succeeded in getting on board. I found him cheerful and much better than I expected. His wound, though severe, was not dangerous. Sam was a brave soldier and all who saw him on that day testified to his coolness. I assisted him in every way possible and then uttering a fervent wish for his recovery and safe journey home, I returned to camp. Sam had been a true friend to me and I parted from him with deep regret. During the day our regimental dead were brought in. We dug a long, deep trench near our camp and buried them in one grave.

April 10th.

It was a painful task. Months passed before I recovered from the effects of it. Now we turned our attention to the rebel dead. We noticed that the faces of all of them had turned black. On examination, we found that their canteens contained whisky and gunpowder which was, no doubt, the cause of it. It seems that this had been given to them just before going into battle to make them fight. This was the cause of the rebels fighting so like demons the first day. It took two days to bury all of them. I will not attempt to give much of a description of this battle-field. It was Ft. Donelson on a large scale. I will leave the imagination of the reader to furnish the picture. On one spot of ground, where we generally had our reviews, an artillery duel was fought and the ground was so thickly strewed with dead horses that you could walk nearly all over it on the carcasses. In another place, a ravine, as the rebels were marching up to flank us, a battery was placed at its mouth and it mowed the rebels down in heaps. Almost every spot on that wide-extended field showed some battle mark. The official report of Grant showed upwards of thirteen thousand killed, wounded and prisoners. Nearly all of General Prentiss' division, with himself, were taken prisoners. Lew Wallace's division suffered the least. He was at Crump Landing when the fight began and did not arrive in season to participate in the first day's fight. The losses of the other divisions were about equal. Only one regiment in the fight showed a greater proportion of killed and wounded than the 15th. Our loss footed up two hundred and fifty-two, killed and wounded, and there was only one man but what was accounted for. Gen. Hurlbut issued a very complimentary order to us. We had in our camp about thirty wounded prisoners, and they received every attention from us that we could bestow. They were Louisiana troops and gloried in the name of "Louisiana Tigers." Judging from their looks and the arms they carried, they did not belie the name.

April 20th.

Colonel Turner now arrived and assumed command of the regiment. He seemed to be very much affected at the loss our regiment sustained, and, in a speech that he made to us, he complimented us highly, but never mentioned the brave Ellis. This omission to do justice to a brave man brought the Colonel more into disfavor than ever. We now began to prepare for an active campaign. We were reviewed and we knew that the ball would open again soon. Gen. Pope's army, the heroes of Island No. Ten, had now arrived, and, with Buell's army, our numbers were increased to one hundred thousand men. The enemy was also receiving large re-inforcements and were busily fortifying at Corinth.

April 21st.

Everything betokened an active and bloody campaign. Gen. Halleck, Commander of the Department, now arrived and assumed command in person. In the meantime important changes had taken place in our Company. Fred, now promoted to Captain, had gone home, and Col. Turner had nominated a private for the office of 2nd Lieutenant, who was on detached duty and was not with the regiment in the fight. Our indignation knew no bounds at this gross outrage. Our new Lieutenant's authority was respected just about as much as we respected him. We knew how he had figured around headquarters to obtain the position, and the boys could hardly keep their hands off from him. Our Captain, hearing how matters stood, came back long before his wound was healed. Sergeant Waldock was the one entitled to the position.

April 22d.

I was agreeably surprised one morning when I awoke to find Uncle Washington in my tent. My friends had sent him down to see if anything was needed. Although his services were not required, his company was very acceptable. He stayed a couple of weeks with us and then returned home. The roads were in an awful condition at this time and it was impossible for the army to move. If there was a prospect of an immediate battle, Uncle Wash was to stay until it was over.

May 1st.

We left Pittsburgh Landing about the 1st of May. We were both glad and sorry to leave a place where had been both pleasing and painful associations. We marched five miles the first day, but it took all day, the roads were so bad. We halted for several days. During the time, we drew new Enfield muskets. The 53rd Illinois was here added to our brigade. We were called out one morning to prepare for a fight. We formed a line but the enemy did not make its appearance. It was probably a scouting party of rebel cavalry.

May 4th.

We kept hitching along now from one-fourth to two miles a day, generally marching it in the evening. Before going to rest we built earth-works in front of the regiment. Each regiment was required to do this before going into camp. Two hours was sufficient for us to throw up breast-works that would stand the test of light artillery. We were required to be up at three o'clock A. M. and form in line for battle and remain with accoutrements on until daylight. The General usually rode along the lines every morning, accompanied by his staff. General Halleck made a poor appearance as a military man. He usually wore a slouched hat, pulled low down over his eyebrows. His general appearance was ungainly and unprepossessing.

May 8th.

When the army came to a strong position, they would throw up strong works, irregular in shape, and commanding every possible position. These fortifications were considered secure places to fall back upon in case of disaster. The whole intervening space between us and the Landing was one continual series of fortifications. General Halleck was one of those old fogy commanders with more caution than spirit. We will admit that the enemy had taught us to respect their bravery, but with the army that Halleck had, he should have marched right up to their stronghold and sat down before it and expended labor in besieging the place instead of so much in the rear to provide for contingencies.

May 10th.

Gen. Beauregard knew what kind of a man he had to deal with and shaped his plans so as to completely fool Halleck. If Sherman, Grant or Thomas had had command of the army, Beauregard would not have gotten away as slickly as he did. The nearer we approached to the enemy, the more cautious he was— so cautious, that it seemed more like cowardice than prudence.

May 12th.

We got very poor water now and the consequence was that some of the boys were taken sick. Charlie and myself amongst the number. Milton had cut his foot badly and he was put on the sick list. A sick and convalescent camp was established and we three were left behind, much to our disappointment. The army had got so far advanced that there was skirmishing daily. Our situation in our sick camp was anything but pleasant. Those whose business it was to draw rations for us, sold half of them, thus making money out of sick men's necessities, but we had the satisfaction of seeing some of them brought to grief by this outrage.

May 14th.

As Milton and Charlie were wandering away from camp one day, they discovered where a dairy was kept. Our mess, five in number, conceived the idea of having new milk added to our scanty fare, so three of us arose before daylight, went out and milked and got back to camp before it was astir, thus keeping others off the scent. We hid our milk after we brought it into camp. After a few days the owners of the dairy discovered that someone had kindly milked their cows for them, so they laid in watch for us one night and caught us at it. High words followed but they knew better than to meddle with us. After that, they would set their dogs on us, but as we went armed, a few shots put a quietus on them. Milk we wanted and milk we would have. We were sick and it was a military necessity and they had to submit.

May 16th.

We were now getting nearly well and requested the doctor to send us to the front but did not succeed at first. We had one of those ignoramuses for a doctor that was a disgrace to the profession. He used quinine in powder or pills for all diseases from a fever down to a sore finger—in fact, he considered it a panacea for all the ills that flesh is heir to. I believe that he did have a little blue mass and calomel which he gave to persons in a dying condition to make them die easier. You need not look incredulous, reader, we had just such men for doctors in the army. One day, our regimental teams came along, having been back for rations. We hastily gathered our things together and "slyed" off and that night we slept in camp. We were now within four miles from Corinth and one-half mile from the enemy's lines. Skirmishing was going on all the time. One-half the company was on picket every day. The rest helped fortify camp. There was sharp fighting at times, but the enemy seemed to avoid a general engagement. Pope was pitching in very lively on the left. The boys had a lively time on picket. There was just fighting enough to make it interesting.

May 18th.

The picket lines of the two opposing armies were within hearing distance, but as each side managed to keep pretty well concealed, the firing did but little damage, although occasionally one would get wounded. The night watch was the more dreary and dangerous.

We knew not how many secret foes were lurking around to take advantage of every movement. There were no lights to penetrate the gloom and all of our conversation was carried on in a whisper. The videttes who were placed in advance had a most trying and responsible position. It was on such occasions that a soldier's thoughts would wander back to home and friends and in the dread silence, his imagination would weave bright pictures of fancy for the future. Thus between watching and waiting, the time passed until the cautious tread of the relief smote on his listening ear and then another dreamer would take his place.

May 20th.

My health was so far improved now that I reported for duty. Capt. Smith had gotten back and the company now began to assume its old buoyant spirits. There was a log house in front of our picket line and each side had tried to hold possession of it, so one day the General thought that he would decide the matter. The rebels occupied it at the time.

May 22d.

A large force of our men went and drove the rebels out. In return, the rebels soon returned with large re-inforcements and our boys were compelled to give it up again. Then we had the whole division in line, supported by several batteries, and charged the rebels and again they were compelled to give way. This time they did not renew their attempt to take it as it would likely have brought on a general engagement. The next day we moved our lines forward again, but we had hard fighting. The enemy contested every inch of the ground.

May 26th.

We were now in hearing of the rebel camp. We could plainly hear the drums beating, the heavy lumbering of the cars as they came into Corinth. Matters seemed to be approaching a crisis. We advanced our lines a little every day and the enemy slowly and sullenly fell back. We could hear the cars arriving and departing rapidly. It was evident that the rebs were either receiving large re-inforcements or were evacuating the place. The latter seemed the most plausible to us. But still Halleck with that extreme cautiousness, crept slowly up and allowed the wily foe to slip from his grasp. The enemy kept up a heavy skirmish line to make it appear that they were still there in strength, but subsequent events showed that they were rapidly evacuating at this time. We had

now begun to suffer for want of water and it became absolutely
necessary for the army to move forward where they could get
water or retreat. The latter was not to be thought of. We were
furnished one-half gill of whisky a day. I mixed it with my drinking water, thus partially neutralizing its bad effects. General Pope
was now thundering for admittance into the stronghold of
Corinth.

May 27th.

Finally on the 27th of May, after sharp skirmishing, we established our line in sight of the enemy's outer works. We could see
that they were strongly surrounded by a heavy abattis and
mounted some heavy guns though afterwards some of them proved
to be wooden ones. We now set to work to fortify our position,
the enemy the meanwhile shelling us, causing us considerable
annoyance, yet, we perseveringly kept at work and soon had a
formidable line of earth-works in front of us. Our regiment was
detailed to support a six-pounder gun rifled battery. The enemy
now commenced throwing grape and canister at us. A charge
struck the ground in front of us, throwing the dirt in our faces;
another passed over our heads, but another dropped in dangerous
proximity to us, and some of the boys were wounded. In the
meantime, there was sharp fighting on the skirmish line. Companies A and B were out. One from Company B was killed. The
rebels suddenly broke cover and charged our men, yelling like
demons. Our skirmishers were driven in, but in good order. Our
battery had placed their guns in position and as soon as the rebels
were in range, six pieces simultaneously opened upon them. The
effect was awful. Some of the shells dropped in their very midst
and men were blown into atoms. The rebels suddenly came to a
halt, turned and fled in dismay in every direction except toward
us. The concussion of the discharge was terrific. We were lying
down, but the jar fairly raised us off the ground. The rifled gun
had a sharp ringing sound which jarred severely on the nerves.
Simultaneous with the discharge, we all rose up to note its effect.
It was all that we could wish. This was the last effort that the
rebels made on our part of the line. Pope kept up a continuous
cannonading all night. We fell back two or three miles and went
into camp and were relieved by another division.

May 28th.

Early next morning we received ten months' pay, and we

immediately started for the front again. On our way there we learned that the enemy had evacuated and that our forces held possession of the place. Soon we heard of a terrible fight in Virginia and that McClellan was defeated. The bulk of Beauregard's army was in the fight, so the campaign against Corinth was a drawn game. The rebels gained the battle in Virginia but lost possession of the stronghold of Corinth. We entered the place about ten o'clock. The rebels had destroyed everything they did not take with them. Huge piles of provision were strewed around, thus confuting the statement that the rebel army was starving. We saw where some of their magazines were that were blown up during the night. Corinth is a small city of about two thousand inhabitants and at this time was a place of considerable military importance, being the junction of the Charleston & Memphis and Mobile & Ohio railroads. The town wore a desolate looking aspect. The fire from our heavy siege-guns had driven all the inhabitants out. Some of our shots had set the depot on fire and it was a smoldering mass of ruins. Several engines and a large number of cars were burnt also. We went into camp about one mile south of Corinth.

June 1st.

Gen. Pope commenced a vigorous pursuit of the enemy on the line of the Mobile & Ohio railroad, but after a few days returned, with poor success. The rebels had destroyed all the bridges in their retreat. We lay in camp a few days and then took up our march on the line of the Charleston & Memphis railway. It was generally supposed that we were going to Grand Junction, a station at the junction of the Charleston & Memphis railway and Charleston & Mississippi railroad, where it was reported that a large force of the rebels were fortifying. This place is forty-seven miles from Corinth and fifty-three from Memphis. We marched one day and went into camp, where we remained over a week, building bridges and scouting. We finally resumed our march and the second day we passed Grand Junction and camped one-half mile beyond, in the wood, between Grand Junction and Lagrange.

June 12th.

We lay in camp here some time. It was blackberry season and they were very plentiful around our camp and the boys just feasted on them. The tedium of our camp life was now relieved by an order to be ready to march by daylight with three days'

cooked rations in our haversacks. Our destination was Holly
Springs, a beautiful city just across the State line in Mississippi.
It was reported that the rebels were here in force. The second
day at noon, we halted for rest and refreshments on the Coldwater, six miles from Holly Springs. Our march had been so
rapid that a number of the boys gave out, William and myself
amongst the number. It was the first time in one and one-half
years' hard service that my feet failed me. Now they were raw
and blistered.

June 16th.

We were left here to recruit. We also answered the purpose
of rear guard. Near our camp was a rank old rebel planter. He
was very kind and affable while the army was there and one
would think, to hear him talk, that he was one of the best Union
men in the South. He said that the rebels had taken nearly all
of his personal property and he prevailed on the General to grant
him a safe guard, but no sooner had the army left than his sneaking, traitorous disposition showed itself. Two of our boys, nearly
worn out, stopped at his house and requested a drink of water,
which he refused, and then commenced abusing them. He did
not know that we were camped just across the river. When the
boys told us how they had been used, we vowed to have revenge.
Seeing a fine drove of hogs near by and naturally supposing them to
be his, the boys went in and commenced killing them. The old
rebel soon saw what was up and in a towering rage came down to
stop it, but gun in hand, I stepped upon the bridge and halted
him and kept him there until the boys had got what fresh pork
they wanted and then I let the old fool go. He was livid with
rage. The next evening the command returned to Coldwater.
The rebels had evacuated the place the day before and pursuit was
deemed impracticable. We got a good joke on Milton here.
Just before the army started back, he took some canteens and
went for water and before he got back the army had left. To
lighten his load, he gave the canteens to a cavalryman to carry
and he never saw them again. We boys knew better than to loan
or give anything to a cavalryman unless he was a friend. It
taught Milt a lesson.

June 21st.

We suffered considerable on this march for want of water. We
arrived back in our old camp three and one-half days after we

left it, marching sixty miles during the time. We did not remain
here in camp long but moved one and one-half miles below Lagrange. This was a very pleasant village and in time of peace
contained fifteen hundred inhabitants. The weather now was
very hot and the dull monotony of camp life began to be quite
irksome.

June 30th.

Picking blackberries was an agreeable pastime and to this
luxury we added sweet potatoes. The boys had to get the latter
on the sly as General Veatch had forbidden them to forage for
them unless under proper authority. Some of the boys paid little
heed to this order. Two from my mess were out one day and
found where there was a large pile of them. They loaded themselves down with them and started for camp, but in order to elude
the picket and get into camp, they had to pass the General's headquarters, and in doing so, got caught. Their potatoes were confiscated and they put under guard. The guard proved to be a
negligent fellow and they succeeded in slipping away for a few
minutes and took their potatoes to camp. Then spying a nice lot
that the General had laid up for his own use, they stole every one
of them and took them to camp. They did this, they said, in
revenge for being arrested, but they went back to their old place
and the stupid guard never knew but what they had been there all
the time. After awhile the General called them up and gave them
a good talking to for disobeying orders. They affected to be
very penitent, promised to be good soldiers in the future, and so
he let them off, but I imagine that if he had known that the rogues
had stolen all his "taters," they would not have gotten off so
easily. The boys were highly elated with their adventure.

July 1st.

On July 1st we received orders to make another descent upon
Holly Springs. The boys received the order in no enviable frame
of mind. The weather was extremely hot and there was a great
scarcity of water on the route. After the first six miles we had to
travel fifteen miles before we came to a pure stream of water;
besides, we had little hopes of our march amounting to anything,
and like its predecessor, proving a weary and fruitless one.

July 3d.

On the 3d we arrived at Coldwater and went into camp. Gen.
Lauman, who now commanded the division, sent forward a recon-

noitering party which returned and reported no enemy near. We
camped on an old cotton field. We were without tents and a
heavy storm coming on, added greatly to our discomfort. We
were also short of rations. William, Rollin, Milton and myself
got permission to go out in the country. We soon made a descent
upon a large plantation and came down upon the proprietor for
dinner, and he knew better than to refuse us. Hungry soldiers
will not stand upon ceremony when their inner man is constantly
crying "Cupboard." Soon we had the satisfaction of sitting down
to a very good meal, and our host who desired to propitiate us,
entertained us by telling stories. He told us that the owner of
the plantation we were on lived in Holly Springs in grand style,
and was a rank rebel. He entrusted the management of his large
estates to an overseer, and he, our host, was acting in that capacity
now. To use his own words, he was a person of considerable
importance. After awhile he brought out some delicious beer
made of corn and molasses. As some of my readers may never
have heard of this kind of beverage, I will state the modus
operandi of making it. To one barrel of corn add four gallons of
molasses mixed with water, and let it ferment until ready for use.
We filled our canteens with it and returned to camp satisfied with
our expedition. On our way back, we marked a large flock of
turkeys at a plantation, which we designed should be our property.
So, when night had spread her mantle over the earth, we silently
crept forth to secure our prize, but to our amazement, we found
that the General had posted a large safeguard over the premises
and we had to give up our undertaking. I am not one to justify
this indiscriminate foraging, but I do think that it was a burning
shame for our General to post safeguards over rebels' property,
thus depriving the soldiers of what justly belonged to them, and
the moment that our backs were turned, these men that our
bayonets had protected would lay in ambush to waylay our tired-
out soldiers who could not keep up with the command. This I
know to be so.

July 4th.

The glorious old Fourth was now upon us, and the boys chafed
and fretted not a little to know that they were where they could
not celebrate the day as became Americans, but for the sake of
amusement, a wrestling match was gotten up in our brigade, and
the champions of each regiment were placed in the ring. After a

long contested struggle, in which the champions on both sides showed great dexterity and skill, the 15th bore off the palm. The victor was Fred Kellogg, of Company H, a slight, active fellow, weighing only one hundred and thirty-nine pounds. Just after dinner the camp was suddenly startled by the cavalry coming in pell-mell with the report that the enemy were advancing in force. We were in line of battle and under arms in less time than it takes me to write an account of it. A skirmish line was immediately thrown out. Soon the cause of alarm became apparent. One of our scouting parties was returning and our timid cavalry supposed them to be rebels and were scared out of their wits. Our contempt for the cavalry had been great, but now it knew no bounds and the crest-fallen cavalrymen had to submit to our satire and jokes which were unsparing and not few. On the evening of the Fourth, we started on our return. I now saw the effect the want of tobacco had on tobacco chewers. The men had gotten'out and it could not be gotten for love or money. It was really pitiful to see the suffering occasioned by the want of it. I saw soldiers offer five hundred dollars for one chew. I thanked fate that I had never used the noxious weed. On the third day we were back in our old camp, and the boys were soon up to their old tricks.

July 6th.

Soon we were ordered to Balls Bridge to guard that. Only the 15th was included in the order. We had a fine camp here. The duty was light and as we were just outside the main army, we had a better chance to forage. I was detailed to go out one day with a forage train, and a squad of us, in charge of Captain Kinyon, was left at a crossing to guard against the approach of the enemy in that direction. Near us was a large farm-house, situated back in the fields. The captain went out that way to reconnoiter. He was gone a long time—so long that we became alarmed for his safety. Several of us went out to see what was the matter. As we approached the house we noticed several horses standing near, and we supposed that the rebel cavalry had taken him prisoner; so we made immediate preparations to attack them. We crept up cautiously toward the house, and when near we made a charge, but, to our chagrin, we found that our supposed rebel cavalry was only several horses standing in the yard, but we found that the captain was indeed a prisoner, captured by the bright eyes and handsome face of a young miss whom we found lecturing him

soundly on his Yankee principles, while the captain replied in play-
ful good humor.   When we broke in upon them they both seemed
surprised.   When I told the captain what we came for, he laughed,
and we joked him considerable about his heart being captured by
a rebel miss.

CHAPTER IX.

1862.

The City of Memphis was captured on the 6th of June by our gallant naval fleet under Com. Foote, after a sharp fight with the rebel navy in front of the city. Jeff Thompson was in command of the rebels and from the portico of the Gayoso House conducted the fight. So confident was he of victory that he invited the prominent citizens to take their position at the Gayoso House to see the Yankees run. Our navy soon made its preparations. The rams, under command of Ellet, steamed rapidly down the river and made direct for the rebel fleet. The rebels tried to evade the shock but it was useless. Their ships were struck by the ram fleet and instantly sunk, while the gunboats steamed up alongside and poured broadside after broadside into the enemy's fleet, and in less than an hour the rebel fleet was annihilated. Then, by way of compliment, a shell was thrown at the crowd of spectators on the house. They did not wait for a second compliment. They thought "discretion the better part of valor" and took to their heels, Jeff amongst the number. So the rebs had the satisfaction of seeing the Yankees run, but it was close to the flying heels of the chivalry. Our fleet sustained little damage. Four of the rebel boats were sunk, the Beauregard and Van Dorn, in shallow water. Our forces took possession of the city and the glorious old stars and stripes were soon floating where the rebel rag was.

July 16th.

On the 16th of July we were ordered to prepare to march, our destination being Memphis. The sick and surplus baggage were sent around by way of Columbus on railroad and river. This march was very severe on the troops. The heat was intense and water very scarce, and the dust nearly suffocated us. The 19th of July was the hottest day we had yet experienced. The army moved very slowly, resting ten minutes every half hour, in the shade, when we could find it, but notwithstanding, scores of men would drop down, some dying instantly, other so far gone as not to be able to move. It was a common sight that day to see dead soldiers by the roadside. I came very near going under, but by exerting every nerve I managed to get along, but it injured me.

5

The next day, when within but six miles of the city, I had a touch of sunstroke. The doctor was near by and put me in an ambulance, so I did not experience its worst effects. The army halted when within a few miles of the city to clean up as much as possible, so as to make as decent an appearance as they could, while passing through.

July 20th.

A large number of the boys had become so immodest as not to care for appearances. Indeed, the whole army was in a deplorable condition for want of clothing. If a soldier had a sound seat in his pants, it was immediately noticed, it being an exception to the general rule, and not a few of the soldiers marched through the city with pocket handkerchiefs hanging out behind, but despite our appearance, we were greeted with cheers and laughter. Many a fair damsel came out to see us pass, and if they wondered at the manner in which some carried their handkerchiefs, they did not say much, but occasionally we could see a smile lurking around their dimpled cheeks as they noticed some who were more conspicuous than others. The boys felt rather proud of their rags. It caused so much notice to be taken of them. We went into camp one and one-half miles south of the city. We found all our sick here who went around by water, except Milton—but more of him soon.

I will now relate a trick that three members of Company D played on the secesh in order to get good living and lodging. They left the company and went in advance of the army twenty or thirty miles. Two of them played rebel soldiers, while the third they held as federal prisoner. They stopped at the most prominent rebel houses on the route, where they were received with open arms and furnished the best that the houses afforded. So well did they play their game that they were not even suspected; but the boys were brought to grief when they rejoined the company, by being held in durance vile for leaving the company without permission; but as their punishment was so much lighter than the good they experienced by the offense, they submitted graciously.

July 21st.

The first thing we did after being settled in camp, was to draw clothing and then Gen. Hurlbut, in consideration of our having so long been deprived of the luxuries and associations of civilization, granted five passes a day from each company to go to the city, said pass lasting twenty-four hours, to be returned to division head-quarters when the holder returned. If he failed, he was put under arrest. Each soldier was required to go armed with a bayonet or revolver. The rebel citizens were very violent yet, and the soldiers would not brook insult or hear our flag spoken lightly of. Some of the boys became so impatient they could not wait the slow process of passes, but would steal away and have a spree and then pay the penalty. The evil disposed now began to plunge into all kinds of dissipation, frequenting drinking saloons and other places of infamous resort. If a soldier came back before the expiration of his pass, he was hooted at and made the laughing stock of his company. William and I waited until the last before we accepted a pass, although we could have had one at any time. Some of the boys dogged our steps to see where we would spend the night. We were conscious that we were watched and we took measures that completely fooled them.

August 6th.

We were considered by all the company to be perfect models of propriety and morality, and some were very anxious to detect something improper in our actions so as to get a laugh on us, but we were determined to give them no such opportunity, and, to this day, very few know where we spent the evening or where we passed the time. For the benefit of my readers, I will tell them. We spent the day strolling around the city seeing what was to be seen. In the evening we went to hear the Campbell Minstrels perform, after which we repaired to a lumber yard and, having found a good place, stowed ourselves away for the night. When we got back to camp, all efforts to find where we stayed proved unavailing.

I now began to be considerably alarmed about Milton. No one had seen or heard of him since he took the cars at Lagrange, and as more than three weeks had passed since then, I had almost given him up as lost. I supposed that he had got off the cars and had strayed away so far that he got captured or killed. I informed his folks of my fears, at the same time promising to use my utmost endeavors to find where he was or what was his fate. Milton, though a little wayward at times, was a boy of noble qualities, and feelings of friendship as well as duty, prompted me to take an interest in his welfare. We inquired of the post-surgeon at Columbus if any such man had been there, but we did not receive any answer. Mr. Mackey's folks wrote to me frequently and manifested great anxiety concerning him.

August 12th.

But our anxiety was relieved one day by Milton's shining, chubby face, sparkling all over with mirth, presenting itself to us. He had a bundle of newspapers under his arm, as usual, peddling. He was without coat or vest, shirt-sleeves rolled up, collar turned under, and, to use a camp phrase, "looked rather seedy." He stalked in amongst us, grinning and joking as though nothing had happened. Of course, we were all glad to see him. He soon told us his story. It seems that he was taken quite sick in the cars and crawled into one of the baggage-cars and lay down. When he arrived at Columbus he was nearly helpless. The other boys, not knowing where he was, went on and left him. He was taken to the hospital and cared for, but had a run of fever. When he was convalescent he wrote to me, but I never received the letter. He said that he wrote to his folks and they did not get the letter until after they learned of his safety by way of me. As soon as he was able, he had gone to cooking in the hospital. He said he hated to leave it as he was having first-rate times and was living high.

We now shifted camp to a more eligible situation, on a high bluff by the river; opposite from camp the bed of the river made an abrupt bend, running west for several miles and then gradually resuming its natural course. A small channel kept straight on and joined the other miles below, forming a beautiful island, which was the favorite resort of the boys. Plenty of melons, tomatoes and other vegetables grew there and nearly every day some of us would go over and get a fresh supply. 'Neath the shade of a large tree overhanging the bluff was a favorite resort of mine. I have sat there for hours in the heat of the day and in the twilight hours, watching the noble steamers plowing the dancing waves of the Father of Waters. From that spot we had a splendid view of the river for miles each way. Closely hugging the Arkansas shore was the rebel gunboat, Beauregard, about half submerged in water. A little above and farther in the stream was the Van Dorn.

August 20th.

We were situated now so as to enjoy ourselves and we hoped to pass the short summer months in quiet and repose. Our duty

was light.   Col. Turner now undertook to put the regiment
through a course of drill, but he made such bungling work of it
that he soon became the laughing stock of the whole regiment.
This galled his proud spirit deeply.   There were plenty of privates
who could beat him manoeuvering the regiment.   Capt. Rogers
had been promoted to Lieutenant-Colonel and Raney to Major.   We
now made quite an improvement in our camp by raising the tents
about four feet from the ground and making sleeping bunks.
This arrangement made it cool and nice.   Every morning before
the sun rose I used to get up and go down to the river and bathe,
and hundreds did the same.   A good many waited until the heat
of the day and then they would stay in the water for hours.   The
consequence was that many were taken sick.   Col. Turner issued
an order regulating the hours of bathing, but the boys paid little
attention to it and several were drowned.   The hours passed
swiftly and pleasantly by.   We drew the best kind of rations and
plenty of them.   To these we added extras, such as hens' eggs,
potatoes, fresh fish, etc., etc.   There was not a meal but what
some of these articles were in.   We saved enough of our regular
rations by selling them to nearly buy all of these things.   So con-
tented were we that we almost wished we might spend the rest of
our time here, but for the good of the regiment, it was necessary
that it should move.   Too many of the boys were becoming too
dissipated to attend to their ordinary duties.   So foul had the
pestilential breath of the city become that decent ladies were not
seen on the streets.   The city itself was beautiful but it harbored
more vice and was more steeped in degradation and filth than any
city I had yet seen, but we will draw a veil over this scene.   At
some other time I will write more about the City of Memphis.

August 25th.

We used to make frequent excursions over into Arkansas.   On
one of these occasions, Roll and his comrade came across two
darkies flying for their lives and struggling for their freedom.
Panting and breathless, they plunged into the river just as their
pursuers with their bloodhounds appeared upon the shore.   Fortunately the arrival of Rollin and his comrade put a stop to all
further proceedings.   Seizing one of the shotguns which the
darkies carried, Rollin fired at the bloodhounds and they went
howling back, and their masters, realizing the state of things,
thought "discretion the better part of valor" and fled in haste.

The delighted darkies were overjoyed at their deliverance. One had traveled all the way from Texas, traveling nights and hiding day-times. My dear old friend, Samuel Cooper, now came back to us, but he was looking quite feeble. He soon had to go to the hospital and did not leave it until he received his discharge. Samuel was a good soldier and a man of inflexible integrity and moral worth and the company lost one of its best members when he left. My correspondence now had become quite voluminous and I occupied a good deal of my time in answering letters

August 31st.

My health was quite poor now. William was also quite feeble. A great number of the boys were sick. Near our picket line was a large farm house where a dairy was kept.

It was my usual custom to go there for my meals when on picket and get fresh milk. We also had plenty of fruit. Peaches were just in their prime. Under this diet, I soon recovered my usual health. There are a great many large dairies around Memphis. The country is adapted to grazing. The soil is fertile and the general appearance of the country splendid. There were some almost palatial residences.

September 6th.

Our division was now reviewed. It marched through the principal streets and made an imposing and splendid appearance. Our quiet dream of repose was now broken up by orders to prepare to march. The enemy was concentrating a large army at Davis Mills, near Lagrange. We were ordered to Bolivar on the Columbus railroad. Soon the earth echoed again to the tramp of the fourth division. There was work for us ahead, and with determined spirits we pressed forward. Frequent reconnoissances were made.

September 10th.

Our march lay through a swampy country, threaded by muddy creeks and rivers. The rebels had destroyed most of the bridges, hence our progress was very slow. We were obliged to take a circuitous route to avoid the enemy, who was liable to pounce upon us in overwhelming numbers any day. Guerrillas lurked in our track, picking up stragglers. Lon Howe and Emory Hiner of our company were captured within one mile of camp.

September 15th.

As we approached Bolivar, the country became more open and

beautiful. We found Bolivar to be a fine looking village of two
thousand or more inhabitants, surrounded by a fertile country,
watered by the Hatchie river which flows within one mile of that
city. We found the 17th Illinois Volunteers here, our old companions in arms at Alton. We stayed here one night, then we
went to Dunlap Springs, five miles from Bolivar. There had been
a fierce cavalry fight here and Col. Hogg left a glorious record to
his country. He fell while leading a saber charge on the rebel
cavalry. A hospital was situated here so that the people could
enjoy the medicinal properties of the Springs. These Springs
were famous, and hundreds of persons made a journey here yearly
to receive the benefits of their life-giving power. The grounds
were tastefully laid out, being dotted with fine covered arbors and
shady walks. There were several springs, and it is a curious fact
that no two springs had the same medicinal properties.

September 20th.

We supposed that this was to be our permanent camp and we
went to work accordingly to fix it up, but the very next day we
were ordered back to Bolivar, as it was not considered safe for so
small a command to be so isolated from the main army. We went
into camp in the suburbs of the town and went to doing provost
guard duty. This was very heavy and it required all the men
that were able for duty. Some of the most prominent southerners
had lived here. There was a splendid cemetery, and on some of the
monuments were carved the names of prominent men, amongst
which was that of James K. Polk. The ravages of war had dealt
lightly with this place. Merchants still continued to trade and
other branches of business were still open. Our 1st Lieutenant,
Shapley, now resigned and there was an exciting contest for the
vacancy. The aspirants for the position were 1st Sergeant Mike
Schoonmaker, and 2d Lieutenant John Waldock. We were all
well aware that Mike would be the choice of the company. It
was well-known that I would cast my vote for Waldock. Not
because I did not like Mike, but because I thought it rightly
belonged to Waldock. Mike received all the votes but six, but
notwithstanding, Gov. Yates gave the position to Waldock. The
same day the non-commission ranks were filled up and I was surprised to find my name heading the list of newly-appointed corporals. Lieut. Waldock had before asked me if I would accept of a
corporalship. The captain wanted him to recommend one. I told

him that I did not desire it and so I supposed that the matter was settled. The greatest objection that the boys had to Waldock was on account of his John Bull proclivities, he being an Englishman. We were now relieved of provost duty and we removed our camp one and a half miles out of town into a cotton field. We went to work in good earnest, fortifying. An attack on Bolivar was strongly apprehended. We made frequent reconnoissances. On one of the occasions, a portion of our command came upon some rebels and a sharp skirmish ensued. Our troops fell back to our fortifications and the enemy made no further demonstrations. Soon after a body of our troops surprised and captured four hundred rebels. We now had battalion drill every day. We were reviewed several times by Veatch and Hurlbut.

September 21st.

Our picket duty was quite heavy. Our regiment had a certain place to picket and the companies took turns. It required two companies a day. About this time, a little twelve-year old boy ran away from his rebel uncle and joined us. He was a bright and staunch union boy. He remained with us all through the war. His name was George King.

CHAPTER X.

October 3d.

On the 3d of October, we were ordered to march in light marching order with no train except an ammunition and ambulance
train. It was very evident that we were going on a forced march
and that something of unusual moment was afoot. To our division
was added the 12th Michigan and 68th Ohio Infantry regiments,
making in all a fighting force of a little less than four thousand
men. General Hurlbut starting in command of the expedition.
Veatch and Lauman were his brigade commanders. Bolton and
Burnap commanded the artillery. We marched twenty-eight miles
the first day and camped near the Hatchie river. Tired out, we soon
went to rest, little dreaming of the events to be enacted in the
morning. If we had known then that on the morrow we would
meet the combined armies of Price and Van Dorn, numbering
twenty-five thousand strong, our rest might not have been so
sweet.

October 4th.

Just as the streaks of day began to tinge the east, we were on
the move. We had not proceeded far before we met the rebel
picket. After a slight skirmish, they hastily retreated. Our
brigade was immediately deployed in line of battle and slowly and
steadily advanced, our skirmishers feeling our way for us. The
enemy was prepared to receive us. They were strongly posted
along the river to dispute our passage. Soon the shells were scream-
ing through the air, bursting over our heads. We rushed like the
speed of the wind to the high hill beyond and soon the crest was
gained. The enemy in rapid succession was pouring in their shot
and shell, but they generally flew wide of the mark, passing over
our heads. Soon Bolton and Burnap planted their artillery on the
crest of the hill and its hoarse notes replied to the rebel thunder.
For fifteen minutes a furious cannonading was kept up. With
rapid precision and deadly aim, our well-trained battery men
poured in their death-dealing charges upon the enemy. Gradually
their fire slackened as one after another their guns were dis-
mounted and most of their horses slain. During a temporary lull

in the fight, the second brigade was ordered forward, marching in echelon, with the 14th Illinois in advance. We swept across the field toward the river. This was a thrilling military sight, such as one seldom sees. With colors flying, with well-dressed ranks and measured tread our gallant lines moved on. There was no wavering, no shrinking back; but as calmly as on dress parade or review, we moved forward. Our firm, undaunted bearing struck terror to the hearts of the enemy. After a few irregular volleys, they broke and ran. We poured in our fire at short range and with a fierce yell rushed forward to the charge. Some threw down their arms and plunged into the river and escaped to the other side. Some were drowned while attempting to cross. Some threw themselves before us and plead for mercy. Yes, the boasted Southern chivalry knelt at the feet of the despised Northern mud-sills and plead for mercy. A guard was detailed to take them to the rear and we again moved on.

We now had a very difficult and dangerous task to accomplish. On one narrow bridge, in face of a terrible fire of grape and canister with which the rebels were raking it, our troops were to cross and form on the other side. Maj.-Gen. E. O. C. Ord had arrived on the ground and took command and he, being ignorant of the nature of the ground on the other side, got the troops mixed up and thrown into confusion. At this point the river makes an abrupt bend and the regiments were ordered to cross and form on each side of the road, but the bend in the river prevented them forming on the right. Gen. Ord was now wounded and taken off from the field and Gen. Hurlbut was again in command and he, understanding the situation, ordered the troops to deploy to the left. We were the third regiment to cross. The 53d Ohio preceded us but being met by a withering volley of grape and canister, they fell back in some confusion. Our regiment was then ordered to cross. We trailed arms and at a double quick we swept across the bridge without the loss of a man. The 53d made another attempt and succeeded, though they suffered severely during the time. The enemy's shots were mowing down our men with fearful rapidity. During the confusion, our regiment became entangled with others and a portion of Company D was left on the bank near the bridge, William, Rollin, Milton and myself being amongst the number. The grape shot and canister were tearing up the ground in front and around us, making a general havoc amongst us. In order to reach the regiment, we had to cross an open field, raked by the enemy's fire. It was our only hope, so we made the attempt, and strange to say, only one man, James Eagan, was wounded and he succeeded in getting across. Our line of battle was now perfect again and we commenced paying back the rebels the damage which they had inflicted upon us. At or near the bridge, four hundred and fifty of our boys lay weltering in their blood. Gen. Veatch was struck by a spent ball and forced to leave the field. The rebels were now strongly posted behind a rail fence, a few rods in front of us, but so thick was the underbrush that we could not see them. They poured in withering volleys through the brush but the thickness of the copse saved us many lives. Our regiment was protected by a long log behind which we lay. William and I first got over it, but concluding that it was too warm, we hastily scampered back. The bullets pelted against the log like hailstones. Philo Handy, my right hand man, was shot and badly wounded. Soon our batteries were across the bridge and their well-directed shots soon put the enemy in rapid retreat. In solid phalanx and beautiful order, we now marched forward, pursuing the flying foe. In front of us was a large open field, toward the center of which arose a large elevation extending in a ridge across the whole space. To rush forward and secure this position was but the work of an instant. Beyond the hill the ground gradually sloped until it reached the belt of wood which skirted the field on the east. Just in the edge of the field, and running parallel with it was a road with an embankment of four or five feet on which was a rail fence. Behind this naturally strong position, the rebels had concentrated their entire force and made their last desperate stand. Our skirmishers were thrown forward and kept up a galling fire on the rebel artillery, while our artillery was being planted on the crest of the hill. We had twenty-four pieces in all and they were extended along the whole length of the line, the muzzles of the guns just clearing the top of the hill so that the recoil would put them back out of range of the enemy's fire. Behind the artillery, our whole force was now posted in its support. By peering over the brow of the hill, we saw a long, dense line of rebels evidently preparing for a charge. Each man grasped his piece firmly and with compressed lips awaited the dread moment. Cautiously the rebels began to advance. Oh, the

awful, deathlike silence of the fearful moment. Our artillery men
stand ready and at a given signal, a sheet of fire and flame burst
forth from the muzzles of those twenty-four pieces, 'shaking the
earth for miles around. It was impossible for the rebel officers to
make their men face the music. They broke and sought the cover
of the woods.

A rapid and continual cannonading was now kept up on each
side for nearly an hour. That hill seemed to be ablaze with fire
and glory. Our chief of artillery, Maj. Campbell, with hat off
and sword waving rode furiously along the line of artillery,
encouraging the men and anon directing the aim of some particular
piece. His eyes fairly scintillated like coals of fire. Perfectly
regardless of danger, he rode back and forth, a conspicuous mark
for the rebel sharpshooters. From our position, we could see the
effect of every shot. It was truly a grand sight. Gen. Hurlbut
watched the battle and directed the movements as coolly and
calmly as though he were on review or parade. Col. Hall of the
14th Illinois, who now commanded our brigade fretted and chafed
because the General would not let him charge the enemy with his
brigade. Lieut-Col. Rogers, commanding the 15th, won honors
for himself. He was fierce as a lion. Always where danger was
thickest, but always cool and collected and ready for any emergency. Before us was a veteran army of twenty-five thousand
men, commanded by their ablest Generals—Price and Van Dorn.
Opposed to them was our own little, gallant division, numbering
scarcely four thousand men, henceforth to be known as the
"Fighting Fourth." The dispirited and discouraged rebels were
not proof against our vigorous attack. They soon were in rapid
retreat, but we did not pursue them any farther. Soon the
echoing notes of Rosecrans' artillery told us that the rebels had
met their victorious foe of the day before. There was but one
road for them to escape by, and leaving their baggage train and
throwing away everything, the terror stricken enemy broke up in
squads and ran for dear life. Thus ended the memorable battle
of Corinth and Matamora. Col. Turner, who had not been able to
march with the regiment, after the fighting was over, came up and
took command. We never ascertained the rebel loss in this
engagement, as they succeeded in carrying off all of their wounded
and burying most of their dead, but it must have been far greater
than ours which was four hundred and fifty, killed and wounded.

Only seven of the 15th were wounded, and when General Hurlbut was asked how it was that his favorite regiments, meaning the 14th and 15th, escaped with so little loss, he replied that they were so near the enemy's guns that the shots all went over their heads and fell amongst the rear regiments, and this was true, for certain it was that we were in the lead all day and suffered the least of any regiment. This battle was fought Sunday, October 4th, 1862, the birthday of sister Zine. We now busied ourselves taking care of our wounded and burying our dead, which took us until nearly dark. Rollin, Milton and Simon Smith came in with a good porker for supper. It was a welcome addition to our scanty rations. In emergencies like this, we could always depend upon Roll and Milt to replenish our stock of provisions. They could not be beaten in the foraging line.

On the 5th we started on our return and on the 6th we were in our old camp highly jubilant at our success. As was usual on such occasions congratulatory and complimentary orders were given. In Gen. Hurlbut's order he paid a high compliment to the 4th division and did credit to himself by declaring that whatever military fame he possessed was due to the 4th division and not to any special merit of his own. One day a citizen asked Hurlbut what name he was going to give the late battle. "Hell on the Hatchie" was his prompt reply, and Col. Rogers had it inscribed on the battle flag of the 15th and although it did not show good taste, it suited a majority of the regiment.

The chaplain expostulated against this inscription, but it was in accordance with the Colonel's nature and he would not change it. The inscription pleased Gen. Hurlbut. The General was heard to say that when he received his orders previous to the battle, he never expected to get through with his command. He was ordered to relieve Rosecrans at all hazards or sacrifice his army in the attempt, but thanks to his generalship and the fighting qualities of his 4th division, he came triumphantly back.

CHAPTER XI.

October 14th.

Gen. Hurlbut was now relieved of his command and ordered to report to Jackson, Tennessee, to assume command of the military district embraced in that section. It was with unfeigned regret that we were forced to part with him. Brevet Brigadier-General James B. McPherson was ordered to assume command of the division, a soldier who in every respect proved himself worthy of the best honors a grateful country could bestow. From captain and chief of artillery on Grant's staff, he rapidly rose in position until he commanded the invincible army of the Tennessee and finally laid down his life in the bloody battle of Peach Tree Creek before Atlanta. When he assumed command of the division, the boys were nearly all prejudiced against him as they were against all West Point graduates, but when we learned the many noble qualities that he possessed, our dislike changed into esteem and later, when we saw his matchless skill as a military leader, and above all, his great kindness to his soldiers to whose appeals for justice he never turned a deaf ear, our esteem amounted to almost veneration, and soon McPherson's name became synonymous with all that was good and noble—a perfect gentleman in every respect and every inch a soldier. He had few equals and less superiors. Troops began to concentrate here and active preparations were being made for a fall campaign into the heart of the rebellion. Our decimated ranks were being filled up by new troops under the five hundred thousand called in July. We now marched to Lagrange where the final preparations were to be made. We had not proceeded far on the first day's march before Col. Turner received a dispatch announcing that his resignation had been accepted. The regiment halted and with visible emotion, he bade farewell to it. To which, in behalf of the regiment, Col. Rogers responded. Despite the ill-will existing against him by many, he had noble traits of character which any true man could not help but admire. The boys on this march committed those acts of lawlessness which wanton soldiers indulge in. Amongst others, they burned the fences all along the route. All the efforts of the officers to find the incendiaries proved unavailing. On the third day the regiment was back again in its old quarters. The 15th regiment was soon detailed to guard Ball's Bridge, a place one and one-half miles from camp.

October 15th.

This was an agreeable duty as it enabled the boys to forage without being subject to the restraints of picket and camp rules. A good number of the boys went into a private speculation by confiscating cotton and then selling it on the sly. About this time the 95th Illinois joined the army. Seven companies of this regiment were raised in McHenry County and three in Boone, and many of our friends and acquaintances were in it, amongst whom I will mention Asahel Eddy, Wif. Mallory, Dan Mitchell and Jimmie Williams. The 72d Illinois Infantry was now added to our brigade, making in all five regiments, still under command of Gen. Veatch, whom the boys had learned to love as a father, but they had not yet gotten over the disposition to play off jokes on him. One dark, stormy night, a squad of the 15th was on guard at his headquarters, and while some were lurking around to see what they could steal, they spied the General's jug of bitters in his tent and they immediately concocted a plan to relieve him of them and place a substitute in their place. It being quite cold without, the boys felt greatly the need of something stimulating within. So after all had retired to rest, one of the guard cautiously lifted the tent and extracted the jug and under the frequent draughts of the guard, the bitters rapidly disappeared. The boys then filled the jug with water and put it back in its old place. The General arose early, and as was his custom, repaired to the jug to take his morning beverage. The boys could hardly refrain from laughing outright when they saw the General's perplexed look. He smelled a rat but said nothing then, and he fooled his whole staff by treating them with water, slightly diluted with whisky. They all had a hearty laugh over it. When the General questioned the guard concerning the missing bitters, they were all professedly ignorant, but he was well satisfied as to where his bitters went. Soon after, the 14th, not to be outdone by their brothers as they termed the 15th, one night stole a nice leg of mutton from the General, and the bleeting that greeted his ears when he passed the regiment, told him pretty plainly where his mutton went. On one occasion, I had charge of headquarter guard. The night was very stormy.

A few choice spirits, wearing shoulder straps, had congregated in Dr. Stevenson's tent and were making themselves merry over the Doctor's wine, singing songs and telling stories. They carried on their carousal until long past midnight, and then all except Capt. Cox, the adjutant, retired, but he had just got enough down to make him feel funny, and he came out where I was and entertained me with extravagant stories about his bravery and how much he thought of the rank and file of the army, to all of which I assented. He thought me a very clever fellow and wanted I should go into his tent and take a drink with him. When I told him that I never drank liquor he seemed surprised, and wanted to know what I was made of.

He then went on to tell me a great secret which he made me promise to keep. He said that he knew where there was a large quantity of cotton secreted and he was going now to secure it and hang the rebels who owned it. I did not think that he was in earnest, much less that he would venture out this stormy night, but he roused his hostler and bade him saddle his horse and then roused up a couple of his orderlies to accompany him. There was some tall swearing by the orderlies when they learned what was required of them. Soon his horse was saddled and he mounted and ran up and down the road through mud and water. He said that he was trying his horse to see if it was all right. He then rode his horse into his tent and over his clerk, Ed. Harrison. By this time, his orderlies were ready and off they went in the rain and mud at a breakneck pace, but when he arrived opposite our quarters, he altered his mind, woke up Col. Rogers, dismissed his orderlies, and stayed with the 15th until morning. Such, my readers, is a sample of many of our officers. The next day our division went out on a reconnoisance toward Holly Springs. The 15th only went six or eight miles as it was necessary for us to return and guard the bridge. The enemy was found to be strongly posted at Coldwater. Preparations were made now for a forward movement and soon Grant's army was on the move. The enemy retreated in great haste as we advanced. Near Holly Springs we got a slight skirmish out of their rear guard. When we arrived at that place, Col. Rogers was offered the position to command the post and garrison it with his regiment, but he preferred to accompany the army and that traitor, Murphy, of the 109th Illinois was left in command.

November 1st.

We continued to push the enemy until they crossed the Tallahatchie. Here they seemed disposed to make a stand, and well
they might. The place was impregnable against a direct assault;
bound on three sides by a broad and impassable swamp, with a
deep, muddy river, backed by the strongest fortifications I had
ever seen, but the invincible Sherman soon flanked them with his
division and they beat a precipitate retreat. So rapidly now did
we press them that their rear guard and our advance guard were
constantly skirmishing. Soon the beautiful city of Oxford was
reached and we marched triumphantly through its streets. We
were now within twenty-five miles of Grenada, where it was supposed that the rebels would make a stand. We had them now
where they were compelled to fight us to cover their retreat, but
about this time, the news of the surrender of Holly Springs
reached us. This put a stop to further operations for the
present.

November 4th.

For a week we lay undecided what to do. The boys were
getting discontented. Nothing will annoy a soldier more than to
have his ration line cut off, and Gen. Lauman, who now commanded our division, gave strict orders against foraging, but of
little use were his orders. Some of the boys, to show their appre-
ciation of his orders, stole him blind one night while on guard at
his headquarters. He never again called for a detail from the
15th to guard his quarters. From that time a strong dislike
sprang up between Lauman and the regiment. Gen. McPherson
had been appointed to command one wing of the army. We had
marched fifty miles south of Holly Springs and twelve on the
direct route to Grenada and Vicksburg.

November 10th.

The former was the objective point, and had it not been for the
base treachery of the commandant of Holly Springs in so ignobly
permitting the rebels to come in and destroy millions of rations,
an immense amount of clothing, tear up the railroads, etc., our
campaign would have been a glorious one, and Vicksburg would
have been added to our list of conquests long before it was. Gen.
Sherman's division did not march any farther than the Tallahatchie, but went back to Memphis and took transports and went
down the river to co-operate with Grant from that quarter.

6

November 14th.

We now kept shifting position and performing those uncertain
movements so perplexing to a soldier. Some of the boys became
almost desperate. Restricted on our rations, all communication
cut off, and with no prospects of getting any more very soon, and
surrounded by a relentless horde of rebel cavalry, our situation
was anything but pleasant. The boys commenced an indiscriminate foraging with an avidity that knew no limits. In many places
gold was found which the rebels had buried before leaving for
the war to prevent its falling into the hands of the Yankees, but a
little coaxing would induce the head darkey on the plantation to
divulge its hiding place. On the 15th the whole army was coun-
termarching and the 15th was rear guard. We were harrassed a
good deal by the rebel cavalry who were watching for an opportunity to capture our baggage train. Our knapsacks were carried
and we were in light marching order and the rebs would have had
hard work to have gotten the start of us. Our route lay through
a splendid country, the best in the state. It was well watered and
timbered. On the streams were numerous mills which we made
use of in grinding corn. In this way our army was enabled
to subsist without drawing heavily on our commissary. One
morning, just before marching, a very serious affray occurred in
Company F. Two men, Ser. Hill and Ser. ———, got into a dispute about some trifling matter. Words led to blows and ———
drew his knife and, before any of us could interfere, stabbed Hill
through the abdomen. The wound was supposed to be mortal and
the surgeon left him at a plantation near Springdale. One of his
comrades volunteered to stay and nurse him. It was a noble act.
The would-be murderer was arrested on the spot. A double guard
was placed around him, but notwithstanding, he made his escape.
He went back to his wounded victim, asked and received his
pardon for his rash act; nursed him until he was nearly well and
then left for the rebel army. The other two men were made
prisoners, paroled and eventually got back to the regiment. We
halted when within ten miles of Abbeyville, and camped for
several days in order to repair the bridge across the Tallahatchie.
Our men were reduced to one-quarter rations. Indeed, some were
entirely without hard bread and the pangs of hunger actually began
to gnaw at our vitals. The country round about was poor and
barren. All we could find was the small pea-beans, but luckily

some of our boys made a raise of some meal. So we got along much better than some of the others. The line and field officers shared our privations.

November 21st.

We were soon enabled to cross the river. The cars ran up as far as the bridge. We now got a scant supply of rations, but a good many had eaten their last mouthful before the supply came. We camped that night on an open plain and we had to go a mile for wood to cook our suppers. Soon a train came along. It was a glad sight for us. Visions of plenty now began to float before our eyes and we were content. We now proceeded as far as Watertown, where our regiment was left as a garrison. We found comfortable quarters that the regiment before us had occupied and soon we were comfortably established. This place was now used as a kind of depot for supplies and in addition to guarding this, we had heavy picket duty to perform and it required every man who was able to do duty. Our orders were very strict. Rebel cavalry were prowling about. Every non-commissioned officer in charge of posts received written instructions. The boys foraged here on a pretty extensive scale and they ran great risk of being captured.

November 21st.

But we had got to be pretty bold now and would as soon meet with a little adventure as not. A great many of the boys adopted a new style. Instead of asking now, they demanded, or went right in without saying a word. They would slaughter a man's hogs right before his eyes and if he made a fuss, cold steel would soon put a quietus on him. Although this mode is highly censurable and cannot be justified, yet, there were many rank rebels who had from three to five years' stock of provisions stored away and would lie to the boys and tell them they were in a starving condition, hence some resorted to this summary way of dealing with them. If this practice had been carried out only on that kind of characters it would not have looked so bad, but there were unprincipled soldiers who had not the least particle of humanity about them. They would rob rich and poor, old age and youth, widows and orphans, and weak and helpless alike. I have time and again seen a poor, lonely woman with a house full of little ones, on her knees, begging these wretches not to take the last mouthful from her starving children, and perhaps when they left, she would be houseless and homeless, left with her little ones to starve, unless some kind hand would succor them. With a clear conscience, I can appeal to the Great Judge of All that I never yet defrauded weak and helpless women and that, when possible, I tried to save them. It is not to be supposed that our officers would allow these depredations, and when found out, the wretches were severely punished. It was a great source of mortification to us that Company D possessed one of these characters. No true soldier would ever turn a deaf ear to distress even though it came from our enemy. While we were at Watertown Lieut.-Col. Rogers received his commission as Colonel of the regiment and feeling pretty well over it, he thought, to use an army phase, "he would wet it," that is, treat his friends. So gathering a few (November 30th) choice friends about him, they had a regular "time," and to use a common expression, "got pretty well sprung." Soon after, while returning from a visit to one of his particular friends and feeling pretty well, he thought that he would "cut a swell." He mounted his horse and rode at a furious rate down the railroad, never stopping for bridges or culverts. He would make his horse jump them or walk the stringers, but he came to one place which more than taxed the gallant steed's power. He just cleared the culvert and fell headlong, throwing the Colonel over his head, striking his head on a railroad iron, gashing it horribly. He was picked up for dead, but it is an old saying that "a drunken man was never known to be killed by accident." So it proved in this case. He recovered, but it left a long scar on his face.

CHAPTER XII.

December 10th.

We now rejoined our division and marched to Holly Springs. The rebels had burned the best part of the place, but there was still enough left to make a splendid looking place. It was now filled with a set of regular sharpers, hangers-on of the army. There were a large number of sutler stands and stores put up in antici- pation of the army soon arriving. The 26th Illinois Volunteers, commanded by Col. Loomis, was garrisoning the town. A few of the roguishly inclined boys in our brigade were bent on a spree. They had been to Holly Springs so many times on a "tom fool" errand that they were determined on revenge now. So one night they went to town and raised the deuce generally. The patrol of the town could not do anything with them. Col. Loomis was sent for and he attempted to awe them into submission, but inglor- iously failed. He drew his revolver and threatened to shoot into the crowd and struck one of the soldiers with the flat of his sword. The boys could not stand this, so they pitched in and cleaned out the guard and brick-batted Col. Loomis back to his quarters. In a towering rage, he now called out his whole regiment and was going to arrest everyone, at the same time sending word to our brigade commander how his men were acting.

In the meantime, some of the boys in camp had learned how matters stood and went down and informed the boys in town, so they all hurried up to their quarters. Orders were issued to have roll-call all through the brigade, and report to brigade head- quarters all absentees. The men were all there to answer to their names, and so Col. Hall reported to Col. Loomis that all his men were in camp. Loomis hated our brigade after that. He gave us the name of "Lauman's mob." Of course, all good soldiers were deeply mortified at the conduct of these men. Thus it always was that a few bad characters in a regiment would bring disgrace upon its reputation, but taking our regiment, as a general thing, they were as noble a set of men as could be found. We had men from all the walks of life in the ranks, from the lawyer to the common laborer, authors, poets and mechanics of all kinds, but

there were about a dozen men in the regiment that were a pest and
curse to us and they were continually getting into scrapes. These
rascals, the night before we left Holly Springs, set it on fire, notwithstanding the watchfulness of the guard, and in the confusion
occasioned by the fire, they stole everything valuable that they
could lay their hands on; but one would have thought, to have
seen them, that they were the most active ones in trying to extin-
guish the flames. They would rush into the burning buildings
with the ostensible purpose of putting out the fire, but they were
seen to come out loaded with plunder. After this, if anyone in the
army had anything nice about him he would be asked if there had
been a fire somewhere.

December 29th.

The next day, on the march, one of the staff-officers caught one
of our boys with a plug hat on. He rode up to him, snatched it
off and threw it into the mud. The fellow belonged to our company and not relishing such treatment, he sprang for the officer
and would have thrashed him on the spot if someone had not interfered. The officer drew his revolver and was going to shoot. This
act of his aroused the ire of the other boys and they compelled him
to put it up. A general melee now seemed inevitable, but our
officers finally succeeded in quieting the men. We camped near
Holly Springs for several days longer and then took up a line of
march for Moscow. The 4th division was ordered to guard the
Memphis & Charleston railroad between Lagrange and Memphis.
We supposed that our quarters would be at Moscow, but there was
a misunderstanding and we were ordered to Lafayette, twenty
miles farther toward Memphis, and when within a few miles of
that place, we were ordered to countermarch back to Moscow. It
was late when we pitched our camp and we got into a mud-hole
and could not get out until morning.

December 31st.

The next morning we arose from our watery bed, amidst a perfect shower of rain, packed up and resumed our march.

January 1st, 1863.

I never saw it rain harder in my life than it did that morning,
and it continued to rain the most part of the day. Ravines and
gulches that we passed over dry-shod the day before, were now
filled with water rushing in torrents from down the hillsides and
valleys, and, in some places, the mules had to swim in order to

cross. We had heavy knapsacks to carry, and that, in addition to our guns and other accoutrements and thoroughly soaked clothing, made our load quite heavy, but, for all that, the boys jogged along as happy as larks. The harder it rained the louder would we sing and shout and crack our jokes.

By an unlucky accident I was the means of furnishing a good joke which rather put the laugh on me. When we came up to these streams, the boys usually scattered to find a convenient place for crossing. Some would undertake to cross on rails and would be precipitated into the stream. Charlie Mitchell lost a gun but saved himself. I sat and watched them for a while, laughing until my sides ached. Finally I got up and thought that I would show them a trick, which consisted in a rash attempt to jump the stream, selecting as narrow a place as I could find, some twelve or fourteen feet across. The boys ranged themselves along-side to see me make the leap. So preparing myself and straining every nerve, I rushed forward, and just as I made the spring my foot slipped and I went in on all fours, frog fashion, disappearing entirely, except my knapsack. After floundering about a few seconds I managed to get on terra firma, and such a shout of laughter as greeted my ears I never heard before. After puffing and blowing for awhile I joined in the laugh, for I saw that the joke was on me and I determined to make the most of it. Creeks and rivers did not annoy me any more that day. I waded through regardless of consequences, but strange to say, I did not take cold, although it was midwinter. The river was so swollen that we could not cross to Moscow, so we camped two miles west of that place. We got in camp about an hour before sundown. Near us was a large plantation with a number of outhouses, and no sooner had we stacked arms than the boys made for these buildings, and, as if by magic, they disappeared in a twinkling, before the officers could interfere. My mess got a goodly share, and William and I made us a bunk to sleep on. The officers did not attempt to interfere. They were too glad to get a share themselves, and if any fuss was made about it, the regiment would pay for it. Soon we had a rousing fire built and our wet garments were steaming before its ruddy blaze. Our tents now came up and soon our camp was formed. While we were standing about the fire we spied a fine drove of shoats, about a half mile off, which we thought would make good roasters. So dispatching our most

expert foragers, Roll and Milt, from our mess, they sallied out
and soon every one of those pigs were slain. Our mess secured
four of them, and in less than thirty minutes they were in our
bake ovens, stewing before a hot fire. It was an excellent dish,
and my readers can form some idea of the state of our appetites
when I tell them that our mess of fifteen devoured them. Our
cook, William Underwood, surpassed himself that night.   He
always could get a good meal on short notice, and this was our
New Year's feast.   By the time our supper was dispatched, our
garments were dry, and spending a short time around the camp
fire cracking jokes and telling stories, the time flew by.   Occasionally they had to remind me of my mishap, and Charlie about losing
his gun.   Finally we retired to rest well satisfied with ourselves
and all the rest, and the arms of Morpheus soon held the camp in
its sweet embrace.

January 2d.

On awakening the next morning we found six inches of snow
on the ground, and scarcely were our preparations for breakfast
made before we received marching orders back to Lafayette.   To
say that there was some pretty rough swearing when this order
was received, would but faintly express the truth.   Scarcely an
hour had elapsed after receiving the order before we were travers-
ing the same road we traveled the day before, but now we had to
wade in the snow and mud, and our march was very difficult.
Many of the boys, having shoes, their feet were soon soaking
wet.

We arrived at Lafayette about sundown, and now, as if to add
to our already overcharged patience, a portion of the regiment was
ordered to go on picket, supperless and worn out.   Some of the
boys invented a new string of oaths expressly for this occasion.
Although I did not swear, I thought horrible things and wished
that the inhuman wretch that gave the order was anywhere but on
this earth.   Lieut. Paxton, Ser. Sedam of Company C and myself
were sent out in charge of one company.   We relieved Logan's
men and they marched that very night for Memphis.   Just in
front of our line was a large cotton gin and other buildings, and
our Lieutenant, with a perfect recklessness which was inexcusable
under any circumstances, ordered his men to take possession of
them, which brought his videttes in rear of the reserve.   If any
picket officer had happened around that night, or if I had chosen

to report him, it would have been the last picket he would ever have stood. As if to add still deeper to his disgrace, he permitted his men to go out foraging, leaving only a very few on post, and finally to cap the climax, the men soon returned with a large quantity of old cider--so strong that one good drink would make a person dizzy. Although it almost scorches my pen to write it, yet truth compels me to say that every person except two on that post got drunk and all night long reveled in a drunken spree. The two sober persons were Charlie Mitchell and myself, and on us alone the safety of that part of the line depended. Sleep was far from my eyelids. Any small force could have come in and captured the whole of us. It would have been utterly impossible to have rallied the men in case of an attack. Had it not been for some extenuating circumstances, I would have reported the conduct of the men, but it seems that the picket officer himself was negligent of his duty for he never made his appearance. It was a good thing for us that he did not. I went the rounds at midnight and found a fire at every post except one and all asleep except Charlie. I had a hard job of it to wake up the next relief—all were in a drunken stupor. I finally got them up, but they were no better than dead men. I don't think that there was ever a more disgraceful picket duty performed, but I kept my skirts clear, unless some would have considered it my duty to have reported them, but as I said before, there were some extenuating circumstances, but nothing to justify so total a neglect of duty, thus endangering the lives of a whole camp. I did not like to have anybody's death lay on my hands and death might have been the penalty.

January 5th.

I now unwillingly gave the boys another chance to get the joke on me. Just across the creek from us was a large number of negro huts, and while looking around the night before, I saw several bake kettles lying around, and as our mess stood greatly in need of one, I thought that I would take one. So, just before daylight, I crossed over and got one. While re-crossing the creek on a log, my foot slipped and I fell in. They had it that I was so drunk I could not walk straight and tumbled into the water, but, however, I brought in the bake kettle, and as it was full of snow and ice, I put it over the fire to thaw out, when, to my chagrin and disappointment the bottom came out. This only made the joke more pointed. They said I was so drunk that I did not know the bottom

of the kettle was gone. I bore their raillery in good humor.
Charlie was also implicated with me and had to stand his share of
the joke. When we got into camp, the affair was repeated with
considerable gusto. It pleased the boys amazingly that "Dad,"
as they familiarly termed me, and Charlie should get tight, but
we knew that not one believed it, so we were content. Their own
disgraceful conduct was still too fresh in their memory, and they
knew that we could cause them considerable trouble, so they
did not carry the joke too far, but whenever an occasion occurred,
they never failed to remind me of the bake kettle joke.

The 2d brigade now became fairly established at Lafayette, as
garrison and railroad guard. We built as comfortable quarters
as possible and then went to work and built several forts and put
the place in a complete state of defense. We now had a long
season of rest and the boys were in a condition to fully appreciate
it. Our picket duty was pretty heavy, especially on the non-commissioned officers. I came on three times a week. There was
only one non-commissioned officer to a post except on the reserve,
but we had regular stations and we built good shelters. During
the night, when I knew that I had men that I could fully trust, I
would let them relieve themselves with the understanding that if
anything occurred, to wake me instantly. I stood my regular two
hours with the rest. When the grand rounds were made, they
woke me up. There was necessity of our being watchful, as large
bands of rebel cavalry were prowling about, oftentimes threatening an attack. On several occasions our forage trains were
driven in. Some of the boys now had quite a notion of firing
away their cartridges and very strict orders were given concerning
it. Each one was made responsible for his ammunition, but the
boys managed to get a lot of extra cartridges and they introduced
a practice called "squibbing" by putting in a very light charge,
the gun making very little noise.

While on picket, they would shoot all day long at marks, often
shooting the same ball a dozen times. We were very careful not
to get caught at it. It was supposed that the pickets always wore
their accoutrements while on duty but we sometimes permitted the
boys to take them off, providing they would keep a strict watch
and put them on when they saw any officer approaching. We
were camped in a very rich country and the boys had great times
foraging. When a forage train started out, it was a signal for

the boys to go out with it, and under its protection, load themselves down with the product of the country, such as sweet potatoes, other vegetables and fresh pork. Very often a whole wagon load of fresh pork would come. Our mess got several weeks' supply which we salted down in boxes. At the same time we drew our regular rations of bacon, but this we burned for fuel. We had made a little stove for our tent out of an old iron kettle and our bacon furnished us with all the fuel we needed. At one time, our company had about a cord piled up. Afterward we would have given a great deal if we could have had that bacon which we burned at Lafayette.

January 20th.

Two members of Company D, whom I will not name, performed an act here which in a law-abiding land would have consigned them to prison. The persons referred to succeeded in eluding our pickets and went daily to a farm house within two miles of camp. Here lived a poor and respectable couple with a daughter, a young lady, who soon became the dupe of the rascals. One of them paid his addresses to her, won her affections and she consented to marry him. One day he brought a comrade with him whom he introduced as a chaplain, and a mock ceremony of marriage was performed (January 24th). It was not until the regiment moved that treachery was suspected. Then the outraged father followed the regiment in hopes of finding the destroyer of his daughter's happiness, but by using disguises and keeping out of sight, they eluded his search. I did not know who the persons were that committed this vile act until the father of the girl had left and to the disgrace of the officers of our regiment, nothing was ever said or done to bring the rascals to justice. Indeed, they looked upon it in the light of a good joke and those who looked with horror and disgust upon such conduct were powerless to punish, but if these men's consciences were not entirely seared, they would always carry a festering sore in their base hearts,—the remembrance of having ruined an innocent girl and destroyed the peace and darkened the home of a once happy family.

January 24th.

The holy cause for which we were contending now began to assume a gloomy, forbidding aspect. Disaster followed disaster in rapid succession. Sherman had been bloodily repulsed from before Vicksburg. The rebel Gen. Bragg was invading Kentucky with a large and powerful army, while an imbecile General—Buell—was leisurely taking his ease, allowing the invaders to carry fire, sword and famine in their track and go unpunished. The army of the Potomac had again met with a disastrous defeat and Lee was preparing to invade the free states. To add to our distress, we had enemies, who by their encouragement to armed traitors nerved the arm that struck the blow which was aimed at the heart's blood of their kindred and friends. The weary and dispirited soldiers saw nothing in the future but a dark and lowering cloud which threatened to engulf them. From defeat and disaster in the field, they had hoped to look for succor and encouragement from the masses at home, but instead, a large part of them who should have been their friends, were creating dissensions, and secret foes were plotting our destruction and the ruin of our government. Those that remained true, rallied around our noble President who stood firm and breasted the fearful tide with a heroism and perseverance which was heaven-bestowed. Although his every action was watched and his deadly enemies were continually blocking his way, still he bore up with superhuman energy. He was our rock on which to lean, our star and guide, our noble Lincoln ! With one despairing, heart thrilling appeal, the army sent in their remonstrance against the actions of those men styled "peace democrats" who would barter away our priceless legacy of freedom to slave aristocracy, reflecting contempt upon the memory of thousands of noble souls who had yielded up their lives that the country might live. Many of these malcontents, though loyal, allowed their party feelings to endanger the safety of our cause. They wanted the country saved under a democratic leader. There was a traitorous set under the lead of Valandingham, who were secretly plotting the destruction of government under the sophistical plea of peace, armistice and reconciliation, while at the same time they knew that there could be no peace until the last armed rebel had laid down his arms and acknowledged the authority of the government, and our flag should be recognized and respected on every foot of American soil.

January 30th.

About this time, I wrote home, expressing some of my views and feelings and, to my surprise, some of my friends took the liberty to have the letter published. The powerful and potent voice of the army was not without its effect. The leaders of conspiracies at home, shrank back at the bold front of the army. They had hoped to create division amongst us, but they reckoned without their game. It is a glorious record for our brave army that they stood like a rock through all these trying scenes, by the President and government. If the soldiers who had to bear the brunt of the strife, imperiling their lives and all in the determination to press on to win or to die, why could not those who were rolling in luxury at home, enjoying the fruits of our toil and danger, be satisfied. A letter from father came now announcing Alsera's death. Considerable sickness prevailed in camp, but my health remained excellent. A new chaplain now came to us, the Rev. B. F. Rogers, a brother of the Colonel and a universalist in sentiment. He was a noble and good man. He remained with us all through the war, sharing with us our privations and relieving our wants and necessities when possible. He was indeed our friend and benefactor. I had forgotten to mention that our old brigade commander, Gen. Veatch, had left us.

January 31st.

He was now in command of the City of Memphis. It was with extreme regret that we parted from him. He was a good man and an able General. He never turned a deaf ear to a soldier's complaints nor refused to grant him justice, and when any of the boys had been guilty of any grave offense, a good fatherly lecture from the General punished them more effectually than anything else, and the offense was seldom repeated.

February 1st.

Col. Hall, 14th Illinois, was now in command of the brigade. We were all happy to welcome back to the brigade at this time Major Nase, old captain of Company K. He had been wounded and taken prisoner at the battle of Shiloh and had his leg amputated below the knee. He was finally exchanged and was promoted for meritorious conduct on the battle-field. Never was promotion more nobly earned. After being taken prisoner, he was taken to Memphis where he was so fortunate as to fall into a Union lady's hands. She nursed him with the most assiduous care until he recovered from the effects of his wound or until it was healed. She probably saved his life, and the Major was very extravagant in her praise. While we were at Memphis, she came to camp to see him and she was greeted by all with demonstrations of respect. She was one of the very few genuine ladies we found in the South. About the middle of February, our regiment moved a short distance from Lafayette and scattered along the railroad toward Memphis. Companies A, F, D, and I stopped about three miles from the former place at a stockade. Our chief duty was to protect the railroad from guerrilla raids. Still we found plenty of time to indulge in our penchant for foraging. Just across the river from us lay a large tract of low swampy ground. Beyond it was a rich country which neither party had molested much.

In this swamp was the headquarters of a powerful guerrilla band, but yet, despite the danger incurred in the risk, squads of our boys would go out through this swamp into the open country beyond to forage. Several times, some of them narrowly escaped being captured. Milt and Roll went out with a squad one day, and as they were nearing a house, a woman seized a horn and blew a loud blast. The boys knew well what that meant. They immediately seized or awed the woman into silence, hastily got what they wanted and left just as a party of guerrillas were emerging from the woods in an opposite direction. The boys were a little more cautious after this. On another occasion, the Colonel went out with a lot of us boys and we had several six-mule teams along. We went out some six or eight miles and came to a large, fine plantation owned by a Colonel in the rebel army. This was the place for us. A large drove of fine hogs and plenty of poultry was there. The Colonel gave us permission to help ourselves and soon that drove of hogs was slaughtered and in our wagons, and most of the men exulted in the possession of chickens, and visions of a nice chicken pie when we should reach camp, floated through our minds. The overseer of the plantation looked on with dumb surprise and chagrin to see the work of devastation going on and he powerless to prevent it.

February 15th.

On our way back to camp, the Colonel stopped where lived a rich and blooming young widow. The latter was perfectly fascinated with the Colonel, and she found various pretenses for visiting him in camp. She finally got desperately in love with him, and the Colonel was just wicked enough to permit her attentions. When the regiment finally moved she followed nearly to the city of Memphis. He had hard work to get rid of her. After that the Colonel was joked considerably about his widow. One of our boys, Amos Holgate, a private of Company D, went out into the

country and passed himself off as Captain Legget. In consequence, he received many smiles and favors from the young ladies,
but it was finally found out in camp and his trick exposed and the
young ladies went back on him. He was known after that as
"Captain Legget."

February 20th.

Our time at the stockade passed quickly and pleasantly away.
The weather for the most of the time was delightful. We amused
ourselves by playing ball and indulging in other harmless pastimes.
Our healths were good and our spirits light. The tide of ill-feeling at the north against our cause was gradually dying away and
victory had taken the place of defeat. Our cause began to
brighten and to the future we looked forward with hope and
trust.

February 22.

The 22d of February, the anniversary of the birthday of the
immortal Washington, was celebrated by our brigade at Lafayette.
Speeches and toasts were made and given appropriate to the
occasion. Our worthy chaplain established a lyceum in the regiment and two evenings in the week were pleasantly and profitably
employed in debating. Some of the best speakers in the regiment
belonged to the society. Our chaplain could not rest unless doing
something for the good of the men. Although not a gifted man
or an eloquent speaker, yet, I will venture to say that there was
not a harder working chaplain in the whole army or one that did
more good. With a good education, he combined goodness of
heart with an indomitable energy and perseverance. We were
not molested much by guerillas while here. We had several
chases after them but never succeeded in getting a fight out of
them.

Occasionally they would make threatening demonstrations by
appearing in force, but being mounted, they could evade pursuit.
Our vigilance prevented them from surprising us. We remained
here until the 10th of March when orders came for the 4th division
to march to Memphis to supply the place of troops who were going
to re-inforce Grant down the river. After two and one-half days'
marching, we reach Memphis.

March 10th.

We spent a week shifting about, changing camp, etc. Finally,
we settled down in the suburbs east of the city, on the famous

Merryweather property, then in litigation. We had a very pleasant camp and a splendid review and parade ground.

March 16th.

A strife now arose between the different regiments in the division for the championship in drilling, etc. The 41st Illinois and the 14th Illinois got up a match first. The prize of a silver bugle was to be awarded to the victor, but so close was the match that the judges could not decide. The 15th was then matched against the 41st and in battalion drill and marching we triumphantly bore off the palm, but we failed to come up to time in the manual of arms.

Casey's tactics had now been substituted for Hardee's and we had not yet got accustomed to the change.

March 25th.

Col. Richardson, a noted guerrilla, now began to harass us. Several regiments of the 4th division were sent out to disperse this band. They were strongly posted in a low, swampy ground, accessible only on one side by the artillery. A sharp fight ensued. We lost several killed and wounded. A Major in an Iowa regiment was killed.

April 1st.

Our picket duty here required the utmost vigilance. Rank rebels of both sexes, under the guise of peaceful citizens, obtained passes to go beyond the lines, and citizens outside of the lines obtained passes to go into the city to purchase groceries, etc. These passes lasting one month and subject to renewal by the commander, Gen. Veatch. It was soon discovered that these persons carried on a regular system of smuggling through contraband articles. It became necessary to form a chain picket. Even then, some would succeed in eluding the guard. Things, calling themselves ladies, were caught with quinine and other articles secreted in their crinolines. Gen. Veatch now issued an order that all ladies of suspicious character should be searched before passing out. Of course, these women were highly indignant at this, but their unladylike conduct begat the necessity of the order.

April 5th.

This summary proceeding of Gen. Veatch soon put a stop to this kind of smuggling. Then another queer expedient was resorted to, which was no less than secreting contraband goods in the carcasses of dead horses. Under the plea of removing them out of the way, they got permission to have them taken beyond our lines. This mode of proceeding was soon found out and then smuggling became a dangerous enterprise in Memphis. We probably lived better at this time than we did at any other time during our term in the army. Provisions were cheap and every day our table was covered with delicacies, such as eggs, ham, pies, sausages, etc. Our lyceum was still in operation, considerably enlarged, numbering over eighty active members. The society did me the honor to elect me its president for one month. It was our custom to invite speakers to deliver addresses before our society and Dr. McKim and the chaplain of the 14th Illinois favored us with lectures.

April 10th.

In addition to our lyceum, a reading-room was established and a small tax of five cents a week, for each member, furnished us with all the wholesome reading matter we could digest. A class in bookkeeping was also established; also a sort of normal school for reviewing the common branches of learning. These exercises, with my usual duties, kept my time pretty well occupied and the time glided swiftly and silently by. While we were thus occupied, many were spending the days and nights in the foul atmosphere of the city, frequenting haunts of vice and dissipation. Not satisfied with that, the atmosphere of camp must needs be corrupted with poor degraded women.

April 15th.

So foul had the morals of the city become that Gen. Veatch issued an order expelling two boat loads of fallen humanity. Indeed, matters had come to such a pass that a decent lady was ashamed to be seen on the street, and stringent measures had to be resorted to to remedy the evil. All the bad passions of the naturally dissipated in our division were brought to light here, and too often were the young and noble drawn into this whirlpool of vice.

April 20th.

There was one, in whom I felt more than a common interest, who was one day thrown into the company of roughs who were bound to get him drunk. Too well they succeeded! Late at night he came to camp partially intoxicated. To say that I was shocked, would be too feeble an expression. I knew that it would be useless to talk to him. So I sat down and wrote him an appeal, directed as though it came from home, and handed it to one of my

7

comrades, William Mallory, to hand to him as a letter from home.
I had the consciousness of knowing that my appeal was not in vain.
He was never known to be intemperate after that.

An order from the Secretary of War now permitted the enlistment of colored troops and the appointment of white officers to
command them. I was offered a recommendation by the adjutant of
of the regiment for a commission, but I preferred my present position to any in a negro company. Several members of the 15th did
receive commissions. William, Roll and Milt could have gotten a
recommendation if they had wanted it. Our pleasant life in Memphis was now about to draw to a close. Our lyceum, schools and
other pleasant pastimes were to be abandoned for the time being.

May 1st.

It was with some regret, but no reluctance, that I bade adieu
to Memphis. A sacred duty called us away. Our chieftain had
called for help and his call was the voice of duty. Our brave
comrades, in their grapple with the rebel "Gibraltar of the West"
—Vicksburg, needed our assistance. Henceforth until our banner waved over the towers and steeples of Vicksburg, we knew
there was no rest, but with our matchless leader and an invulner-
able army to back him, the fruition of our hopes was sure to be
realized. So, with cheerful hearts, we packed up and marched to
the levee where transports were waiting to receive us.

May 11th.

As we passed the Gayoso House, our patriotic governor,
Richard Yates, came out and made us a speech. He had just returned from the battlefield of Ft. Gibson, and he pictured in
glowing colors the bravery of Illinois troops in that field. He
predicted that ere long Vicksburg would be in our possession.
After everything was on board our division proudly swept its
moorings, and the noble steamers were soon skimming the crest
of the Father of Waters, bearing us to where honor and glory
awaited us.

May 12th.

The weather was delightful. Spring had on its richest dress.
All was life and animation. The green fields, the feathered warb-
lers, the grazing herds of cattle and sheep, the splendid villa of
some rich planter and the picturesque scenery along the river
thrilled our souls with an intense joy, causing them to vibrate with
an adoration and reverence to the Author of all these beauties,

but when our thoughts reverted inward to the terrible present, a wailing note of agony would creep along our heartstrings at the thought that God's beautiful handiwork of nature was now witnessing a bloody and terrible strife on its very bosom, but through the gloom of the terrible reality we saw the silver lining of the war cloud which soon would spread and irradiate our loved land with gladness, proclaiming peace, joy and contentment. The first day we passed Helena with its rocky crags and frowning precipices, made glorious and historic by the thrilling deeds of valor performed on its crest by freemen beating back traitors. Still on swift wings we sped, following the devious windings of the river, passing splendid plantations, "Old Zach Taylor's" plantation in Mississippi amongst the rest. About noon on the second day, while passing near Greenville, one of our boats was fired into by a band of guerrillas. Our troops immediately landed and laid everything waste on the shore. This mode of retaliation may look barbarous to some, but it was the only way in which we could check these lawless villains in their murderous schemes.

By night we arrived at Lake Providence, Louisiana, where a short time before Grant's army was camped. Halting but a short time here, we pressed on, and on the third day at noon, Milliken's Bend was reached. We passed four miles farther down to where the river makes an abrupt bend, circling around a point toward Vicksburg, and we disembarked. In the distance, the towers and steeples of Vicksburg were plainly discernable, and a cloud of dust rising over the city, indicated that some great excitement was existing. What that excitement was, we could imagine, when we heard that Grant was marching with steady tramp toward their stronghold, hurling back the rebel army as though it were naught.

A brief account of General Grant's movements here will not be out of place. While his army was lying here, the famous canal project was originated, but I believe that it was only a blind. The subsequent movements of the army are too well known to need repetition. The mock Monitor which scared the rebels so running the blockade, the gallant Queen of the West and the Indianola passing through a terrible shower of shell and shot, passed the city of Vicksburg and the subsequent fate of the two noble vessels, the running of six transports past the blockade, manned by volunteers, and their heroism, but the crowning act was moving his army down to Grand Gulf, storming and taking that place, and with six days' rations, he severed communication with his base, crossed the river, captured Fort Gibson, rapidly pressed the enemy back, attacked and defeated Johnson at Jackson and captured that place, then pressing forward, in quick succession he gained the battles of Raymond, Champion Hill, Haines Bluff, Black River, and finally set his army before Vicksburg, completely investing it. These movements were executed so rapidly that it caused the wildest excitement when heard of at the North, and Grant became the hero of the war.

May 18th.

We stopped in camp but a few days, then crossed the neck of land opposite Vicksburg. We took transports for Grand Gulf, but the army was so far advanced toward Jackson that we received orders to return to Youngs Point and join the army by the way of Haines Bluff on the Yazoo. About midnight on the day of our arrival at Grand Gulf, we again embarked and were speeding on our way back to Vicksburg. We approached within four miles of the city, nearly opposite Ft. Warren, but the enemy commenced shelling us and we were forced to disembark farther down the river. Before sundown, we were back at Youngs Point and again on transports. Soon we passed into the mouth of the Yazoo which empties into the Mississippi at this point. We received a large mail that night, and a long letter from Let announced his betrothal to Mary Bartholemew. We arrived at the Landing about nine o'clock P.M. Our regiment was detailed to guard five thousand prisoners captured the day before. The prisoners were ragged, dirty and disheartened, still they were called the "flower of the rebel army." The next day we went into camp on the bluff. This bluff was considered the key to the rebel position, and they determined to fight it out here, but a flank movement compelled them to abandon it in haste, leaving all their heavy artillery behind. The fort was manned to resist an assault from the front. They little dreamed that Grant would come up in the rear. We were ordered to hold this place. There was danger of Johnson attempting to capture it.

May 22d.

It was fifteen miles to Vicksburg, and we could plainly hear the heavy notes of artillery. On the 18th and 22d, when the charges were made, the hills fairly shook with the shock of artillery. Grant saw what a sacrifice of life it would cost to take the place by storm, so he waited the slower and surer operations of a seige. Our officers now asked and were granted permission to take their commands to the front, and on the 24th of May, we took up our position on the extreme left of the line, near Ft. Warren, below Vicksburg. The rebels were now completely hemmed in. There was no possible chance of escape except by cutting through our lines, an attempt they dare not undertake. Our gunboats effectually guarded the river side. The flanks of the army rested on the river, one above and one below the city. Thus contrary to the instructions of President Lincoln, Grant had completely invested Vicksburg. Lincoln wanted him to co-operate with Gen. Banks and reduce Ft. Hudson first, but with a magnanimity seldom equalled, the President acknowledged his error and highly complimented Grant. It was a perilous move—a move few military men would have dared undertake, but Grant was of that bold, sanguine nature, ever confident of success.

CHAPTER XIII.

May 26th, 1863.

Now began one continual series of thrilling events which lasted until the glorious consummation of our labor, which gave the Fourth of July additional luster to the American people in the surrender of the rebel "Gibraltar," Vicksburg, thus virtually raising the blockade of the Mississippi, and from Itasca Lake, in Minnesota, to the broad bosom of the Gulf, could our commerce teem, uninterrupted by traitorous foes. Each day, each night, yes, each hour, now brought to us danger, excitement and mirth. The boys entered into the spirit of the siege with a recklessness and gaiety which totally drove *ennui* from our minds. There was just excitement enough to make it pleasing and danger enough to excite a spirit of daring. I cannot enumerate all the daring enterprises conceived, but will mention one, and let that suffice. We were now within one and one-half miles of the rebel line and two and one-half miles from Vicksburg. In our immediate front was a strong fort, a little isolated from the others, mounting heavy siege guns.

May 31st.

From this fort an annoying fire was kept up on our camp. All efforts of our guns to silence it, proved ineffectual. The fort was surrounded by heavy abattis, strengthened by several lines of sharp pickets, protruding out of the ground several feet, slanting outwards, called *cheval-de-frise*, making it a very perilous enterprise to attempt to capture the fort, but Col. Rogers, chafing under long inactivity and, anxious to distinguish himself and win a proud reputation for the regiment, asked, of the commanding General, and received permission to attempt to surprise and capture the fort, spike the guns and return before re-inforcements could arrive to succor the garrison. Ten picked men, from each company, with one commissioned and two non-commissioned officers, were selected to carry out this enterprise. Rollin, Milt and I were among those selected from our company. Lieut. Waldock was to command a squad from D Company. At that time we did not know what was required of us, although we knew that something of importance was afoot. We got ready and waited for the order to fall in, but fortunately for us, an order came at this time countermanding the former order. The plans were so far matured, that each officer was instructed as to what was required of him and what he should do in certain contingencies. Files were ready to spike the guns. The men were well satisfied at the turn of affairs, though not one would have flinched from the undertaking had not the order been countermanded, yet, the idea of one hundred men capturing such a fort, in the face of twenty thousand men, was preposterous. I always found my courage equal to any duty required of me, but certainly I had no relish for such fool-hardy enterprises where a whole command would have been sacrificed. Pride is a potent word with the true soldier, and rather than be stigmatized as cowardly, he will face a cannon's mouth and suffer himself to be torn limb from limb.

June 1st.

We now received orders to move farther to the right. We kept changing position every few days, gradually drawing nearer the rebel lines, fortifying as we advanced. One day we were on the skirmish and picket line and the next in the trenches. There was no rest for us, but labor, fight and dig was the order. Occasionally we would make a charge on the rebel picket to drive them back and secure a more eligible position for ourselves. From noon until night for days, weeks and months, the rattling of musketry and the heavy notes of artillery were heard. Perhaps while lying concealed in some thicket or copse watching for the foe, the dull thud of a bullet striking a bush or log near you, would apprise you that in the same thicket lay concealed rebels.

Our rifle pits were built in the night. So noiselessly did we work that the enemy, perhaps not more than ten rods off, would not know what we were about until the next morning when perhaps a new line of works, nearer than the others, would extend around the line. Conversation was carried on in a whisper. Sometimes the enemy would find us out and fire on us, causing us to abandon the works for the present. Our picket was relieved in the evening. Sometimes we had to march miles to get forty rods from camp in order to avoid the rebels. The ground was cut up by deep ravines, winding around in such a manner that we could march almost to their lines without being seen. Some of these ravines were covered with a dense thicket. We often passed where the least misstep would have precipitated us hundreds of feet

below. Often we would approach within a few rods of the rebe.
picket and the breaking of a twig or slight rustle of the bushes
would betray our presence. From our position, we would watch
for the enemy and whenever one of them would venture to lift his
head above the rifle pits, a score of bullets, sped by the unerring
hands of the Yankee boys, was sure to greet him. Sometimes for
amusement, we would fire at the men on the fort from one-half to
one mile distant.

June 4th.

One day General Grant rode along the line and told the boys
that he had plenty of ammunition and not to be afraid to use it.
This was a signal for firing. Some of the boys expended over two
hundred rounds that day. The rebs lay in their trenches, whist
as mice, not daring to show their heads. Some evenings when not
on duty, we would crawl to the top of the hill near camp and
watch the gunboats shell the city. From the instant the shell left
the gun, we could trace its progress through the air. The shell
had a rapid rotary motion and the burning fuse with its red glare,
showed its course, describing a semi-circle in traveling four miles.
When at its highest altitude, we would hear the report of the gun.
When it neared the earth, we could see the flash as it exploded,
and after several seconds, we could hear the report. The terrified
inhabitants sought safety in caves from these terrible engines of
death. A practical engineer could so time the fuse as to explode
the shell whenever he wished. Sometimes the rebels would make
a charge on our picket line in the night and try to force it back.
In one of these charges, they surprised the 14th Illinois, killed and
wounded seven and took twenty prisoners, Lieut.-Col. Cam
amongst the number, and filled up their rifle pits. All this was
done so quickly that we, only a short distance from them, were
unable to render them any assistance.

Soon the whizzing of bullets over our heads apprised us that
our presence was required in our own trenches, but the rebels
seemed satisfied with their work and did not molest us further that
night, although we stood with guns cocked, expecting an assault
every moment. On another occasion it was required of the 15th
to dig a rifle pit across an open field in full view of the enemy's
works. It was a moonlight night and we could be plainly seen
from the rebels' lines. Each men of the fatigue party took a
spade and set vigorously to work, and before the astonished rebs

recovered from their surprise, there was enough earth thrown up to protect them from the rebel fire. Each man dug a hole for himself, and as self-preservation was his motive to work, he was not slow about it. Soon after this our regiment was ordered to dig a rifle pit in front of a fort, not more than fifty yards from the rebel picket. A part of the regiment kept watch to prevent being surprised, while the rest worked. Our vidette crawled out a few paces in front of us, lying flat on the ground, ready to give the alarm on the instant, if occasion required. The *modus operandi* of building these rifle pits was this: Long baskets, made of withes in the shape of a cylinder, were placed on line and filled with dirt, the man standing behind one while he filled the next, thus protecting himself from the enemy's fire. On this occasion I was assigned to the working party. There was a rebel picket a few rods in front of us who annoyed us somewhat by his close firing. His shots would strike the baskets and one boy had his hand grazed by a bullet. Anxious to know the whereabouts of this unseen foe, in company with Tommy Huston, I scaled the fort and stood on the top watching for his fire. We presented too tempting a mark for him. Instead of firing on the working party, he drew bead on us. We saw the flash of his gun and attempted to dodge the bullet, but it struck the ground at our feet before we had time to stir. As we did not like to be treated in that uncivil manner, after telling the rebel to shoot higher next time, we hastily "scrabbled" down. Before daylight our work was completed and we returned to camp. It would not have been safe to have attempted to get away from there by daylight. The garrison had to remain there during the day. They could only be relieved in the night.

June 20th.

We had now got so close to the enemy that in several places along the line we were at work undermining their forts with the intention of blowing them up, by digging a deep trench from our works to theirs. Our boys protected themselves in their work by placing cotton bales before them, shoving them along as fast as they dug. When up to the fort the rebs attempted to stop our work by throwing hand grenades over at our boys, but generally they would get out of the way before they burst. Some of the boldest would grab one and hurl it back before it burst, exploding it in the rebel ranks. The chief engineers were bent on under-

mining Ft. Hill, the strongest works that the rebels had. Finally
everything was in readiness, the troops were under arms, ready
to make a charge if a breach was made and our boys went in.
The concussion was terrific. Rebels were thrown twenty feet
into the air and buried in the ruins, but so strong were the works
that the explosion failed to make a breach. A fierce hand-to-hand
encounter ensued over the parapet, bayonets crossed over the
works and thrusts and stabs were made. Our boys finally retired,
confident that victory wonld soon crown our efforts. The 45th
Illinois stood the brunt of this engagement.

June 25th.

The next day we were ordered to hold ourselves in readiness
for action. The artillery received orders to look to their ammunition. On the morrow, at four o'clock A. M., a general cannonading along the whole line was ordered and to be kept up until ten
o'clock A. M. The 15th lay just in the rear, supporting several
heavy siege-guns and some twenty-pound Parrott guns. We waited
with impatience for the ball to open. Soon the signal gun was
fired; then, as if by magic, the hoarse notes of hundreds of pieces
of artillery shook the ground. It seemed as though the very earth
was going to open and swallow us up. The chief of artillery in
in our division offered the prize of a field-glass to the one that
would make the best shot. We lay where we could note the effect
of this cannonading. Our solid shot would strike the rebel works,
filling the air with a cloud of dirt. The air was full of screeching
shells, crossing each other's track and finally bursting in town or in
the rebel camp. For six hours this terrible cannonading was kept
up but it failed to elicit a response from the rebels. They remained
quiet as the grave. We never ascertained the amount of damage
done. A shot from a gun in front of us, cut the rebel flag-staff in
two and the dirty rag came tumbling to the earth. The fellow
that fired that shot received the field-glass. On other occasions a
general cannonading occurred, but with little effect. The situation was now getting decidedly interesting. The two armies were
so close to each other that they could almost shake hands, while in
our rear was a powerful rebel army under the rebel General Jobn-
son watching for a favorable opportunity to pounce upon us, but
the brave Dutchman, Osterhaus, with his command, kept a vigilant eye upon him and he dared not cross Black River. Rumors
that Johnson was going to attempt to raise the siege and relieve

the garrison at Vicksburg were rife in camp, but still he did not
try it. While our regiment was on picket one day, Company I
caught eleven rebs trying to steal through our lines. They had
two hundred thousand percussion caps and a dispatch from Johnson to Pemberton in cipher. The rebs were sadly in need of percussion caps and Johnson took this method of supplying them, but
our boys couldn't see it, so they snailed them in. The dispatch
was deciphered. It stated that if Pemberton could hold out two
weeks longer, he would be there to relieve him, but somehow or
other, he failed to keep his promise. I suspect that the brave
Dutchman interfered with his plans. Occasionally we would succeed in getting hold of a paper printed in Vicksburg. It was
printed on wall paper and with a miserable type, fit emblems of the
waning fortunes of the Confederacy. This paper would have flam-
ing editorials telling about Johnson, how that, at the proper
moment, he would attack and annihilate Grant. It also stated that
Marmaduke had captured Milliken's Bend and cut off our supplies,
and by a general system of lying had made the rebel soldiers believe
that we were as good as "goners." The opposing armies were so
near each other now that the soldiers of each could not resist the
temptation to blackguard each other, and for the sake of gratify-
ing their minds in this respect, they would agree upon a cessation
of hostilities for an hour or so.

The time usually selected was just as the day was deepening into
twilight. Then the two armies' pickets would commence a regular
system of blackguardism. We liked to remind them of their situation and that in all probability they would soon be our prisoners.
Then, perhaps, we would ask them how their mule meat was holding out. In return they said that Joe Johnson would soon make
us "hunt our hole." In reply, we would tell them that Johnson
was annihilated and hosts of other answers. They would retort by
asking how we liked to have our hard-tack-line cut off. They actually believed, until we undeceived them, that Marmaduke and
Dick Taylor had taken Milliken's Bend and cut off our supplies.

The rebels were both pleased and surprised to learn that we
felt no ill will toward them personally, but that we wholly blamed
their leaders for deceiving them and bringing this war upon them.
They had been taught from the commencement that we entertained
a deadly hatred toward them and that we were prosecuting the
war to free the negro and to get plunder. They had been told

that it was a vindictive and mercenary war on our part, with the sole object of ruining and desolating the South, and as they had no means of gainsaying them, they were compelled to accept them as facts, but when they came to converse with us and found out that the restoration of the Union, founded on mutual justice, was our sole purpose, a better feeling sprang up and their cause became decidedly unpopular. Desertions became quite frequent from the rebel lines. They would have deserted by regiments, if they could have gotten away. Some of the most scrupulous on this point have been known to come over and drink a cup of coffee with our boys and then return. One evening, while conversing with the rebs, we found a man from our neighborhood in the 27th Georgia, in front of us, whom I used to know. He began to question us first by inquiring what regiment we belonged to, and when he learned that we were in the 15th Illinois, and from Marengo, he asked if such and such persons were in the company. Being answered in the affirmative, we then asked him his name. It was Charles Rice, a boy well-known to many of us. He assured us that he espoused the cause of the South because he thought they were right. Maj.-Gen. Herron's division had now taken up its position on our left. That impetuous commander was ever wide awake, seeking some vulnerable point in the enemy's lines and pouring a continual stream of fire from his artillery with telling effect.

July 1st.

One day I saw some of Herron's pickets march up and surprise and capture a rebel picket post, right in face of the enemy's big guns. Before the astonished rebs could recover their senses, our boys were well on their way back, but a sweeping discharge of grape and canister laid some of the brave fellows low. The siege of Vicksburg was noted for such daring and bravery on our part. We had a splendid signal corps camped on the highest point of observation in our lines, and not a movement the rebels could make of any importance, but what was signaled to head-quarters.

Grant had high towers or look-outs built where he could look down into the city. It seemed now as if the decisive moment must soon arrive. Johnson was strongly threatening an attack, and Grant had determined, if he was hard pressed by Johnson, to charge and take the enemy's works by assault. This could be done, but it would involve a tremendous sacrifice of life, and it was only to be resorted to in the last extremity. We now had several of their forts undermined and about ready to be blown up, but General Grant thought proper to demand a surrender before proceeding to extremities. Accordingly it was made with the request, that in case of non-acceptance, he, Pemberton, would have the women, children and non-combatants removed, as he should shell the city. He received the haughty reply from the commander that he was placed there to defend the women, children and helpless, not to turn them off, and the blood be on their own heads for the sacrifice of the women that were killed in the terrible bombardment which followed. They sought shelter in caves, but they were built to protect them from fire from the river side. From the rear it afforded them sorry protection. So sharp was our target shooting that a rebel could not even show his head above the works, but that a dozen bullets would speed after him. There was not a spot in the sand-banks, which formed their loop-holes, but what was pierced with bullets. The rebels lay in their trenches forty-eight hours without scarcely stirring. They dared not attempt to leave. Food and water was brought to them in the night. They showed a perseverance and valor worthy of a better cause, but it was not possible for human flesh to hold out much longer. Their last ration was nearly consumed before the rebel general asked for an armistice to arrange terms of capitulation.

July 3d.

The two Generals met beneath the wide spreading branches of a stately oak between the lines. These two Generals had been companions at West Point Military Academy. Both received their education and were sustained by the fostering care of the Government. Behold them now! Comments are unnecessary. The picture suggests its own sequel. General Grant gave him until the next morning to accede to his unconditional terms of surrender. In the meantime, he informed him that if he did not surrender, he would again open on the town and would not cease until it was in smoking ruins or he showed the white flag. While the truce was being held, the pickets of the two armies met and conversed on friendly terms on neutral ground between the lines. Blackberries were very thick there and friend and foe picked from the same bush and vied with each other in acts of civility. Our regiment was on picket duty in the rear at this time and we lost this occasion of enjoyment. Pemberton did not at once accede to

Grant's unconditional terms.   He was given until ten o'clock the next day to consider.

July 4th.

The morning hours of the Fourth of July were slowly dragging toward ten o'clock and still our strained visions could detect no signs of surrender.   A deep silence prevailed.   Finally the order came for the troops to be under arms, but just then a white flag was seen to flutter from the rebel works, which proclaimed that the finale had been reached.   Then one long, joyous shout echoed and re-echoed along our lines.   Its cadence rang long and deep over hill and valley until we caught the glad anthem and swelled the chorus with our voices in one glad shout of joy.   It was a glorious opening for the Fourth of July, this day sacred to every American heart as a day that gave Freedom birth, was made more glorious, more hallowed by witnessing the severing of the strongest link in the chain which was riveting slavery, despotism and ruin upon our fair land, dimming the bright luster of our proud American escutcheon.   On the wings of the wind, the glad news was borne to anxious waiting hearts at our firesides in the North, until every hamlet, town and city pealed forth its notes of joy at the great victory.   Could we at that moment have rent aside the veil which hides from our view the glory which surrounds our revolutionary sires in the spirit land, methinks we would have seen smiles of gladness radiate their countenances as they mingled their congratulations with the martyr heroes of this war who had yielded up their lives to preserve the freedom for which they sacrificed theirs.   This great victory gave us thirty-one thousand prisoners, three hundred pieces of artillery and fifty thousand stand of small arms, and an immense amount of ordnance stores.   Gen. Grant paroled the prisoners and they were permitted to go home.   They left singly and in groups and by companies and battalions.   The enemy's camp showed plainly the ravages of war.   In front of our picket line was stationed the 27th Georgia regiment, and eleven newly made graves could be counted, showing that our random fire did some execution.   We hoped now to enjoy a short season of rest, but scarcely had the excitement begun to abate, consequent upon the surrender of the city before we received orders to be ready to march immediately.

July 5th.

The indomitable Grant, never easy when any armed traitors

were within striking distance, immediately upon the surrender of Vicksburg, turned upon Johnson, hoping to give him a blow before he heard of the fall of Vicksburg, but that wary General had no desire to measure swords with Grant just then and so he beat a precipitate retreat, closely followed by our victorious army. Only one corps was left in and around Vicksburg, except the sick and wounded. I was feeling quite unwell at this time and the doctor advised me to stay back with the sick, but I thought that it was only temporary illness, so I concluded to start with the regiment. Early on the morning of the 5th we were on the move. The weather was excessively hot. I came very near giving out the first day, but I got permission to fall out from the ranks and take my own time. In this manner, I got along quite well. We camped near Black River the first night, having made only nine miles. Here we had to wait until other troops crossed, and it was not until the morning of the sixth that we crossed.

July 6th.

On this day we halted at five o'clock P. M. on the battle ground of Champion Hill and supposed that we were going into camp. Our regiment was detailed for picket duty. We had scarcely been posted before orders came to resume the march. The night set in dark and stormy. The rain came down in torrents. We were soon wet to the skin. The water in the road was ankle deep, and we had to pick our way by the flash of the lightning. In this way we continued on until after midnight, when we halted on a high hill to seek rest and sleep.

July 7th.

A huge fire of rails was soon built, and stretching ourselves on a few rails before the fire, we soon fell into a profound slumber, from which the rain beating upon our faces failed to arouse us. The cause of this sudden move was this: Our advance had encountered the enemy's rear near this place and a prudent commander like Sherman, kept his men well in hand for emergencies. By daylight, we were on the march again, but the roads were so bad we only made fifteen miles that day.

July 8th.

Our advance were continually skirmishing with the rebs. The next day we halted within fifteen miles of Jackson.

July 9th.

On the 9th, when within six miles of Jackson, our brigade was ordered to halt and guard a large train which was left here. Our provisions now failed us and we subsisted for three days on green corn. Salt was very scarce and it set a good many of the boys into a diarrhœa. I was lucky enough to have some salt with me, and Roll, William, Milt, Charlie and myself had a good dish of succotash. The boys foraged the country for miles around but failed to find anything good in the eating line. Jeff Davis' plantation was only a few miles from our camp. Some of the boys visited it and brought away relics. Some went to his library and brought away some of his books. Others would bring away a piece of a carpet for a blanket. William got a piece of the latter, but the most valuable of all was Jeff Davis' private correspondence. These private letters of the rebel chieftain opened our eyes to the deep duplicity practiced by the leading rebels long before the final outbreak. This correspondence embraced letters to the leading men of the South of the Yancey and Rhett school. There were also letters from ex-president Pierce implicating him in a great measure as being in sympathy with Southern fire-eaters.

At the time these letters were written, from 1852 until 1860, Jefferson C. Davis was a senator of the United States from the state of Mississippi. His speeches at that time, both in congress and in public, pompously proclaimed his great devotion to the Union. In Faneuil Hall, in Boston, he used the words: "Palsied be the hand which attempts to sever the ties which bind the American Union," yet, at this time, he was concocting his hellish plan for the disruption of this government. To Governor Rhett, of South Carolina, he urged the necessity of more vigorous action. He accused him of lukewarmness. Secret circulars were issued, poisoning and prejudicing the Southern mind and heart against what they called the tyranny of the North and with the poor, ignorant classes, they too well succeeded. At the time of Buchanan's election, in a letter to his brother, Davis used the words: "We have now four more years to prepare in," that is to say, that while James Buchanan is President of the United States, we have a friend and ally who will not interfere in our traitorous schemes. At the same time, the language implies that at the next presidential election the tide would turn against them and that they must mature their plans during Buchanan's administration. The leading rebels, to further their schemes of secession, made the grossest misstatements and resorted to the vilest depths of treachery. To our laboring female population, such as worked in factories, etc., they gave the name of prostitutes. Our mechanics, men of genius, were nothing but mudsills, still, these despised mudsills, as they were termed, built their cities, railroads and all their manufacturing establishments, and to them, more than to any other class of people, are they indebted for whatever of prosperity they have enjoyed. In comparing the resources of the South with those of the North, they claimed that the little State of North Carolina was equal to five of the New England States or to Pennsylvania or Ohio. They also claimed that the resources of the South were inexhaustible while the North was already pinched with want. Thus, by a system of lies industriously circulated, they succeeded in uniting the South against the North in a deadly warfare. While the poor deluded victims bore the brunt of the battle, the chivalry bore off the spoils. This boasted chivalry represented the North as carrying on the war for plunder; that our purpose was to pillage, burn and destroy their homes, free their slaves and spread general ruin and desolation in our track. The fiery appeals of their leaders found a responsive echo in the hearts of the deluded Southern people. This picture is not overdrawn. I have the evidence of my own senses that this devilish deception was practiced upon the ignorant, and to Jeff Davis more than any other man, do I ascribe the guilt of producing this state of affairs, and ever since, I have had a strong desire to have justice meted out to him. I am sure that he will get it sooner or later.

July 14th.

Much to our satisfaction, we now received orders to march to the front and join our division. Before night we had taken our position in line of battle. Johnson had made a stand at Jackson. Gen. Sherman concluded not to sacrifice the lives of his men by assaulting their works when a safer and surer method was open to him. So we commenced fortifying and gradually extending our lines toward the rear of the enemy with the purpose of surrounding him and cutting off his retreat. Our division-commander, Gen. Lauman, now made a blunder which lost him his command. In his strong desire for popularity and promotion, he overdid the thing. He misinterpreted an order to move forward our line for a charge on the rebel works. The charge was made and the rebels finding it unsupported, concentrated their whole available force against us. Unfalteringly we swept up to within a few rods of

8

their works, but their fire was too terrific for flesh and blood to
stand. We were forced to retire with fully one-fourth of the
boys placed hors de combat. A flag of truce was sent in asking
permission to bury our dead. It was refused. They lay where
they had fallen until the stench became so offensive to the rebels
that they were forced to do something with them. So without any
regard to decency, they scooped out shallow holes and rolled them
in and left a great many arms and legs in sight.

July 15th.

By the 15th, we had them nearly surrounded. One more day
would have cut off their retreat, but that wary General, Johnson,
was not to be caught napping. Silently, and in a masterly manner,
he effected a retreat and our troops took quiet possession of the
place and at once proceeded to gather up the spoils of war.
Tobacco seemed to be the greatest spoil, but some succeeded in
getting the genuine "yellow dogs" (gold). We pursued the foe
as far as Brandon, ten miles from Jackson, and then returned.
My health, which had for some time been quite poor, now entirely
failed me. I had a run of fever. I was sent out one day in
charge of a fatigue party, to clear the ground in front of our
works, but before it was finished, I was forced to give up and go
to camp. I found Dr. Myron Underwood there looking for me.
He was assistant surgeon of a regiment camped near by. He
advised me to take medicine immediately and try and break up
my fever. I was sent back to Vicksburg in a sick train and
started one day in advance of the army. We went by way of
Raymond and the army took the old route. Near Raymond is an
artesian well, celebrated for the medicinal virtue of its waters.
The existence of the water was made known to a man by a vision,
and under the influence of that vision, he proceeded to put down
the well, but his means failing and meeting with other discourage-
ments, he abandoned it for a time. He again had the same vision
and again went to work and finished the well and his vision was
verified. Hundreds of invalids visited the well yearly and its
waters proved to be a great benefit to them. The weather was extremely hot and our wagon being uncovered, I suffered excru-
ciating tortures from the burning rays of the sun.

July 16th.

When within ten miles of Vicksburg, I left my hot bed and
went the rest of the way afoot, though so weak I could scarcely

walk. I got into camp about six hours before the regiment. We expected to enjoy a short season of rest during the hottest part of the season, but our expectations were poorly realized. An order now came to grant furloughs at the rate of five per cent. of all enlisted men. In consideration of the state of my health, I was proposed as one of the favored ones, but there were some men who had families at home which needed their presence and I yielded my claim to them, and my friends, Stockwell and Thompson went. We now moved camp inside the rebel works, one mile south of the city. The ground was still strewed with the filth of the rebel camp and the air was pregnant with noxious odors. The water was very poor. We drew a great portion of it from the river which was more than a mile from camp. As a consequence of our foul camp and the impure water, the sick list increased rapidly, endangering the organization of the regiment. It became necessary to move camp to a more healthy position in order to preserve the organization. Every day the solemn strokes of the muffled drum told the requiem of departed comrades.

July 17th.

I was attacked with a dysentery but by being very careful, I managed to keep around. One day I went to the city and called on John Eddy, who was clerk in the purveyor's department and he got me up a dinner which did me good. Vicksburg is situated on a series of bluffs commencing at the river and extending back. Each bluff rising above the one in front. Aside from its commercial importance, it is an inferior city. Its population is about six thousand. Jackson is situated forty-four miles east of Vicksburg on Pearl river. It is a fine looking city and surrounded by a splendid looking country. The State Capitol, situated in the center of the town, is a fine looking structure. The rebels burnt the best part of the city before Sherman occupied it. Much to our satisfaction, we now received orders to take transports and go down the river to Natchez. We were now transferred from Logan's command, 15th corps to the 16th corps, Maj.-Gen. E. O. C. Ord commanding.

July 20th.

But a few days elapsed before we were transferred to the 17th corps, Maj.-Gen. James B. McPherson commanding. We were still on the 4th division, Brig.-Gen. M. M. Crocker, commanding. This worthy officer succeeded Gen. Lauman when he was displaced

at Jackson.   Gen. Lauman carried his hatred of our regiment so
far as to prejudice Gen. Crocker against us, but after being with us
for awhile, he changed his mind concerning us and we became the
favorite regiment of his command.   In conversation and appearance, Gen. Crocker was a very rough appearing man.   Swearing
was second nature to him, but a braver officer never drew his
sword.   (He has lately died.)   We found the 95th Illinois at
Natchez doing garrison duty.   We camped on the levee the first
night.   The next morning we marched one and one-half miles
north of the city and went into camp.   The U. S. marine hospital
is situated here and is a fine looking building.

July 21st.

We hardly got established in camp before an order came for
our brigade to guard a train of wagons to Kingston, twenty miles
east of Natchez, to secure twenty thousand bales of cotton.   Our
troops captured the place, but fearing an attack from overwhelming numbers, sent back for re-inforcements.   I had been left at
Natchez sick when my regiment went out.   I went out with the
re-inforcements.   I found the boys having a jolly time and living
on the top shelf.   We were in a rich country.   Our tables were
loaded with fruits, jellies, vegetables, etc.   A company of the
95th got a keg of beer, and of course, they had to treat their
friends in the 15th, and together, some of them had rather a jolly
time, and some of their heads got so heavy that they could not
walk straight.   It rained a great deal of the time we were out
here, and having no tents with us, we got wet.   I took cold.
Finally the last load of cotton was secured and we started for
Natchez and it rained hard all day.   I got thoroughly drenched.
I now had to give up.   A fever set in, commencing with ague and
terminating with an intermittent fever.   For two weeks I did not
leave my bed.   This was the first time that I had been confined to
a sick-bed for any length of time since. I enlisted, and it seemed
tough to bear.   Just as soon as I was able to be around, I went
back to the company.   I paid dearly for my imprudence.   I had
a relapse, and for several days I lay in a precarious state, insensible
to anything.   The doctor considered my case doubtful, but not
liking the idea of a doctor getting seven dollars for burying me, I
determined to disappoint him, but it was a long time before I was
well enough to resume my duties, and to this day, I have
never fully recovered from the effects of that illness.   While

insensible, the doctor got a dose of calomel down me which salivated me.

August 1st.

Our division again received marching orders. They crossed the Mississippi into Louisiana and proceeded as far as Washita river and captured Ft. Beauregard. The fort was six miles from Natchez and our boys made the trip there and back in five days.

August 10th.

My health still continued poor. I went back to the company, but was still kept on the sick list. I reported for duty but was not accepted and all the while that I was at Natchez, I did not do any military duty except voluntarily.

August 15th.

We now went to work to prepare better quarters, supposing that we would pass the winter here.

August 20th.

We built a square frame four or five feet high, boarded it up and set our tent on top. On one side we built our bunks, one above the other. This left over one-half of the tent for spare room. We had a writing table and several camp stools. In one corner was a door and in the other a cozy little fire-place with the chimney built on the outside. Just as we had got the chimney built, Captain Smith notified me that my name had been sent in for a furlough, but perhaps it would be several weeks before it got around.

August 25th.

While here, Col. Hall, who now commanded the brigade, ordered matched drills between the different companies comprising the brigade. As a reward for the best drilled company, it was to be excused from duty for ten days. This was quite an item, as our duty was quite heavy.

August 30th.

The different companies now set to work drilling, cleaning guns and improving everything that would make a good military show. Each company knew the day of its trial. Judges were appointed from each regiment, and in case of their disagreeing, Col. Hall was appointed umpire, but jealousies and ill-feelings were soon created. Col. Hall was accused of favoring his old regiment, the 14th.

September 8th.

Company D acquitted itself creditably and the judges were unanimous in the opinion that we excelled in drill and manual of arms, but one or two of the boys were dressed slovenly and a speck of dirt was discovered on their guns, so we were counted out, and so it went until finally the judges awarded no decision. The only good the drill did was getting the arms in number one order and perfecting our drill a little more.

September 10th.

Col. Crocker was present at these drills and warmly applauded our efforts. My health had so far improved that I was able to walk. I went down to the 95th quite often to see Asahel Wiff and other friends. Occasionally I attended church.

September 15th.

I went to the catholic church one morning and was quite amused with their performances. It was quite galling to these rebel divines not to be permitted to pray in public for the success of the South.

Natchez is one of the most beautiful cities of the South. It was nearly destroyed by a tornado in 1820, but has been rebuilt. It is a very wealthy place, its principal inhabitants being large planters whose plantations were in the surrounding country. Its streets are neatly laid out, wide and well shaded. There are a good many splendid residences in the suburbs. "Natchez under the Hill" as it is called, is situated on the levee at the foot of the bluff and it was a perfect cess-pool of vice. It had always been the resort of the worst characters and was noted for the amount of crime which had been perpetrated in its midst.

September 30th.

There were camped here about twenty thousand negroes. Their condition was distressing in the extreme. The small-pox broke out amongst them, carrying off as many as one hundred daily. They just rolled in filth and rags, dependent upon the Government for support. A good many earned a little by washing clothes for the soldiers. Most of the able bodied males enlisted and several regiments were formed here. Some of our boys went in as officers of companies.

October 5th.

Tidings of the bloody battle of Chickamauga now reached us. It came first through rebel sources. There had been a rebel regiment formed from the principal young business men of Natchez, which was in the fight and only about thirty escaped unhurt. There was weeping and wailing in the city. These men were the flower of the society there, and although our foes, we could not but sympathize with their friends in their loss.

October 10th.

We now commenced fortifying. One of the best houses in the city was pulled down over the rebel owner's head and a fort built on its site. The rebel General Rodney threatened an attack, and for two days our troops were kept under arms. We finally marched out to meet him and he retreated in hot haste. There is a peculiar feature in the country around Natchez which deserves mention, viz: deep gulches or a sinking away of the earth. These sink-holes are sometimes abrupt and are from eighty to one hundred feet deep and are very irregular in shape. They used to be hiding places for thieves, etc., the thick cane brake and caverns affording good concealment.

Some supposed that these gulches were caused by earthquakes, others by quicksand settling away. The ground is very sandy, and when heavy freshets occur, it caves in. Plantations have been badly injured and the graveyard at Natchez partially destroyed in this manner. Millions of dollars have been expended in building something to prevent this destruction.

October 25th.

My furlough had now gotten around, duly signed and approved by Gen. McPherson. The date was left blank and Col. Rogers gave me permission to fill that but not put it beyond the present month, so I dated it the 29th, thus gaining four days' time. I now felt in excellent spirits at the thought that I would soon be at home. To a war-worn, sick soldier, the shelter of home, where love and kindness only greet him, is a heaven upon earth. It was with feelings of regret that even for so short a time I was to leave the boys. The sacred ties of friendship, cemented and strengthened by sharing mutual toil and danger were strong. On the 29th of October, I was on board a steamer with my face set homeward.

October 30th.

On the 30th I arrived at Cairo. When my feet again pressed the soil of my adopted State, feelings of joy filled my soul. Every little delay annoyed me exceedingly. My heart filled with pride, viewing as I passed along, the thrift and plenty which prevailed wherever the eye might look. Large fields of golden corn were bending 'neath the weight of their autumnal load. Huge ricks of grain and hay bespoke the plenty with which the country abounded. The villages were teeming with busy life. A stranger, to pass through the State, could not realize that a terrible civil war was raging in our land and that one hundred thousand of the brave yeoman of the soil of Illinois were battling with vehement energy and bravery to save this fair land from disruption and desolation.

November 1st.

I could not help contrasting this busy scene with the desolation which reigned in the South. On the one hand were the friends of freedom and free labor, and thrift and plenty reigned supreme. On the other hand, were the friends of slavery and secession, desolating the land which fostered them and seeking to involve the whole in one common ruin. The next day's light revealed to me the spires of the Golden City. I was just in time to take the morning train. With lightning speed, I passed old familiar objects, and, at noon, I arrived at Marengo. I had hoped to surprise my friends but they had been expecting me. Kindly faces and warm greetings met me on every side. I hastened to my old friend, Billy Holgate, to get barbered before presenting myself to my friends, but Nivvie, my darling, impulsive sister, who was attending school at Marengo, heard of my arrival, traced me to the barber shop and regardless of consequences, threw her arms around me, sobbing like a child. What matter to her that my bearded face was all lather! It was enough that I was there, and for awhile good Billy had to stand back. Other school girls had come peeping in at the door. All shy, yet, anxious to greet me. I now started for uncle Lorenzo's, but news of my arrival had preceded me. My good old grandfather could not wait for me to get there but came out to meet me, with faltering voice and tear-dimmed eyes, he reached out his aged hands to bless and welcome me. Dear old man! He is at rest now! If all mankind had been as sinless as he, this horrid war would never have been. Equally warm were the greetings of the others. After dinner, I hastened up to Mr. Crissey's to see Cinda who was there on a visit. On my way, I encountered Let Eddy who was teaching school at Marengo. I had the satisfaction of completely surprising Cinda. One would have thought to have seen how she acted that she was a little demented. Just as twilight was folding her curtain over Mother

Nature, I arrived at home. I tried to steal upon them unawares, but Manda's watchful eyes caught sight of me and when opposite the weeping willow, her arms were twined around my neck, she weeping and laughing by turns. Mother heard the glad cry and a fervent "Thank God" escaped her lips and she was soon weeping on my neck. No less affecting was father's warm greeting. Rose, too, had her cry and Amory, very dignified, came forward, hardly knowing whether to laugh or cry. Lester was absent at the time, but when he returned and found that I was there, something quite moist was seen to gather in his eye and brother and brother were clasped in a strong embrace. Father, mother, brothers, sisters, I am with you once again, but in my joy at beholding you, I cannot forget that there is one who is not here to greet me (in body). One loved voice, one loved form is absent, but if angels are permitted to visit this mundane sphere, Alzina was there and enveloped us all with her great love.

CHAPTER XIV.

November 10th.

I will pass over briefly my stay at home. My readers are already familiar with it, but I cannot omit to again acknowledge the unceasing kindness and care during the illness which succeeded my arrival. In the rough usages of camp life, a soldier learns to rely a great deal on self during trouble, but to be suddenly transferred to where every wish is anticipated, to be petted and indulged unceasingly, formed so striking a contrast that I thought it was taking away my military pride to submit to it. For every peevish and fretful word, I humbly crave pardon. Kindness will conquer the most rebellious nature. I now learned from letters from the boys that our division had moved up to Vicksburg. After the first glad excitement of being at home began to subside, I began to long for the companionship of old friends and comrades, but my protracted ill-health made it necessary for me to stay longer than I anticipated. My furlough had been extended twice. I had been at home over two months. I felt that to remain longer would be a neglect of duty. But here I must beg pardon for omitting to mention the nuptials of Lester and Mary. I owe them many thanks for having that interesting ceremony performed while I was there to witness it.

December 1st.

Government had offered large inducements for the first three years' men to re-enlist, and by letters from the boys I learned that a good portion of the 15th had re-enlisted for three years longer. Roll, Milt and Charlie Mitchell amongst the number.

December 10th.

This produced a feverish state of excitement in my mind. I longed to be with them. I did not say much about it to my folks for I knew that they would oppose me. Perhaps it was foolhardy to think of re-enlisting in my poor state of health, but I believed that one year would see the end of the Rebellion and I thought that I could stand it that length of time.

I had a strong desire to see the end and nothing but absolute physical disability would prevent it.

January 5th, 1864.

January 5th was the day set for my departure. I felt that the Star of Destiny which had so long protected me would still continue to shield me and that when peace had dawned upon us, would return me safe home at last. The last good-by had been spoken and I stepped on board and was soon rapidly whirling toward Dixie.

January 10th.

On arriving at Cairo, I found the river so blocked with ice that it would be impossible for a steamer to leave for several days. The first steamer that left, the Illinois, bore me as a passenger. We were soon beneath the frowning batteries of the forts at Columbus, Kentucky. The next day we touched at Memphis. On the same evening we passed Helena, and on the ninth day after leaving home I landed at Vicksburg. I found the 95th here but Asahel had been transferred to the invalid corps. Russell Mallory and Dan Mitchell went to my camp with me.

It was situated eight miles from Vicksburg and named Camp Cowan.

January 15th.

I found the boys all well and in excellent spirits. They were in comfortable quarters. They had log cabins sixteen feet square. I found mess No. 4 all quartered together, but they had a place left for me. We had a very pleasant camp and we passed three months of contentment here. Soon after getting back, I enrolled my name as a veteran and got my enlistment dated back to the 1st of January. The other boys enlisted the 15th of December. My health was now much improved.

January 20th.

Camp life and out-door exercise brought strength to my frame. Every day we engaged in the pastime of playing ball, jumping, etc. We occasionally had battalion drill.

January 25th.

A good many of the boys were engaged in making keepsakes out of "Pemberton's oak" as it was called, the wood being gotten from the tree under which Pemberton and Grant sat when the final terms of the surrender of Vicksburg were agreed upon. There was not a root or branch remaining.

A great deal of dissatisfaction began to be manifested now amongst the veterans. Government had not fulfilled its promise.

We were to have thirty days' furlough and one installment of
bounty immediately after enlisting.

January 31st.

There was no immediate prospect of either, but instead, a long
and arduous campaign was marked out for us. A good many
would have backed out if they could, but they had signed their
enlistment papers and there was no help for them. We were to
receive four hundred dollars government bounty, to be paid, one
installment of sixty dollars when sworn in and another two months
after, the rest in semi-annual installments of fifty dollars, unless
honorably discharged before the expiration of our time, in which
case, we were to receive the residue in full.

February 1st.

We broke up camp at Cowan on the 31st and removed to Camp
Hebron, near Black River bridge. The enemy here made a dash
at our picket line but was easily repulsed. We now made our
final preparation for the campaign. The command comprised the
greater portion of the 16th and 17th corps, the former commanded
by Maj.-Gen. Hurlbut, the latter by Maj.-Gen. McPherson. Gen.
Sherman was in command of the expedition. Each corps had a
train of over five hundred wagons with ammunition and provision.
We went in light marching order, carrying only one blanket
apiece and no tents.

February 3d.

We left camp on the 3d, halted awhile at Black River, where
Gen. McPherson issued an order which was read to each regiment.
He predicted that this campaign would be short and glorious. He
regretted the necessity that compelled the veterans to go on this
march before they had had their furloughs, but he promised them
that they should have them as soon as they returned. This satisfied the boys. We were still ignorant of the object of the campaign, but it became manifest as we advanced. Sherman had cut
entirely loose from his base and all communication from the outside world. The whole nation looked on in wonder at this bold
move. Various were the conjectures concerning his movements.
Some supposed that he was going through to Mobile. Others
thought that he was going to join Grant. We camped near
Champion Hills the first night and our regiment was detailed to go
on picket. The next morning our brigade was in the lead. The
cavalry went ahead as skirmishers, but they soon came flying back

in disorder. They had met a large force of rebel cavalry and been completely routed. Gen. McPherson ordered Gen. Crocker to send forward his best regiment and deploy them as skirmishers, and the 15th was ordered to perform this duty.

Without delay, we proceeded to the front. We advanced one mile uninterrupted and then came upon a brigade of Wirt Adams' rebel cavalry. It was strongly posted in the woods across the open space in front of us. Without any delay, we opened fire upon them, which they returned. They being concealed in the woods had the advantage, but we had good backing and did not hesitate to attack them. The 14th was in line of battle a short distance in our rear as support. Gen. McPherson rode up and took a survey of the field and said that he would soon rout them out of that. Just at this time a rebel officer mounted on a beautiful white charger rode out toward us. We were ordered not to fire, supposing him to be a bearer of dispatches. He rode up to within easy range, coolly drew his revolver and fired several shots at Col. Rogers who was on horseback, then wheeled his horse and fled. A perfect shower of bullets was sent after him, but strange to say, he escaped unhurt. His very boldness insured his safety. We were petrified with astonishment. Now the order came to advance and we swept across the field in quick time, expecting to meet a withering volley of musketry, but the rebs deemed it prudent to retreat, and just as we gained their first position, we saw them posted in another. The man on the white horse was riding up and down in front of the line, encouraging the men. Shot after shot was fired at him but he still remained unhurt. He seemed to bear a charmed life. A sharp firing was kept up on either side for about fifteen minutes. We took the trees for shelter and their firing did us little damage.

We again moved forward and again the rebels retreated. The rider of the white horse rode furiously up and down the line, waving his sword and vainly trying to rally them. As we advanced, we passed seven dead rebels, thus showing that our fire was not without effect, and by the track of blood we knew that many were wounded. The rider of the white horse again succeeded in bringing them to a stand. Again we charged them and again they fled. A very melancholy incident now occurred. The rebs had taken a position just beyond a dwelling house where lived a widow with three small children. She came to the door to

see what was going on when a ball struck her, killing her instantly.
When our boys got there, they found her form rigid in death,
lying in a pool of her own life's blood. Her little children were
clinging frantically to her, not realizing that she was dead. Gen.
Sherman caused a notice to be immediately posted on the house,
specifying the manner of her death and ordering the premises to
be held as sacred. I do not know from which side the shot was
fired that killed her. About three o'clock the rebels made a
determined stand by a stream of water which they supposed we
would want to camp by. The stream was bordered by thick
underbrush in which the rebels lay concealed. In order to get at
them we had to cross an open field two hundred yards in width.
The rebels now opened upon us a furious fire from which we took
shelter behind a rail fence. They had now brought artillery into
play. They had evidently received re-inforcements, but it was
necessary to dislodge them, and we prepared for this dangerous
charge. We fully expected to leave one-half of our number dead
and wounded on that field, but good luck showed it otherwise.
At a given signal we trailed arms and with a yell that made the
welkin ring, we rushed across the field. The rebels, terrified,
hastily retreated, after giving us one volley which passed harm-
lessly over our heads. Only one man was severely wounded,
Lieut. Allison, of Company H. The regiments in the rear
suffered more than we did, quite a number being killed and
wounded. The rebels had planted their artillery so as to rake the
bridge, and they commenced pouring in their grape and canister
upon us but the thick bushes prevented it from doing any harm.
One shell dropped in our midst and exploded, but strange to say, it
did not injure any one, although it flew into a hundred pieces.
Col. Rogers asked permission to charge the battery but Gen.
McPherson was not willing to make the sacrifice of lives which would
necessarily follow such a charge. He had a surer and safer
method of dislodging them. He sent out our skirmishers and
they flanked the battery and poured in so hot a fire that it was
forced to retreat. We now quietly crossed the stream. The rebs
did not annoy us much more that day. We had marched fourteen
miles in line of battle, through swamps and creeks, through dense
woods, valleys and over mountains. We had made charge after
charge and steadily driven the enemy before us. We were now
completely tired out and the 12th Wisconsin took our place for a

short time. We did not march much farther that night. Generals McPherson and Crocker paid us a high compliment for our work that day. The reputation of the 15th from this time for fighting qualities was second to none in the army. During the day Col. Rogers received an injury in one eye by a piece of shell throwing dirt into it, and as we were going into camp, he was struck by a spent ball, fired by a rebel in ambush, and he fell from his horse insensible, but he recovered and would not relinquish the command of the regiment.

In the last charge that we made, we did not notice the rider of the white horse, but we found the white horse dead by the side of the road and the citizens said it was one that Wirt Adams rode, but whether the rider escaped uninjured, we could not tell. During the night, the rebels received large re-inforcements and they boldly resisted our march on the next day. A sharp and severe fight of fifteen or twenty minutes' duration in which a number were killed and wounded on both sides, resulted in a total rout of the rebels. They did not oppose us in a body after this, but hung on our flanks and rear to pick up stragglers and attack foraging parties. Our route lay through a splendid looking country, remarkably level, rich soil and well watered and timbered. The most prominent places we passed through were Brandon, Decatur and Hillsboro. At Decatur, Hurlbut's train was attacked by a band of guerrillas and twenty wagons were captured and destroyed. The leader of the assault was a resident of Decatur. His splendid residence and the principal part of the town were burned in retaliation. The country through which we passed was bountifully supplied with bacon and cured hams, and the citizens, in order to put them out of the reach of the soldiers, secreted them in swamps, but it was impossible to get them out of the reach of the soldiers. When our keen scent and argus eyes failed us, it did not require much coaxing to get some confidential darkey to reveal the hiding place, and sometimes from out some swamp, load after load of the nicest hams was taken. The Southern people surpassed the North in curing hams. I never ate so sweet meat as in the South. They use a great deal of saltpeter and molasses in curing them and smoke them but little. I stood the march very well until one afternoon, about the tenth day out, I had a violent shake of the ague. However, I kept on. When my fever was at its height, I lay down in the edge of the woods to rest and fell asleep. I must

have slept several hours. When I awoke all the troops had passed
and the ammunition train was then passing.

Hailing a driver that I was acquainted with, he took me on his
wagon. That night I took a heavy dose of quinine, which broke
up the fever, but I felt miserable for several days. I got my things
carried, so got along very well. One night, as we were going into
camp, Gen. Veatch, who now commanded the 4th division, 16th
army corps, passed us with his command. The regiments fell in
line and lustily cheered their old commander. He seemed very
much affected at this mark of our esteem. The army arrived at
Meridian about the 17th. When within twenty miles of there, our
provision train was left back and a strong guard with it, also the
sick, myself among the number. Rollin, who had a felon on his
hand, also remained. Left to our own resources, we did just about
as we had a mind to. Rollin or I went out foraging nearly every
day, but usually Rollin went, as he always had better success than
I did. We always went with a forage train and thus enjoyed the
protection of the guard. Roll seldom came in empty. A porker,
some chickens, sweet potatoes, always came within his grasp. We
drew plenty of hard bread from the provision wagons near by,
charging the same to Uncle Sam, and for shelter and covering, we
appropriated the chaplain's blankets to our use. So, all things
considered, we were faring remarkably well—a great deal better
than many of the others. The 17th New York, for instance. This
regiment was composed of Wilson's old zouaves and roughs from
New York City, and they were a rough set. Their officers claimed
that in order to keep them in subjection, they had to use harsh
measures. I never before saw men tyrannized over as they were.
In the first place, they started out with heavy knapsacks and half
rations.

After marching hard, the Colonel, before he would allow them
to sit down or rest, had a camp guard detailed and picket also, if
required. They went through the regular formula of guard
mounting with knapsacks still on. The Colonel kept a guard
walking back and forth before his tent, with his load still on, for
two hours. The poor fellows looked completely drilled out, but
yet there was not a better fighting regiment in the whole division
than the 17th New York. When we arrived in camp, if any
picket duty was required of us, the detail was made and we were
allowed to break ranks, but we were to be ready to fall in when

the bugle sounded. The 17th New York got so reduced in rations that they suffered from the pangs of hunger. They were left back as guard to the wagon train, and their officers would not permit them to forage. They would come around our wagon and pick up the mouldy, hard bread and devour it with avidity. On one occasion one of them spied a goose which we had thrown away. It had begun to smell pretty bad, but he eagerly seized it and bore it off with a look of triumph. In the meantime, our boys had arrived at Meridian, and were playing havoc with the enemy's lines of communication. Meridian was a central place for railroads from all parts of the South. Each division was assigned a certain portion of the track to destroy, which they effectually did by tearing up the ties, piling them on the rails and then setting them on fire. After the rails were red hot, they would twist them around the trees, utterly unfitting them for further use. In this raid our army destroyed four hundred miles of railroad and burned over twenty engines and a large number of cars. They set fire to Meridian, and Gen. Sherman had his headquarters burned over him. He said that he thought that the boys might have waited until he got out before burning his quarters. A remarkable instance of revenge was perpetrated here. In Sherman's first disastrous fight at Vicksburg, a federal soldier was taken prisoner. His guard stopped at a residence here for food and refreshments. The woman of the house, after heaping all manner of insults upon the prisoner, finally spit in his face. It happened that the soldier soon after made his escape and rejoined the army. After arriving at Meridian, he proceeded to the house where he had been insulted, piled up the furniture, and told the woman that if she did not want to burn up in her own house, she would have to leave, at the same time reminding her of the insult she had given him. She implored, but to no purpose. Her house and furniture were burned. Thus may it be with all who descend from their high pedestal of womanhood and disgrace themselves by spitting upon helpless prisoners.

February 20th.

One day the Quartermaster came in and said that the army had started, and that he had orders to break up camp and move also. He went as far as Hillsboro and then waited one day for the arrival of the command. The boys had their faces set homeward and they made quick time. We had only ten days' rations on

9

hand now, but a dispatch had been sent through for a provision train to come out and meet us. Forage was not so plentiful now as on our out trip, but a few days after we left Hillsboro, we took a new road and we found forage in abundance. Large parties were sent out daily. Oft-times they were attacked and forced to come in empty. I believe that Col. Rogers made the largest haul of any. He was not easily scared out and his team usually came in loaded down. Sherman's army left fire and famine in its track. The country was one lurid blaze of fire; burning cotton gins and deserted dwellings were seen on every hand. I regret to say it, but oft-times habitations were burned down over the heads of occupants, but not by orders. Those gangs of ruffians, who always follow in the wake of armies, to pillage and destroy, seemed on the march to give loose reins to their passions. I have seen the cabin of the poor entered and the last mouthful taken from almost starving children. No one, who has a heart that beats in sympathy for the sorrows of others, can look on these things without the strongest feelings of compassion for the victims. The wretches who caused this suffering were brought to punishment as often as caught, but the most vigorous measures could not always stop it.

February 26th.

We crossed Pearl River thirty miles above Jackson. We halted here for a few days. After everything had crossed, our company was detailed to go back on the other side to do picket duty. This was a dangerous business, as hordes of rebel cavalry were prowling about, looking for a chance to pounce upon some detachment. Two of our boys went out a few rods from the post and narrowly escaped being captured. They were fired at but were not hit. Some boys were captured in sight of camp. A party of twelve or fifteen went out foraging, one day, from the 15th, and they were all captured but two. Gen. Sherman had now opened communication with the outside world and the whole country was electrified at the brilliancy of his exploits. The great apprehension that existed, as regarded the safety of his army, was removed by its returning with victory on its banners. We now moved to Canton and camped again for a few days. Canton is twenty-five miles above Jackson, on Pearl River, and forty-five miles from Vicksburg. It is surrounded by a splendid country. Its thrift is more of the Northern style than any city I had yet seen in the South.

Taking it all in all, the country through which we passed, on this march, was fertile, well watered and timbered, and remarkably level. We captured fifteen engines and a large number of cars at Canton, all of which were burned. The rebels now began to be pretty saucy. They came up in full view and threatened to attack us, but, when any force was sent out after them, they were sure to keep out of harm's way. Their object was not so much to attack us as it was to annoy us, but they failed entirely.

February 27th.

We took our own time and were neither hurried nor delayed by the manœuvering. When we left Canton, they hung on our track like blood-leeches. Oft-times we would have to turn around and fight them. One afternoon, after we had all gotten into camp, the rascals drew up in line and showed themselves. This touched the pride of our cavalry and they formed and charged them with drawn sabres. The rebs stood their ground for awhile, but, before our force got to them, they broke and ran in confusion.

We had planted artillery so as to rake their flank and help them along in their flight.

February 29th.

The next day our regiment was rear guard. The rebs still kept in sight, fighting our cavalry all the time. We were where we could see the whole performance. The only effect these attacks of the enemy had on us was to keep our men from straggling. Towards night they began to lag and finally ceased to annoy us at all.

This gave the rebs a chance to give a great puff in their papers that their troops had utterly routed Sherman and driven him back across Black River.

March 3d.

We arrived back in our old camp March 3d. On this our last day's march of the campaign, we started at six o'clock in the morning and at eleven A. M. we were in camp, having marched twenty miles, or rather ran. It could scarcely be called marching. So eager did we become to get back to camp. Our brigade was in the lead and perhaps we were a little vain of our marching and wished to exult over the rest of the command. We left them far in the rear and it was not until five o'clock P. M. that the rear regiments arrived. Our first thought after arriving was to secure our mail. I found a goodly number of letters awaiting me. My readers may rest assured that their contents were eagerly devoured.　My next move was to doff my travel-stained attire and substitute a clean suit from my knapsack.　We had made this march without a change of clothing.　We left our knapsacks in our tents.　It made us feel almost like new men to once more be clothed in a clean and wholesome suit.　Looking|back as we now did upon our campaign as one of the most remarkable of the war in its boldness of conception and brilliancy of execution, fraught with such happy results, the large extent of country traversed, giving a deeper insight into the interior of the rebellion, the enjoyment of the thrilling events which daily transpired and the good feeling and enjoyment which generally prevailed, we could not regret our trip, but were proud of it.　It added one more wreath of fame to our already glittering array of achievements and by generations yet unborn will the story of this march be read.

March 8th.

Active preparations were now made to furlough the veterans, and many a weather-beaten, war-worn cheek lighted up with a smile of joy at the prospect of once more beholding home and friends.　On the 10th of March, those of us who had not been sworn in our new term of service, duly took the required oath and received our discharge from first term of service, dating back to time of re-enlistment.　The non-veterans took a deep interest in these proceedings.

No less patriotic than the veterans, home ties had a stronger claim on them.　For three years they had served their country faithfully and well.　There were thousands yet at the North whose duty it was to enlist and it is no wonder that we thought it was their turn now.　On the 16th of March, we bade adieu to comrades, marched to Vicksburg and embarked on board a steamer for St. Louis where we were to be paid off.　On arriving at St. Louis a grand ovation was given us.

March 20th.

A deputation of the citizens presented each soldier with a badge of welcome.　We were then marched to a capacious hall where a bountiful feast had been prepared for us.　After dinner, we all adjourned to the saloon where all who chose were treated to beer. While we remained in St. Louis, every attention was shown us. It was not until the second day of our arrival that we were paid off. During the interval, we were allowed our liberty and took this occasion to see the sights of the city. I attended the theatre both evenings. We were paid on the 22d. We received our pay in full on our first installment and one installment of bounty on our second term and one month's pay in advance. I received two hundred and eighty-seven dollars.

March 24th.

We took the steamer for Alton that evening, where we disembarked and took the cars for Chicago, arriving there the next evening. A telegram had been sent apprising the authorities of our approach and we found a warm supper awaiting us at the Soldier's Rest, prepared by the good ladies of Chicago. We received our furloughs here and each took his own way homeward. At the expiration of our furloughs, we were all to rendezvous at Freeport preparatory to returning.

March 26th.

At seven o'clock on the evening of the 26th, we arrived at Marengo. Roll, Milt and I found a load of Riley friends waiting for us and a jolly load of us were soon on our way home.

March 31st.

We will pass briefly over the time spent at home. Suffice it to say that time passed on swift wings and each moment was laden with joy.

April 24th.

All too soon the time passed and our time came to go. Our farewells were spoken and we started for Freeport. On arriving there, we found that the regiment would not leave until Monday, So we got permission to spend the time at home. Of course, our folks were surprised to see us back again so soon. We had a party at Aaron Sears Friday evening, and we made ourselves merry until morning. We left Freeport Monday morning. Just before starting, we were drawn up before the Brewster House to listen to a farewell speech from our old Colonel, Thos. J. Turner. He spoke with considerable feeling. In behalf of the regiment, Col. Rogers briefly responded. Col. Turner then treated all who wished to a glass of beer. He then shook hands with each one of us.

April 30th.

We then got on board the cars and were soon rapidly whirling toward Dixie. The next day we arrived at Cairo where we found that a regiment of non-veterans had been there, but had left a few days before and had gone up the Tennessee river to Clifton where we expected to join them and then march through the States of Tennessee, Alabama and Mississippi and join Sherman's army in Georgia. We stopped but a few days in Cairo and then set out to join our comrades.

May 5th.

We went up as far as Paducah and then waited for the rest of the fleet to come up. We arrived at Clifton on the 6th of May. The boys had left the week before. They drove a large herd of beef cattle through to Huntsville, Alabama. We camped here four or five days. The scenery on the Tennessee river at this time of the year is very beautiful. The shores were lined with splendid groves and woodlands, with scenery unsurpassed in beauty. Now they were dressed in the most gorgeous attire of spring. Our command was composed of detachments of the 17th army corps, numbering eight or ten thousand, commanded by Brig-Gen. Leggett, of Ohio. On the 9th of May, we resumed our march, our first point of destination being Pulaski, in Tennessee, on the Coosa river.

May 10th.

We drove through a large drove of beef cattle. We had considerable sport. There were numerous rivers to cross and some of the boys who could not bear the thought of stripping and wading would mount a young steer, but the wild and frightened animal would generally land them on all fours in the river. It was amusing to see us crossing these rivers. My readers may imagine several thousand men, stripped naked, their clothes wadded up in a bundle and held high over their heads, wading the Elkhorn river. At times the water would be too deep for the short ones to wade. They would stretch and walk on their tiptoes to keep their heads out of water. The current being too swift for some, they would be submerged. Those who had crossed would stand on the bank and laugh at the others' mishaps. Two darkies were drowned and some of the boys made sport of the occurrence.

A tragical occurrence happened in an Iowa regiment the morning we started. Two soldiers got into an altercation about a certain young lady to whom both were paying their addresses. The foolish men agreed to settle the matter, privately, by fighting a duel with their rifles. At the first fire both fell dead. Young misses, let this be a warning to you to never have more than one sweetheart. On arriving at Pulaski we found that the boys had been gone several days. We came up with the rest of the command at Huntsville, Alabama. We found the boys well, but terribly chafed in spirit, but that did not prevent them from extending to us a cordial welcome. The non-veterans had been shamefully misused. It seemed as though some of the officers wanted to vent their spite on them because they would not re-enlist. The idea of marching them two hundred miles just as their term of service was about to expire, when it was of no earthly use, was an outrageous one. They were treated more like dogs than like patriot soldiers, which they were; and, finally, to cap the climax, on the very day that their term expired, they were ordered to drive a drove of cattle through to Chattanooga, a distance of one hundred and fifty miles. This was more than they could bear, and, in their just indignation, they revolted. They had the sympathy of all the veterans, and the officers found that they could not stem the tide of wrath which was setting against them and the order was rescinded. The procuring of this order was attributed to Colonels Hall and Rogers, who represented to headquarters that the boys were willing to go. After Gen. Crocker found out the facts of the case, he declared that the boys should not go.

May 24th.

While these things were transpiring, the veterans received orders to march, but I cannot leave Huntsville without telling my readers what a beautiful city it is. It seemed like a paradise situated in a wild country. Its cottages were neat and tasty and closely entwined with ivy. The streets were deeply shaded, making it a nice, secluded spot. In one edge of the village was one of the largest springs of pure water in the United States. It gushed from the foot of a rock one hundred feet high. A deep basin formed a reservoir. A stream of considerable magnitude ran from this spring and it furnished water for the whole city. The morning we were ordered to march, the regiment was consolidated into three companies, A, F, I and J forming one, called Company A; B and G forming another called Company B; K, H, C and D forming the other, called Company C. This last order took us by surprise. We were dumfounded, indignant. It was the deepest wrong that had yet been done us. It was utterly violating their faith.

We re-enlisted with the understanding that we were to retain our company organization and have the privilege of electing our own officers, and now, in a most arbitrary manner, they had taken both of these rights from us. After voluntarily re-consecrating ourselves to our country for another term of three years, it was a small favor to ask to be permitted to retain our organization and elect our officers, but small as it was, it was refused us. Officers were forced upon us who were obnoxious to us. Those officers who had our welfare at heart, and whom we would have liked to have stay with us, had the magnanimity to leave. Not one of Company D's officers remained. While we were indignant at the wrongs done us, the non-veterans were having their trials and, while the cloud was over us, we parted. Nothing could dispel the sadness we felt as we parted never more to meet as comrades in arms on the tented field.

Having shared alike a common danger, linked together by the strongest ties of friendship, it seemed like severing the strong ties of our being to part with these, our old comrades, but the last lingering pressure of the hand was given and each party started off in the path marked out for them, one leading to freedom from war and bloodshed and the weary bivouac to the quiet home circle, surrounded by the dearest earthly friends, whose hearts would be made glad by their safe return; the other leading to the dim, uncertain future of civil strife, to face again the whizzing bullets and flying shells, to plod along through storm and sunshine, through summer's heat and winter's cold, with the earth for our bed and the broad canopy of heaven our covering, but yet, in the distance was a bright star of hope which beckoned us on,—a hope which o'ermastered fatigue, hunger, sickness and want, which will not meet its full fruition until dove-winged peace again broods over all our country, saved and regenerated.

May 26th.

Our first point of destination was Decatur, Alabama, on the Tennessee river. The country here was low and swampy. On the fourth day we arrived opposite Decatur. The army crossed on pontoons at five o'clock P. M. and marched ten miles farther that night. The country on the Alabama side was higher and more beautiful than on the Tennessee side. Our cavalry had a fight with the rebel cavalry. Gen. Rosecrans started on his famous raid through the States of Mississippi, Alabama and Georgia. The

Cumberland railroad bridge crossed the Tennessee river at this point.

May 30th.

We now began to come to a more mountainous region and our marching became more difficult. The farther we advanced, the more rough did it become. The road wound around in the valleys. On either side of us loomed up high, craggy cliffs, with ragged edges of stone and sparsely covered with dwarf pines. Amongst these ragged cliffs, the enemy's scouts, secure from all danger, sat and watched us, closely calculated our strength and the number of wagons in our train. This I got from their own lips afterwards.

The country was very thinly settled. The inhabitants generally were poor, but a strong Union sentiment prevailed among these sturdy mountaineers and many had to leave their homes and families and flee to the mountains to escape from their merciless foes. They were hunted like wild beasts. The valleys abounded in large springs of the purest kind of water. Often we found deep caverns. We were now approaching a range of the Cumberland mountains which we would have to cross. It was a stupendous undertaking with our immense train. The road was very stony and often wound around the mountain where the least mischance or misstep would have precipitated us thousands of feet below. Several teams went over these precipices and were seen no more.

June 10th.

There were scarcely two hours in the day but what troops were on the move. The rear never got into camp until past midnight, and then they would take the lead the next day and march before daylight. I remember distinctly on one occasion when the 15th was rear guard. It was two o'clock A. M. before we got into camp and the wagon that carried our knapsacks got lost and did not come up until an hour later. Then we found the knapsacks scattered all over. Some of the boys never found theirs. We camped one and one-half miles from water, so it was out of the question to make coffee that night. We lay down in our wet garments in a rain-storm, to get a few minutes' rest before resuming the march. At five o'clock A. M. we were again on the move, being minus coffee for breakfast. After this, when our regiment was rear guard, when night came, some of the boys would go ahead several miles, lie down and take a nap before the regiment came up, and as we moved very slowly, they sometimes slept several hours.

When the regiment came up, they would fall in and someone else would go ahead, but we were always careful not to go beyond our camping ground. On one occasion, some of the mess, including Charlie, Roll and Sime Smith stopped and lay down in the exact spot where our regiment camped and they were in the right spot for our company. Our mess used the camp fire they built to cook our supper by. Scarcely a day passed but we lost at least a score of mules. If there had not been a drove of extra ones along, a portion of the train would had to have been abandoned.

June 15th.

About the 15th, we arrived at Rome, Georgia, and were once more in communication with the main army which was thirty miles distant. We continued our march in the track of Sherman's army until we arrived at Allatoona Pass. Our brigade—second —was left here to garrison this important post. Sherman's army was now before Kennesaw mountain which loomed grandly up in the distance, eighteen miles.

The rebel army was stationed on and around the mountain. This was one of the strongest positions that Mother Nature ever formed, and held as it was by a veteran army, commanded by one of the ablest Generals that the rebels had, it seemed an impossibility for our brave army to gain possession of it, but with undaunted courage and perseverance, seldom equaled, never excelled, under the leadership of that great leader, Sherman, our army went resolutely to work to gain the rebel stronghold or die in the attempt. We camped at Allatoona only one week, when we were ordered to Etowah Bridge to repel an anticipated attack. We put the place in a state of defense and left the 45th Illinois there as a garrison. Then we were ordered back to the Pass. We took up a different position this time. On top of one of the highest mountains, we fortified ourselves. The whole rebel army could not have driven us from this position. From here we had a most magnificent view of the surrounding country. To the north, east and west as far as the eye could reach, mountain upon mountain rose up in the distance like huge billows of the sea, their cragged peaks piercing the very clouds. To the south, Kennesaw stood out in bold relief from all the rest like a pyramid in the desert.

June 25th.

The cloud of curling smoke which hung around the mountain,

and the hoarse, heavy notes of the artillery, plainly told us that our boys were still pushing bravely on, despite the rebel thunder and the fierce storm of iron hail rained down upon them. It was the ambition of our gallant army to see our glorious flag floating from the highest peak of Kennesaw, where the rebel rag now waved. No artifice was left untried, no opportunity missed, where fighting would avail, but what our boys took advantage of it and pushed forward their lines. Slowly but surely Sherman was weaving a web of fate which would place the rebel army in his power, but it was at a fearful sacrifice. Charge after charge was made on the enemy's works. Close, fierce and deadly was the fighting. The rebel army clung to this as their last hope. If they could not hold Kennesaw, they felt that their case was hopeless, and they fought like demons. We were soon summoned from our dizzy height on Allatoona mountain to repair immediately to Etowah, as an attack was anticipated on the railroad bridge at that place. If the rebels had succeeded in destroying that, they would have inflicted incalculable damage upon us. This bridge was three hundred yards long and one hundred feet high, and it had just been completed. In seven days from the time that they commenced operations on the bridge, a train of cars passed over it. Such was the dispatch with which Sherman's engineers did their work. They had dimensions of every bridge from Chattanooga to Atlanta, and as fast as the rebels burned them and fell back, we would advance and rebuild, and the cars followed close in Sherman's wake. It was our duty to guard the railroad between Cartersville, one mile above us, and Allatoona Pass.

June 30th.

At first we patrolled the railroad, but that got to be too dangerous business. Two of the 45th Illinois were shot dead only a few nights before by rebels in ambush, waiting for them. So we adopted the plan of stationing pickets at intervals along the railroad so that the videttes of each post could see each other. We took our position in the most concealed places and placed our videttes where they could see and not be seen. Then all night long we lay on our arms, scarcely moving and never speaking above a whisper lest it might betray our position. Ever and anon, the sharp crack of a rifle would ring out on the midnight air, which would cause us all to silently grasp our pieces and await the issue of events. In most instances, these were false alarms.

Some timid sentinel would be on post, and his imagination would conceive a black stump or a bush gently waving in the evening breeze to be some rebel creeping upon him, and in his fright would discharge his gun; but sometimes the danger was genuine, and skulking rebs could be distinctly heard, but they were very cautious about approaching within range of our rifles. Vigilant eyes were watching for them from every picket, but in spite of our utmost caution, they did once in a while succeed in tearing up a rail. Besides this duty, we had our regular picket to stand on other roads and by-paths. We built us comfortable shanties on the bank of the river, and despite our arduous duties, we enjoyed ourselves. The country abounded in whortleberries and notwithstanding the danger we incurred, we would go outside the lines to gather them. Some of our mess, No. 4, went out every day and we kept a supply constantly on hand, besides selling a good many. Milton would make berry pies and puddings, and with the other luxuries we procured, we lived pretty well. Three of our mess now left us. They had been detailed to corps headquarters. Charlie Mitchell and Underwood and Tom Smalldridge by name. The welcome news now came that our army held possession of Marietta and Kennesaw Mountain. By a sudden flank movement, Sherman had compelled Johnson to evacuate in hot haste. An unfortunate occurrence now happened to a party of our boys out foraging. They were surprised by a party of rebs and three were killed, one wounded and one taken prisoner. One David Stokes of Company I and a quartermaster at brigade headquarters were killed. Jack Gaynor of Company B was captured, but he happened to have a canteen of whisky with him and he got his guard drunk and effected his escape. Rollin, Milton and myself went out foraging one day. Four or five miles outside our lines we came to a deserted plantation. It was evident from the appearance of things that they had not been gone long. We found the garden in a thriving condition and we helped ourselves to all the vegetables that we wanted. Amongst other things, we found raspberries. I also found a lot of fresh eggs and a sack of flour. After we got back, we cooked some of the flour and it made us all sick. It operated as an emetic on me. Some of the boys were sick several days. There were others in the regiment affected the same way. The flour had been poisoned.

July 1st.

It had now been ascertained that some of the citizens who had professed Union sentiments had been engaged in plots to tear up the railroad, attack foraging parties, etc., and an order was issued to banish all citizens five miles outside our lines, under penalty of having their houses burned if not complying within a certain length of time. Severe as this order may seem, the circumstances justified it.

July 4th.

The glorious Fourth now dawned upon us and we celebrated it as well as circumstances would permit. At the front it was celebrated by the firing of cannon and musketry and the glittering of cold steel. It was no child's play there. It was fitting for them on this hallowed day to show their devotion to their country by fighting traitors in arms against it. After leaving Kennesaw, the rebs made a stand at Chattahoochee River. They were now driven from that into their last stronghold around Atlanta. We were always within hearing of the fighting. At times could see the smoke of battle. A regular siege was now commenced. The rebels confidently hoped that they could hold Atlanta, the Gate City of the South. In truth, it did seem almost impregnable, so well was it fortified. We now received marching orders and we hoped that it would be to the front. We were heartily tired of guarding communications in the rear. The continual harassing alarms and the vigilant watch it was necessary to keep, added to the enormous duty to perform was worse than to be at the front where we knew what we might expect, and in truth, there was less danger there than in the rear, but our hopes were doomed to disappointment. We halted at the foot of Kennesaw mountain near Marietta and went into camp.

July 8th.

Again the annoying and fatiguing duty of picketing and railroad guarding had to be performed. One picket post was stationed on the top of the mountain. We stood picket two days here before being relieved. Sometimes we would 'go out five or six miles. It was blackberry season and we feasted on this delicious fruit to our heart's content. Marietta in time of peace was a model city. Its dwelling houses were so closely shaded by vines and shade trees as to be hardly visible. The yards and flower gardens were nicely laid out, the sidewalks nicely paved and shaded and everything bespoke comfort and elegance. The business part of the town was nearly destroyed. A military college was situated here and Gen. Sherman was at one time teacher in it and some of the Generals in the rebel army now fighting him were once his pupils at this institute. I suppose that he little thought then that he was training the hand that would be raised against this country and himself, yet, so it was. Marietta was once a city of several thousand inhabitants and liquor was not permitted to be sold within its limits unless on a doctor's prescription. I suppose this was mainly to keep temptation away from the students attending military college.

July 10th.

There was to us one important event that happened that I have omitted to note and that was the consolidation of the 14th and 15th Illinois Volunteers into one battalion to be known as the 14th and 15th Veteran Battalion of Volunteer Infantry. This was done by order of Gen. McPherson in pursuance of instructions from the War Department. This did not take us by surprise for we had long expected it, and since it had become known that such a consolidation must take place, we were desirous that it should be with our brothers, the 14th. The whole battalion numbered only six hundred men, with six companies, three to each regiment. This organization took effect July 1st. I will now give a passing notice to Kennesaw mountain. It is situated one-half mile southwest of Marietta. From its base on the east to the top is a gradual ascent at an angle of about seventy-five degrees. On the north and south its sides are steep, almost perpendicular. To the west it gradually slopes until it reaches Little Kennesaw which extends some distance to the west.

We had a single corps stationed on top of Big Kennesaw, from which place we had a magnificent view of the surrounding country. Away to the north, as far as the eye could reach, mountains lifted up their heads against the sky, looking like ragged clouds pressing against the edge of the horizon. Down below us to northeast, Pine Mountain looked like a small knoll. To the northwest, toward Dallas, was Lost Mountain, so named from its isolated position. Then sweeping the horizon to the west, one interminable range of mountains meets your vision. Continuing on to the south, the spires and steeples of the "Gate City of the South," Atlanta, meet your view, and as we looked we saw clouds of dust rising, caused by troops moving to the left. We afterwards ascertained this to be the army of the Tennessee, making a flank movement. The country toward Atlanta appeared to be more level, but away to the southeast, full fifty miles distant, Stone Mountain rises like a high pyramid on a level plain. There were some of the oldest inhabitants of Marietta who had never been on top of Kennesaw Mountain. One day, while some of the boys were wandering about Little Kennesaw, they came across a large number of rebel and federal dead, which were yet unburied. From their position, it seemed that our men had made a charge and a fierce hand-to-hand fight had ensued.

The consolidation of the regiment had left a large surplus of non-commissioned officers, hence it was necessary to dispose of them in some way. It was given out that the excess was to be mustered out, and there were plenty who were willing to accept the sacrifice. In our Company C, there were fourteen corporals and eight sergeants. Six corporals and two sergeants had to be reduced. In the old organization I was first corporal. In the new I was second and Rollin fourth. Charlie Underwood was reduced. I was now offered a detail at headquarters as corporal of the guard, but declined to accept it, and got another person to go in my place. Had I known then what transpired three months hence, I should never have had the pleasure of a peep into Andersonville prison den.

July 31st.

The bloody battle of Peach Tree Creek, before Atlanta, was fought on the 21st and 22d of July. In that battle the country mourned the loss of one of its most illustrious defenders, the brave and noble McPherson. When his death became known to the army that he had commanded, many brave and war-worn heroes wept like children. We loved him with a strong, deep love, a love which was born of his kindness to us and the bravery that he displayed on the field. Ohio might well be proud of him. It is said that Gen. Grant wept when he heard of his death. The skill and discipline that he had infused into his army was conspicuously displayed in this fight. Assailed by the whole rebel army, attacked in front, flank and rear, they bravely stood their ground, and would have fought to the last, rather than have yielded. Over one-fourth of their number fell on that bloody field. The defeated and discomfited rebels received a blow from which they never recovered.   The next day McPherson's body passed through Marietta on its way to his home in Ohio.

August 10th.

We began to be very much annoyed now by scouting parties of rebel cavalry who would attack our forage trains and make raids upon the railroads.

We were constantly kept on the move chasing them.   Finally we were ordered to Ackworth, a small village fourteen miles from Marietta, for scouting and picket duty.   We took three days' rations.   After scouring the country awhile we returned, but had not been in camp twenty-four hours before we were ordered to return, prepared to stay a week or so.   No sooner had we left before, than a band of rebel cavalry made a dash at the place and tore up some of the railroad track.   We went back and took up our quarters in some of the vacant houses and established our picket line.   One day a Union citizen came in and reported a large force of the enemy out about twenty-five miles.

August 25th.

Word was sent to Marietta, and Col. Logan, with the 32d Illinois, and Col. Rogers, with his command, started out.   They were to form a junction, about twenty miles out, and attempt to surprise and capture the enemy, but, in an enemy's country, it was almost impossible to do it.   They got word of our approach and hastily decamped.   The forces joined about midnight.   We had marched twenty miles since sundown without rest.   We now started back for Marietta.   We never took any blankets on these forced marches except one rubber blanket to a man.   We arrived at Marietta the next day about five o'clock P. M., having traveled fifty miles, without rest, through the scorching rays of an August sun.   We were completely fagged out, but congratulated ourselves now on the prospect of having a good supper and a night's rest, but hardly was our supper dispatched before an order came for us to get ready to march immediately, in light marching order, with three days' rations.   Unjust and cruel as this order seemed, there was no course but to obey, but it was some relief to find out that we were to take the cars.   The rebel, Gen. Forrest, had made a raid on the railroad near Dalton and was trying to capture that place.   We were hurried forward to re-inforce it, but the next morning, when we arrived at Resaca, we learned that Forrest had been repulsed and was now making his way back.

August 31st.

Our command of about three thousand was sent out to cut off his retreat. We marched rapidly until we arrived at the ford where we hoped to intercept him, but found that we were too late. We had marched twenty-five miles during the day and the sun was tremendously hot. I came near being overpowered by the heat. I could scarcely put one foot before the other. Ever since I had had a touch of the sunstroke I could not stand the heat, but I managed to get through, and a good supper and a bath in the river near by, made a new man of me. At five o'clock P. M. the order came to countermarch. I was better prepared for it than most of the others. In the cool of the evening I could march as far as any of them. We arrived back in camp about two o'clock A. M. It is needless to say that we were in a condition to enjoy a good sleep. In thirty hours we had traveled fifty miles. Instead of going back to Marietta, as we anticipated, our regiment was ordered to halt at Ackworth and remain and garrison the place. So we sent to Marietta for our things and established ourselves in camp. Our regiment was scattered along the railroad, Companies A and B at Big Shanty, D at Moon Station and C, K and E at Ackworth. Each party immediately set to work to fortify their position. We converted the depot into a kind of fortress and barricaded brick houses. Now commenced those series of alarms, midnight tramps and forced marches which did not end until we were finally captured. There were not two days in a week but what some of us were out on a scout. We usually marched thirty miles per day. Our picket duty was heavy, and, in addition to this, we had to patrol the railroad. Scarcely a night passed but what attempts were made to tear up the track or a picket post was attacked. The country was alive with swarming bands of rebel cavalry, bent on mischief. One day while out scouting, a party of rebels came within one-half mile of camp and threw a train off the track by means of a shoe which the rebs had invented for the purpose. This shoe was made to fit the rail and, as the wheel ran onto it, it ran off. It was a simple and ingenious contrivance and was much safer and easier than to try to tear up the track. We took possession of this shoe. This trick of the rebs caused us a great deal of trouble. We had to place our videttes so closely together that they could see the whole railroad. Then woe to the rebel that dared venture on the track.

How we boys longed to get to the front. Most anything was

10

more tolerable than this harassing life. We had only six hundred men to guard thirty miles of railroad which was lined with rebel scouting parties. Our boys at the front had now reached the goal of their ambition. Our flag now waved over the "Gate City of the South" and the rebel army, with ranks broken, was flying before our victorious army. By a bold flank movement, Sherman had marched to the rear of Atlanta and the enemy came out and met him at Jonesboro, thirty-five miles south of the city and they were utterly routed and scattered. The 20th corps, who remained before Atlanta to cover Sherman's movements, now quietly took possession of the city. Gen. Hood gathered together what he could of his broken and disorganized army and halted at Newman, a place fifty miles to the west of Atlanta. Our army was content to rest awhile. Meanwhile the rebel army was not idle. Parties were sent out to intercept Sherman's communication. Our situation was bad before. It was ten-fold more so now. I was now detailed as color-bearer, but never had an opportunity to take my place.

September 1st.

Most of the boys were now boarding with the inhabitants of the village, giving their rations for their board. Rollin and I were boarding with a lady, Mrs. Hunt, whose husband was in the employ of the Government, at Chattanooga, in the machine shop. He was a stanch Union man, but the rebels held him now as a prisoner. Our Colonel also took up his headquarters at her house and was treated with great kindness and civility. These were estimable people. They had stood the test of loyalty. No threats could intimidate them, and, in more than one instance, they had done our cause great service. Great as was the danger we incurred, we would go out foraging. Some of our boys were captured by venturing too far. Roll and Milt went out a little way one day to get some beef. They had not gotten more than one mile from camp before they encountered some rebel cavalry who immediately gave them chase. They took to the woods in different directions and made pretty tall time for camp. They arrived about the same time, breathless. They were a little more cautious after this how they ventured out. We had a novel way now of supplying ourselves with beef. Large droves of cattle were passing through every week to the front. When we would see a drove coming, some of the boys would slip out of the road a piece and when they came along, would select a nice fat one and hurry it out into the bushes until after the drove passed and then butcher it. This trick was played time and again.

September 20th.

One night, from my post on picket, I saw a squad of rebels skulking around. I told the boys not to fire for I thought it would not be prudent to disclose our position and bring down an overwhelming force upon us. It was hard to stand with loaded guns and see the rascals skulking about, but they did not come within good range of our guns and did not try to molest the railroad, therefore, I did not think I would be justified in alarming the camp by attacking them, but we kept a vigilant eye upon them until they disappeared.

September 25th.

We had now about thirty mounted men and they aided us materially in scouting and warning us of attacks. A picket post got nicely fooled one night. A party of horsemen was approaching and the sentinel challenged them. The leader said it was only Col. Rogers out on a scout. This threw the sentinel off his guard and he permitted them to approach. They were instantly surrounded, and every man except one was captured. He lay concealed until nearly daylight, then came in and reported. It seems the rebel officer had had the Colonel's name from some rascally citizen, and so passed himself off for him until it was too late for the picket to escape. There was a whole regiment of rebels near by. The next morning, bright and early, our whole command set out to try to overtake them. We pressed them so close that we came in sight of their rear guard. Sergeant Hooker chased down and captured one man by knocking him off his horse with his saber. Those boys that were captured, were all from Company C. This hard life began to tell upon me. I was troubled with a hacking cough and was feeling quite poorly. Mother sent me a box of Brown's bronchial troches, which helped me.

There was a doctor and one lady in Ackworth, who were suspected of playing the spy. The doctor got passes to go out and in at pleasure to visit his patients, but I believe he was nothing more or less than a spy, although he professed to be a strong Union man. This lady, Jones by name, was a perfect virago. She made pretty free use of her tongue and abused us whenever opportunity would permit. The boys used to go to her house just to hear her rave at the Yanks. The Colonel and several of the boys thought it would be a nice thing to play a Yankee trick on her, and at the same time get some useful information out of her, so the Colonel procured a rebel Lieutenant's suit, and so disguised, presented himself at her house one night, after she had retired. The Colonel gave his name as Lieutenant—somebody—from Forrest's cavalry, and demanded to be admitted, as he had important information to communicate. Mrs. Jones rushed to the door to admit him. (It must be remembered that this Mrs. Jones was a young widow). The Colonel told her that Forrest was out only a few miles, and that very night was going to attack and capture the place, and he wanted to know who were Union men and who were rebels, at the same time telling her that all Union men would be hung and their houses burned. She seized a pen and gave him the names of all the Union families in town. Amongst them were Mrs. Hunt's and Mrs. Crawford's. Before the Colonel came in, he had agreed with the boys on a signal and they were to rush in and capture him. After the Colonel had got all the information that he could, he commenced sparking her, and was progressing finely when a loud knock at the door suddenly interrupted their tete-a-tete. Hastily throwing some bed-quilts over the Colonel, she demanded to know who was there. "Soldiers after a rebel spy," was the prompt answer. "There has been no such person here," was the rejoinder, but they burst open the door and commenced search. The suppressed laugh of the Colonel betrayed his whereabouts, and he was dragged forth apparently much frightened.

The widow scolded, raved and begged of them to let him go, but all to no purpose. When fairly out of hearing the party laughed to their heart's content. It was not until several days after that she found out the trick that had been played on her, and if ever there was a mad woman, she was one. Similar tricks were played off on other rebels, by which means we found out who piloted that squad of rebel cavalry who captured our boys. He was sent under guard to Marietta. We learned now that the rebel army had crossed the Chattahoochee and was making toward Rome.

About this time the Colonel and Adjutant were called to Atlanta; the former on a court martial and the latter on a visit. Capt. Kenyon of Company C was left in command. He put on

more pomp and style than a Brigadier-General. Happening
around to my picket post the next morning and not finding it to
suit him (but I suspect that it was because I did not turn out the
guard to salute him) he commenced to give me a lecture on my
duty. I heard him through, although my cheeks tingled with suppressed anger, for it was wholly uncalled for. It was the first
reprimand that I had ever received in the army and it was not
needed then. He finally wound up with this declaration: "Eternal
vigilance is the price of freedom. Corporal Barber, resume your
duties." The next day I had a good notion to throw that declaration back in his teeth when he so ignobly sold us to the enemy. The
last words the Colonel said to him were that if he were attacked by
a superior force to fall back to Allatoona and save all the baggage,
but self-conceited as he was, he chose to do as he pleased. The
rebel army, instead of making for Rome, made directly for us.
They attacked Big Shanty first, but not until they had killed and
wounded twice their number and the rebel flag was planted on
their works did our boys surrender. Equally firm was the resistance that they met at Moon Station. The evening of October 3d,
they camped within one mile of Ackworth, their camp fires extending in a semi-circle around us. Some of us wanted to go out
and reconnoiter but the Captain would not allow it; nevertheless,
some did go out and reported a large rebel army with artillery, but
the Captain would not believe it. He said it was a force of rebel
cavalry and they were trying to scare us. Contrary to the advice
of all the other officers, he persisted in his foolish determination to
remain. That night or early the next morning, he could have retreated to Allatoona and saved everything. All night long we lay
on our arms in a drenching rain storm awaiting an attack. It
seemed that the rebels were sure of their prey, but rather than
alarm the garrison of Allatoona Pass, they would suffer us to
escape.

CHAPTER XV.

October 4th.

The morning of October 4th dawned bright and beautiful. The rain drops still hanging from the autumn foliage reflected in the bright rays of the morning sun, appeared like a sheen of silver, as if mocking at our calamity and rejoicing at the fate before us. Long before the rays of the sun tinged the eastern horizon, we were astir, watching with strained vision for the approach of the foe. We knew that if Captain Kenyon persisted in his mad course, ere the sun set we would be prisoners in the hands of our foe, but with self-conceit and stupidity, which was wholly inexcusable, he bustled around giving us orders as though the fate of a nation depended upon the issue. As daylight began to approach and still the enemy remained quiet, Captain Kenyon said that if we got a fight out of those rebels, we would have to go out and meet them. So he sent out two companies, C and K, to reconnoiter, and left the remaining company as reserve. We marched out a few rods and deployed in line as skirmishers and cautiously advanced. I was sent with five men on the right to guard against a flank movement but keeping within hailing distance of the line, though quite concealed from it by the intervening woods. We marched boldly up and drove in their light picket and marched up within full view of their camp. They were not yet astir. It seemed that General Loring, who commanded them, was in no haste to open the ball, so he allowed his men all the repose they could get, but our vehement attack soon roused them from their repose and some fell before our destructive fire before they had time to form their lines. When they were fairly aroused, we saw a large army spread out before us. To oppose this host, we had barely one hundred and fifty men. Slowly and deliberately they formed their line. We could hear distinctly every order given. During the time, we made good use of our ammunition, well knowing that when they moved forward our time would be short.

I now stole cautiously forward in advance of my men to get a a better view of the position. A fierce yell now broke forth and I knew that the rebels were making a charge, and almost before I was aware of it, I was cut off from the command. Our boys were swept like chaff back to their quarters. I resolved to make the effort to regain them. In so doing, I had to pass the flank of the rebel line and cross an open space over the rise of a hill. I never expected to get over that hill safe. I rushed forward, casting side glances at the moving line of rebels. I saw a group in advance of the others, halt and fire at me. A shower of bullets rattled around me, two passing through my clothes. I made a desperate effort and got behind the cover of a house beyond, halted and discharged my gun into the advancing foe and then rejoined my comrades who were already sheltered by our frail defenses. Some took up a position in the depot, others around Mrs. Hunt's dwelling and the rest scattered to the brick houses that we had prepared for such emergencies. A portion of Company C took refuge in an old brick store whose walls projected several feet above the roof. On this roof about one dozen of us climbed and took our position. We made port holes through the brick and from there commenced a galling fire on every reb that came within range of our guns. Rollin and Milton were on picket. I did not know what had become of them until I saw them creeping around the corner of a house to get a crack at some rebels behind another house. I heard the simultaneous report of their guns and then saw them safely retreat to the other brick building. This set my mind at ease as regarded their safety. The rebels did not seem disposed to attack us openly while in our fortresses, but they were not idle. They were rapidly surrounding us, the thick wood screening their movements from our view. Finally to the east, where the country was more open; we saw a long line of troops emerge and a large force of cavalry march in our rear, but more fearful than all, a battery had been placed within easy range of our works and in fifteen minutes could level our defense to the earth, but with a reckless courage, we still fought on. Now was seen a horseman mounted on a white steed advancing toward us, waving a white flag. On the instant, the firing ceased, and we waited anxiously to know our fate. I took advantage of this temporary lull to retire to my quarters and fill my haversack with bread and a canteen with water. Then I took a box of hard tack on my shoulders and started back. I meant to provide for a siege if it came to that. Just as I started back, the maddening shout rang out that we had been surrendered. I hastened back and found the other boys boiling over with rage at the manner in which they had been sold. A grand nephew of Patrick Henry, of revolutionary fame, bore in in the flag of truce, accompanied with a demand for the surrender of the garrison with all stores. He gave three minutes for consideration and if the demand was not complied with, no mercy would be shown except to the sick and wounded. We could do nothing else but surrender. A useless sacrifice of blood would have been the result of a refusal. During the parley, Mrs. Hunt had secreted the Colonel's most valuable papers and the boys had entrusted her with their watches and other valuables, supposing that the rebels would take everything from us. She also concealed the mail bag which was filled with letters ready to mail. I had one in directed to Let Eddy. After our forces got possession of our mail bag, some kind friend enclosed the letter in a note to Celestia, telling her that the writer of the letter had been captured.

The rebel army now began to pour in by the thousand. It was Gen. Loring's division. We were fortunate indeed in falling into that humane officer's hands. After stacking our arms and delivering up our accoutrements and stores, he kindly permitted all to get their breakfast and such articles of clothing, etc., as we wished to take with us. He also ordered his men not to molest our private property without our consent but permitted them to purchase of us. This kindness was duly appreciated and we acted in a straightforward manner that won his confidence. This treatment was in striking contrast to that received by our comrades at Big Shanty and Moon Station. The rebels there stripped our boys of almost everything, even to their boots and hat, barely leaving them their shirts and drawers. These wretches belonged to Gen. French's division. The 6th Mississippi infantry was detailed to guard us to Gen. Hood's headquarters which was at Dallas. Gen. Loring gave strict orders to have us kindly treated and recommended us to the favor of General Hood. We found the 6th Mississippi to be composed of a noble looking set of men. They were veteran soldiers and treated us civilly. As we marched by widow Jones', that detestable female rebel clapped her hands for very joy. Our little drummer boy, King, played a sharp trick. He went to Mr. Crawford's and donned a citizen's suit and passed himself off as their son, and the next day when our army marched through the place, he rejoined it. I will here mention that Company A and a part of Company B escaped. The rebels were now busy tearing up the railroad and filling up the cuts. Indeed, the night before, we could plainly hear them at work. As we marched past the place where we first made our attack, we counted no less than twelve newly made graves. We had only one man wounded. We were marched to Gen. Stewart's headquarters at Big Shanty, and from there we marched toward Dallas. As we were marching along we could plainly see our signals flying from Kennesaw mountain. Right over the heads of the rebel army, that signal flag sent an order to Rome for re-inforcements to defend Allatoona Pass, and the consequence was that when the rebels attacked that stronghold the next day, they were bloodily repulsed. We went into camp that night late and within four miles of Hood's headquarters. Although a vigilant guard was kept over us, we were allowed a good many liberties. Early the next morning we were marched up to Hood's head-quarters. We reluctantly parted with the 6th Mississippi here. We knew that we could not get into any better hands, but in all probability into worse. I found amongst them some brother masons, and the strong bonds of fraternal love which permeates our order were held sacred by those arrayed in arms against us. I have to acknowledge many kindnesses extended to me by the brothers.

October 5th.

At Gen. Hood's headquarters, our names were registered and one day's rations were drawn, consisting of one pint of corn meal and a few ounces of raw beef without salt. We were not furnished anything to cook with. Indeed, the rebels did not have anything of the kind with them, so most of the boys made dough of their meal and baked it on a stone and the beef was thrown on the fire and roasted. I and several others of my mess happened to have little pails, and a plate, knife and fork along. We made our meal into mush and as good fortune would have it, we had a little salt also and we fared comparatively well. We now sold considerable of our baggage for which the rebels paid exorbitant prices in confederate money. For instance, for a good rubber such as cost three dollars, they would pay twenty-five. Milt, Roll, Elex and myself concluded not to part with these useful articles and it was well for us that we did not. We sold such things as we could dispense with. I sold my old canteen, knapsack and portfolio for twenty dollars of confederate scrip. My messmates, Roll, Milt and Elex sold enough so that we had about two hundred dollars in confederate money, and between us we had thirty dollars in greenbacks, and as the latter was eagerly sought for by the rebels, we felt that our condition could have been much worse. We found the rest of our battalion here and a sorry looking set they were. Some were minus boots, hats and coats but with a brave spirit they made light of it and we joked each other as freely as we would in our own camp.

The 12th Tennessee cavalry was now detailed to guard us, and with few exceptions, they treated us as kindly as the 6th Mississippi. We left Hood's headquarters about 3 o'clock P. M. and traveled until about 8 o'clock. During the day we heard heavy cannonading in the direction of Allatoona, and we knew that they were having a fierce fight there. We all felt deeply anxious to know the result of the engagement. If they succeeded in capturing the place, it would be an irreparable loss to our army. Toward evening the sound of battle ceased, and to our anxious inquiries as to how the battle went, the rebels remained silent, but their gloomy countenances told us just as plainly as words that they had been defeated. We passed through the whole rebel army, and as a general thing, we found them in high spirits. Their leaders had worked upon their minds and made them believe that victory and the destruction of Sherman's army was before them—that they would carry the war to the banks of the Ohio, and possibly invade the free states, but the bloody repulse at Allatoona rather chilled their ardor. They were out of rations and confidently expected to get the immense supply at that place, but that little band of three thousand men drove back in confusion two divisions of the rebel army, and they were forced to beat a hurried retreat to avoid a clash with Sherman's army, which was now closely pressing them. We firmly believed, and subsequent events justified the belief, that this was a trap laid by Sherman to compass the destruction of the rebel army. My readers need not be told how well he succeeded. There was a great deal of bantering between the rebs and us. They confidently thought that they would regain more than they had lost, and tried to bargain for our coats and blankets. They said they were going North, where it was colder, while we were going South, where it was warmer, so we would not need them. We told them that we did not doubt but what they would go North, and the most of them get up as far as Camp Douglas and other northern prisons. They did not relish this thrust much and had they known how true our prophecy was, they would have relished it less. We resumed our march at daylight. It had rained all night and nearly all day. We halted at 10 o'clock A. M. and drew two days' rations, consisting of hard bread and bacon. Resumed the march at 12 o'clock M. The marching was very difficult on account of the mud. We camped at Villa Ricca, having marched over twenty-five miles during the day.

October 7th.

Resumed the march at daybreak. We camped that night on the south bank of the Chattahoochee, having marched over twenty miles. The rear of the rebel army was camped here. Gen. Beauregard passed during the evening. He was on his way to the front to assume command.

October 8th.

During the night, the rebels took up their pontoon, marched at sunrise, arrived at Newman at 10 o'clock A. M. Here we drew two days' more rations. Newman is a small town on the West Point railroad. We were quartered here in the old court house and remained all night.

During the day, Milton and I were drawn into a discussion with a violent rebel of the aristocratic sort. Our debate grew warm. Milton got his blood up and the guard interfered. Whenever occasion required, we did not hesitate to express our sentiments. We indulged in the hope all along that a speedy exchange of prisoners would be made and we would be free soon. Had we known that we were going to Andersonville prison pen, we would not have gone so quietly along. We had some opportunities to try to effect our escape, but we thought that a failure would subject us all to more rigorous confinement, and if we succeeded, it would be worse for those that remained. So we desisted. Besides, our guard put us upon our honor and trusted us. A mason, one of the guard, allowed me to go out forty rods alone and fill some canteens.

October 9th.

We took the cars at two o'clock A. M. for West Point. Arrived there at daylight. Here we parted with the 12th Tennessee cavalry. I will here mention that at Newman I wrote home and entrusted my letter with Dr. Chafee. It was contrary to the rules of war to hold surgeons as prisoners. The doctor was going home by the way of Richmond, but as he never mailed the letter, our folks did not hear directly from me while a prisoner. We now drew another day's rations and took up a line of march for Columbus in charge of several companies of Alabama militia who treated us more like brutes than men. We halted at sundown and camped. Their insolence was hardly bearable, and we commenced secretly maturing plans for revenge and escape. It only wanted the sanction of our own officers to carry it into effect, but they would not countenance it. Possibly the rebels had an inkling of what was going on for they ceased their abuse. These were men who had never seen active service and they made much ado about their bravery, but they were the most despicable cowards imaginable. Could fifty of our men have got hold of arms, we would not have hesitated to have attacked the whole crew. As it was, they rode along with their pieces ready, fearing that we might attempt to escape. The commander of these brave Alabamians rejoiced in the name of Sir William Wallace. The boys put on the Sir just to excite his vanity. I will note one instance of his bravery. Some of the boys became footsore and weary. They marched us almost on a double quick and some could not keep up. This brave Alabamian would ride back, draw his revolver, flourish it over his head and threaten to shoot them if they did not keep up. One of our boys in Company C, turned on him, drew his form up to its fullest extent and with flashing eye, bared his bosom and dared him to shoot. The valiant Captain was snubbed. He quailed beneath those flashing eyes.

October 10th.

We were on the march again at early dawn and one hour before sunset, the spires of the beautiful city of Columbus were in view. This was a place of some twelve thousand inhabitants and was noted for its extensive iron manufacturing works, they being the most extensive of any in the South. The place at this time was a military post and presented some signs of life. It lies on the Chattahoochee river and is a place of considerable importance. Our eager eyes took in everything, noting its defenses. We were sure that Gen. Sherman would ere long pay his compliments to this city. We were not mistaken. In less than two months after we were there, the federal flag waved over the city. We were marched up before the commandant's headquarters for inspection, where a gaping, eager crowd stared at us. They wanted to know where the rest of the prisoners were. They had read in their papers and heard

by report that there were seven thousand prisoners expected.
When they found out that there were only four hundred, they felt
cheap enough. They inquired for Sherman. Some supposed that
he was along. One man stepped out and pointed out a person of
rather shabby appearance and said that he was Mr. Sherman. The
crowd stared eagerly at him. We could not restrain a shout of
laughter. These poor deluded beings did actually believe that
Sherman was along. Their papers said that he was captured and
of course they believed it. We were marched to the church green
and rested awhile. Our valiant Alabamians were now relieved,
and they returned, covered with imaginary laurels. It seemed as
though the whole population of Columbus came out to gaze at us.
The reigning belles, children and aged, and even the very dogs
eyed us curiously. I suppose that they never saw a Yank before
and they expected to see something like wild animals, but when
they found out that we were veritable human beings, their wonder
ceased and they seemed disposed to treat us kindly. We sent
some of them to the bakery for us and they faithfully performed
the errand and would not take a cent for their trouble.

A detachment of the 39th Alabama infantry now had us in
charge. They were veteran soldiers and knew how to treat prisoners. In fact, in their presence, we almost forgot that we were
prisoners. They allowed us a great deal of freedom and treated
us with the most magnanimous kindness. We were quartered in
an old cattle pen that night and a strict guard placed over us.
They apprehended an attempt to escape. Early the next morning
we took the cars as we hoped for Macon. We had a horrid dread
of Andersonville. The inhuman treatment of prisoners received
at that place had reached our ears, but when we came to the Junction and left the Macon road to our left, then we knew we were
doomed for Andersonville. Our train moved slowly and we had
plenty of opportunities to attempt to escape, and it seems now
almost a wonder that we did not attempt it. The only reason I
can give is that we did not fully realize our situation. Our guards
treated us so kindly, we did not realize we would get into such
fiendish hands as the rebel commandant at Andersonville, and here
I will make a statement that is true and proved true in every
instance, and that is, whenever we fell into the hands of veteran
soldiers who had fought us bravely on the battle-field, we received
all of the kind and considerate attention due a prisoner of war, but

whenever we were in charge of militia or that class of persons who, too cowardly to take the field, enlisted in the home guard, we were treated in the most outrageous manner. Now let it be under- stood that most of the guard at Andersonville were these militia. There were a few veteran troops there.

October 11th.

At 4 o'clock P. M. the Georgia Hell, which clutched in its iron grasp ten thousand Union soldiers, was seen in the distance. We were marched up to the commandant's headquarters, Captain Wirz, where a rigid search was performed before we were put inside the stockade.   This devil in human shape, Wirz, I will briefly describe. Any man gifted with any discernment would pronounce him a villain at first sight. I should judge that he was of German descent; five feet eight or nine inches high; sandy complexion, with a scowling look.   On his upper jaw one tooth protruded, giving his otherwise repulsive features a horrid expression.   As he moved around amongst us, he spit out his vile abuse in the most disgust- ing manner, nearly every word an oath.   It was evident that he had received instructions from his superiors in regard to our search else we would have fared differently.   As it was, they only took away our knapsacks, canteens, haversacks, knives, etc., and allowed us to keep all under twenty dollars in money.   When his subordinate came to search me, I emptied my pockets before him. Amongst other things, I had a box of Brown's bronchial troches. I told the sergeant who was searching me (he appeared to be a nice fellow) that it was some cough medicine my mother had sent me for a severe cough.   He thought that I would be allowed to keep them.   Unfortunately, the captain happened to see them.   He snatched them out of my hand, smelled of them, sniffed up his nose and then scattered them in the dirt at my feet.   I never experienced a moment of such frenzied rage before in my life.   If I had had a revolver I should have shot him on the spot, regardless of consequences, but a moment's sober thought con- vinced me how useless it would be to have remonstrated, for to have said one word, would have been the signal for my death.   We were powerless and in the hands of a merciless foe.   During the search Rollin picked up some of them, so I succeeded in breaking my cough.   I firmly believe, had it not been for them, I would have been added to the long list of victims whose bodies were left to rot in unknown and unmarked graves in this Southern hell.

Rollin also had a box of homœpathic medicine which was taken from him.

About sundown we were marched to the outside gate of hell. One of his satanic majesty's servants stood ready to meet us and to usher us into the inner temple. Its huge doors swung open to admit us and we were in the presence of—I do not know what to call them. It was evident that they were once human beings, but hunger, sickness, exposure and dirt had so transformed them that they more resembled walking skeletons, painted black. Our feelings cannot be described as we gazed on these poor human beings. Equally astonished were they to see us. I presume we appeared to them like heavenly visitants, so white did we appear in comparison with them. Almost the first cry that greeted our ears was "fresh fish," then eager questions as to where we came from, whether there was any prospect of exchange. How eagerly would they watch for the least gleam of hope! How their wan cheeks lit up with intense joy as we told them we hoped to be exchanged soon! Oh, ye who were basking in the sunlight of home and friends, surrounded by comfort and plenty, how little you could realize the suffering and misery that your friends were experiencing in Southern prisons, confined in loathsome dungeons, or foul pens, starved, sick, meeting with nothing but injury and insult, with no ray of hope to illumine their path, no kind word to cheer, where death would seem an angel messenger to release them from their trouble. No wonder that stout hearts, who had faced death in a thousand forms on bloody fields with unblanched cheek and flashing eye, should now give up and groan in anguish and despair! To face death on the battle-field where, if you met death, your friends would know your fate, and to die with the glorious old banner waving over you would be a blessing indeed, compared to the dark despair which here engulfed us. Entirely forsaken, it seemed, by our Government, what hope was there to comfort us? But, if we would live, we could not indulge in these thoughts. All who gave way to their grief soon sank into the arms of death. I saw what I had to meet and bent my strength and energies to meet it. I knew that if ever I went out of that place alive, I should have to meet everything in a determined manner. I dared not look at the dark picture, but I looked forward to life and liberty. I was determined to conquer my disease and I succeeded, though, that, with the scant rations, left me weak. I thought that I had seen misery in its worst forms, but the worst that I had ever seen was paradise compared to what here met my vision. Such squalid, filthy wretchedness, hunger, disease, nakedness and cold, I never saw before. Thirty-five thousand souls had been crowded into this pen, filling it completely. Poorly clad and worse fed, drinking filth and slime, from one hundred to three hundred of these passed into the gate of the eternal world daily. In fourteen months' time, fourteen thousand found a resting-place in the grave. In hot weather, while in their dying agonies, these suffering soldiers would clutch at the ground to dig a hole in the sand in which to hide their heads from the burning rays of the sun. Andersonville prison originally comprised sixteen acres of sandy soil, covered with pitch pine.

Near the north end, a filthy stream, bordered by a mucky swamp, ran through it. From this stream the prisoners got a great deal of their water. Afterwards a spring broke out in the east part of the camp, north of the swamp, which supplied the whole camp with pure water. In the swamp the men would wade waist deep, to gather a few roots with which to make fires to cook their scanty rations. Some who were unable to get wood, would give one-half of their rations for the sake of getting the rest cooked. Subsequently, our rations were furnished us cooked. Some of the men, while wading in this swamp, caught the disease called gangrene. The bruises or sores they had on them coming in contact with the poisonous filth of the swamp poisoned the affected part. The victim usually died after suffering the most excrutiating agony. If one chanced to recover, he lost the limb on which was the affected part. In these wounds, vermin or maggots would gather, and there was not attention enough paid to the patient to keep the wound purified. The prison was surrounded by a double line of stockades, by palisades protruding ten or twelve feet above the surface of the earth. The palisades were pine logs from one foot to eighteen inches in thickness. On the outside of the inside stockade, platforms were erected for sentinels. In the daytime only every other stand was occupied. In the night, it was doubled. Inside the stockade about twenty feet from its base, was erected what was called a "dead line" and a prisoner that even put a foot beyond that line, sealed his death if the guard chose to shoot him. It is estimated that from two to five deaths occurred daily from this cause alone while the prison was so crowded. Subsequently, when a larger portion of the prisoners had been removed, our treatment was not so rigorous. Before the prison pen was enlarged, the prisoners were crowded so that they could hardly find room to lie down and then perhaps it would be in their own filth. Water became so scarce that many commenced digging wells, and wells thirty feet deep were dug with no other tool than a jack knife or one half of a canteen, the dirt being drawn up in little pails. So thick did the wells become that it was dangerous to walk in the nighttime. As for shelter, very few had any except what they found by burrowing in the earth or building clay houses. The consequence was that many died from exposure. There was no time of day but what we could see some dead men lying around camp while scores of others were dying. Some would be so thickly covered with vermin, or more properly called body lice, as to be perfectly white with them. In fact, they would eat them up alive and they had not the power to rise or get rid of them. We would find some poor soldier almost destitute of clothing, his body resembling a charred mass of flesh and bones, lying with no shelter, sick nigh unto death, with no friends, no hope, longing and praying for death to relieve him. There was one curious phase of human nature exhibited here in regard to helping one another. One would naturally suppose that being thrown together, as we were, that banding together and helping one another would take place, and when a squad, company or regiment was captured together, this was generally the case, but if one was captured alone, put with strangers and became sick, it was ten chances to one that he would die unattended by any human being. His fellow sufferers would pass him with perhaps this remark, "Let his friends take care of him. I have more than I can see to now," and so the poor sufferer expires uncared for and unknown. How many, many homes in our land have been darkened by the uncertainty of the fate that befell their lost ones. Before we entered Andersonville, the prisoners, except about ten thousand, had been removed to other prisons and it had been enlarged to twenty-six acres, bringing the stream in the middle of the prison, and as the spring had broken out, we did not experience near as much suffering as the other prisoners did before a portion of them were removed, but our treatment would have put the wildest, untutored savage to the blush.

11

As soon as we got settled, we went to work renovating the camp and we produced a marked change in its appearance. We were soon organized into detachments and messes, ours being the 6th detachment and 5th mess. A sergeant had charge of each mess. A rebel sergeant charge of each detachment. We had roll-call each morning. If one was found absent, our rations would be withheld until he was accounted for. Sometimes a whole mess would go without rations on account of the delinquency of one man. Our daily rations consisted of a piece of corn bread, about two and one-half inches square, one pint of beans, with pods, dirt and bugs all cooked together, and in lieu of these, some maggoty rice. Sometimes we would get some pork, but one day's rations was not a decent mouthful. We occasionally drew a small piece of skeleton beef, sometimes so strong that we could smell it before it got near us. We usually cooked our grub over to purify it and make it into soup. From the beans we could skim off spoonful after spoonful of bugs, but most of the boys preferred to eat them bugs and all. Such, my readers, is the plain, unvarnished statement of our prison fare; but we were not long in finding out the most favorably disposed guards and they would carry on a traffic with us on the sly, furnishing us with sweet potatoes, corn meal, etc. In this manner we managed to live. I verily believed that we would have starved to death if it had not been for this. There were some rebel sutlers who made money out of the prisoners. A sort of market street was established, and all times of day the most avaricious were trying to speculate. Some would manage to get hold of a little flour and make a few biscuits, and for one little biscuit, about two or three mouthfuls, they would charge ten cents in greenbacks or fifty cents in confederate money. Everything else in proportion. For instance, a teaspoon of salt would sell for fifty cents. There seemed to be a perfect mania amongst some of the rebels to get something that belonged to the Yanks. Our military buttons took their eye at first, and I have seen as high as twenty dollars paid for one-half dozen. We disposed of all these extra and useless articles and took in exchange something to eat. The trade with the guard was made at a certain hour of the night under cover of darkness.

EXTRACT FROM DIARY.

October 13th.

Arose early, washed a shirt, pair of socks and one pair of

drawers and took a good bath. The mortality of the camp is about twenty per day now. Rollin, Milton and Alex Killon are my messmates.

October 14th.

Cloudy and prospect of rain.

October 15th.

Pleasant and warm.

October 16th.

Cool night, pleasant morning. Drew rice and molasses last evening. We got a little wood yesterday for the first time. A piece two and one-half inches through and two feet long being a ration.

October 17th.

Are gathering brick made of wet clay baked in the sun, for the purpose of building a small house for winter quarters.

October 18th.

Pleasant. Busy putting up our winter quarters. Did not draw any corn bread last night. Drew only one pint of beans.

October 19th.

We are having splendid weather; nights getting to be quite cold. Wrote a letter home according to the rules prescribed and sent it on its mission, trusting to the fate of war to reach its destination. Drew our back rations of bread this evening, and the boys are feeling quite well. The number of deaths is decreasing.

October 20th.

Was on fatigue this morning, filling up old wells. Some of the detail carried out the dead to the deadhouse. It is very shocking to human feelings the way the dead are disposed of. They are piled up in a wagon like so much wood, taken to holes dug for them and piled in, with no respect for decency or humanity. We are still working on our little house. The sides and one end are laid up two feet with brick. We are going to put on a mud roof. Will take several days yet to complete it. Its dimensions are six feet wide, seven feet long and four feet high. Four of us occupy this little building. There is considerable talk of exchange of prisoners between Hood and Sherman. A few of us are allowed to go out once in awhile under strong guard for wood. Some of the boys have at such times attempted to escape, but the bloodhounds generally tracked them down and they were caught and brought back. I have seen some of the prisoners so mutilated and torn up by these hounds that it did not seem possible for them to recover. A large pack of these hounds was kept for this purpose. Under command of their master, they are trained to the sound of the bugle and are kept half-starved to make them ferocious. They take a circuit around the stockade every morning to see if there are any fresh tracks. So keen is the scent of these hounds that they can scent the very air through which a person travels, but the scent can be destroyed by using turpentine on the soles of your feet and in your armpits. Some of the boys escaped by using some of this. Or if a prisoner can get twenty-four hours the start, he is safe from pursuit of the hounds, but he is in danger of running across, at any moment, bands of confederate soldiers patrolling the country for deserters and escaped prisoners. Some have been caught and brought back after they got in sight of our lines. The negroes, with rare exception, always befriend these fugitives. They have been known in hundreds of cases to secrete and feed them for months. Tunnelling was now resorted to as a means of escape. Some of my comrades were engaged in this. Only a certain number were let into the secret. They would work it in this way. They would build a kind of shanty over one of the deep wells and then go down some twenty or thirty feet into the well and commence digging, the bottom of the well furnishing plenty of room for the dirt. One tunnel was so nearly completed that one night's work would have finished it, when someone proved traitor and exposed them. Thus, from the highest pinnacle of hope to the lowest depth of despair were they plunged. After these attempts had been discovered, the commander sent for the ringleaders and told them that if any such thing were attempted again, he would open fire on the prisoners with grape and canister and not cease while one was alive. We knew that his disposition was none too good for such an outrage and it operated as a restraint. At one time a plan was nearly perfected for a revolt, but it was discovered by a traitor divulging the plan. One of our boys, Wolford Hotchkiss was shot at one day for stepping a second beyond the dead line, but the shot did not hit him. For every soldier that the guard shot for for stepping across the dead line, he was to receive twenty days' furlough. This is as we got it from their own lips.

There is one important event that transpired in prison that I had forgotten to chronicle. While the stockade was so full, there was a desperate set of scoundrels and blacklegs ready to pounce upon anyone that had any valuables about him. So bold did they become that murders were committed in broad daylight, and one man was known to murder even his own brother, although he did not know it at the time. A vigilance committee of our own men was formed. Six of the ringleaders were arrested, tried by an impromptu court martial, condemned and hung on the spot. This wholesome proceeding had a good effect and effectually crushed the gang. We had a police force of one hundred men whose duty it was to see that the camp was kept quiet and clean. Had a touch of the ague to-day. The accommodation for the sick is a little more humane than heretofore. A shed has been erected for their accommodation. A good portion of the prisoners belong to the Army of the Potomac.

October 21st.

We are still blessed with pleasant weather. Do not feel well to-day. Drew rations of beans last evening and one teaspoonful of salt to each man, the first we have drawn. My stomach rejects the beans. They are so foul. We still have a little money and can buy what is necessary for our subsistence. If it were not for this, we would starve. Are not doing much on our quarters to-day. Have it all completed except the roof and chimney. Rollin and Milton have gone now to get some straw to thatch it with. The report is that Richmond is taken, but we cannot put much credit in it.

October 22d.

Pleasant. Everything quiet. A poor soldier ended his sufferings this evening within a few feet of us. The nights are quite cool and it causes untold suffering amongst the poorly clad soldiers who are without blankets, shoes or coats and some without any shelter.

October 23d.

Had a very poor night. The coldest we have had, but it is a very fine morning. In the past few days, quite a number of soldiers have been brought back who tried to effect their escape. Some nearly reached our lines before being caught. One man in particular, by the name of Davis, of the 4th Iowa infantry, lived three weeks in a cave near the rebel army and within three miles of our lines. He was well-fed and otherwise provided for by negroes. This man used to live in Coral and worked for Mr.

Bartholemew. Drew beans last night and rice the night before. We buy a ration of rice, corn bread and some meal daily. We have made some beer of corn meal and molasses to keep off the scurvy. Its effects are very beneficial. We are getting along very slowly in completing our quarters. Milt baked some corn bread for dinner which was very good.

October 24th.

Pleasant day. Very cold night. Drew rice last evening and one pint of molasses to a man. The rice was very poorly cooked. We had to cook it over again before we could eat it. Have not done anything on our shanty to-day. Could not get out to get material.

October 25th.

Pleasant. Commenced putting on a mud roof to-day. We cannot get out to get any more straw. Captain Wirz has prohibited any more prisoners going out on account of so many trying to escape, and for trading with the guard. Drew beans last night.

October 26th.

Cloudy and prospect of rain. Am not doing much to-day. Drew rice last evening. One man went to hospital to-day from our mess.

October 27th.

The morning set in rainy. During the afternoon it rained very hard, completely destroying our mud roof, which proves to be a complete failure. Toward evening, it cleared off and was quite pleasant. Drew beans last evening. Only two deaths during the day. Some of our regiment have tried to escape within the past few days but all were caught and brought back. We have been talking of trying it but the ill success of the others discourages us. Caught a severe cold yesterday. Feel some better to-day. Prison fare is gradually reducing my strength. I am getting to be quite weak.

October 28th.

Pleasant and cool. Considerable talk of our being sent to another prison at Millen, twenty miles from Savannah. Drew rice last evening. Bought four quarts of sweet potatoes to-day for five dollars confederate scrip. Also bought two quarts of meal this evening for two dollars. It takes ten dollars confederate money as an equivalent for one dollar in greenbacks.

October 29th.

A little cloudy this morning.   Market street is unusually active this morning.   Notice several articles for sale that I have not seen before, such as pies, radishes, apples, etc.   The price of pies is one dollar and a half in United States money.   Drew rice last evening.   Washed shirt and socks this afternoon.

Sunday, October 30th.

Pleasant and warm.   Six prisoners came in last evening, captured near Atlanta while out foraging.   They report the capture of Petersburg and that Sherman was whipping Hood badly.   Trains were expected through from Nashville the day they were captured.   Only two deaths occurred in the hospital yesterday.

October 31st.

Cloudy and prospective rain.   The 1st and 2d detachment and two hundred of the third left this morning.   We suppose that they are going to Millen, Georgia, whither we expect to go as soon as transportation arrives.   The reason for removing us, we are told, is for the purpose of repairing the stockade and putting up barracks for winter quarters.   We may come back again.   Three or four hundred carpenters remain on parole to work on barracks.   This is a good place for a prison if it was properly laid out and accommodations made for the prisoners.

November 1st.

Weather still continues cloudy and cool.   I made my first visit to the hospital to-day.   Found it nearly deserted.   They are removing all the sick to the hospital outside of the stockade.   All that are able, return to their respective detachments.   I think it is evident that they intend to clear the camp entirely of prisoners.   There remain here now besides the sick, four detachments, five hundred men in each, and two hundred in the fifth detachment.

November 2d.

Morning rainy and cold.   Rained very hard during the night and our mud walls caved in completely, soaking our blankets with mud and water.   We passed a rough night.   For the past few days our rations have been cut down a little.

November 3d.

Rained all night and still continues raining.   Two detachments left last evening.   We have orders to be ready to leave this evening at ten o'clock.

November 4th.

Very cold and cloudy. Rained a little during the night. Our rations were very scant last evening. It is impossible to keep warm to-day unless bundled up in clothes or huddled around a warm fire.

November 5th.

Another day has passed and we still remain in this miserable pen, and get rations barely sufficient to sustain life. One year ago this evening, after nearly three years' absence, I crossed the threshold of home. Friends and plenty there surrounded me. How great the contrast now! A prisoner of war, penned up in a loathsome prison, and would gladly grasp for the food thrown to the dogs; but it is the fate of war and I submit without murmuring.

Sunday, November 6th.

Pleasant and warm. No prospect of moving to-day. Drew full rations of rice and molasses but only three-fourths rations of corn bread.

November 7th.

Cloudy and warm. We expect to move before to-morrow morning. Several of our boys scaled the stockade by means of ladders while the guard was warming by the fire and tried to escape, but the hounds were put upon their track at daylight and most of them have been brought back. Did up some washing to-day.

November 8th.

This day, fraught with so deep an interest to every American heart, dawned unpleasant and rainy. The great issue to be decided to-day will engross the whole attention of lovers of liberty and free government throughout the civilized world. A monstrous and wicked rebellion has thrown its iron grasp upon the freest and best government that ever existed, and is trying to plant upon its ruins a government whose chief corner-stone is slavery, totally ignoring that which every true American holds dear, trampling upon the sacred ties that should bind American hearts together in bonds of fraternity. Traitors still defiantly proclaim their treason and affect to scorn and trample upon our emblem of national unity as though it were a rag unworthy the homage of a loyal heart. To suppress this monster rebellion, Abraham Lincoln, as President, has labored four years, expending millions upon millions of treasure, sacrificing thousands upon thousands of precious lives until every household is draped in mourning for loved ones slain; yet, after all these sacrifices have been made, treason still shrieks defiance in our ears and horrid civil war still throws its damp and bloody chill over us. The issue this day will decide whether another man will be placed at the helm to guide the ship of state. Trusting to an overruling power, we anxiously await what the unborn future has in store for us, hoping and praying that the right may triumph, and our nation, one and indivisible, survive forever. A vote was taken in our detachment. There were two hundred twenty-four votes cast. Lincoln received one hundred eighty-eight and McClellan thirty-six. Over one-half of the men did not vote. Our rations still continue very scarce and our prospect of moving is gradually dying away.

November 9th.

Cloudy and fleeting. Rather warm. Traded off my scissors last evening for one pound of salt. Traded for four pounds more this evening and gave five dollars in confederate money for it.

November 10th.

Pleasant and warm. Washed a shirt this morning. At eleven o'clock we received orders to get ready immediately and march to the depot. Seventy-eight were put in one car, which made it so full we could scarcely stand up. We remained in this condition twenty-four hours, but anything was a relief to get out of Andersonville. We were the last to leave. We drew one day's rations. During the night several of the boys jumped off the train and tried to escape. Only one succeeded.

November 11th.

We arrived at Macon at 9 o'clock P. M. and stayed until 4 o'clock A. M. Father is fifty-seven years old to-day.

November 12th.

Arrived at our new prison, five miles from Millen, at 3 P. M. Here we found the boys of our regiment who were captured a few days before we were. They were Houston, Lowell, Irvin and Shaffer. They had had hard usage and were looking thin, but had been in good health most of the time. We were glad to meet them again, even though it were under such painful circumstances. Our camp here is much more pleasant than it was at Andersonville or Sumter. It consists of an inclosure of about forty acres, surrounded by a single line of stockades. A splendid stream of pure water runs through the center. The ground is well adapted for a

camp. It gently slopes gently from the east and west toward the
stream. Below, at one side of the stockade, a privy is built over
the stream, and all filth is thus carried away. At the upper portion of the stream we get water for cooking purposes, and a little
below we do our washing. There are at present nine thousand
prisoners here, all camped on the west side of the stream. They
are divided into divisions of one thousand men each. Each division is divided into detachments of two hundred and fifty men.
Each detachment is divided into messes, two of one hundred men
each and one of fifty. Then these messes are divided to suit the
taste of the soldiers. A rebel sergeant has charge of the division
and one of our own sergeants charge of detachments, messes, etc.,
and draws his rations from division sergeant. Our rations to-day
consist of beef, rice, beans and meal. We get double the amount
of beef that we did at Camp Sumter, and of a great deal better
quality. Our rations are drawn uncooked. We get one pint of
meal to a man, which is sufficient to sustain life. We are bothered some for wood to cook with, but by digging up roots of
stumps we manage to get along. We expect to be allowed after
awhile to go out and bring in wood. This camp is named Law-
ton. An exchange of sick and wounded is going on now, and
there is a prospect of a general exchange soon. Was on Market
street to-day. Noticed that they sold thing a great deal higher
than at Camp Sumter. Some of the rebel officials are in league
with the sutler, and charge outrageously for everything.

November 13th. Sunday.

Pleasant day. Very cool night. Passed the day in looking
around camp.

November 14th.

Pleasant. Suffered with cold last night. Have had no chance
yet to put up a shelter or bring in wood. We have drawn no
rations to-day, and the pangs of hunger are sharpening our appetites to the keenest point.

November 15th.

We were aroused before sunrise and ordered to move over to
the other side of the camp. Nearly one thousand sick and
wounded leave here to-day for Savannah to be exchanged. We
drew rations of sweet potatoes. Prisoners captured at Richmond
one week ago report the capture of that place by Gen. Grant.
Prisoners captured near Sherman's line within a few days report

that three of his army corps have returned to Atlanta preparatory
to a forward move to the Gulf, and left Gen. Thomas with forty
thousand fresh troops to watch and take care of Hood.

November 16th.

Removed back to our former camp last evening. The report
is that we will be exchanged soon. Drew sweet potatoes again
to day. Removed across the stream again this morning. Two
car-loads of sick arrived last night from Andersonville. We have
not had a chance to go out since we came in here, and we are
greatly bothered to get wood to cook our rations. The sutlers ask
such an enormous price for their articles that we cannot buy.

November 17th.

The night was warmer than any night for a week past. The
day has been pleasant and warm. Several car-loads of paroled
rebel prisoners have passed through this place within a few days.
Twenty-five hundred are reported to leave this camp to-morrow—
mostly sick and wounded. Drew meal, rice, beef and salt this
evening. Meal sells at ten cents a pint, rice sixty cents a quart,
salt five cents a teaspoonful, sweet potatoes twenty dollars per
bushel. Went out to-day for the first time for wood. Roll and
Alex went with me. Only thirty can go out at a time. Forty
squads go out in a day. If one man fails to come back with the
rest, the division to which he belongs does not go out again until
he is brought back. A Dutch captain by the name of D. C.
Vowles commands the prison. He is a harsh commander. The
mortality of the camp averages about ten per day. My health
continues good, though I am conscious of growing weakness.

November 18th.

The sick continue to leave daily. About three thousand have
left. By paying the doctor a good sum, from twenty to fifty dollars in greenbacks, he will put a person on the sick list, and thus
they will get out of prison. Those who are fortunate enough to
have money and who are disposed to use it in this manner, succeed
in getting out, and many of the sick are actually crowded out to
give place to those who have bought their freedom. The doctors
are making quite a speculating game out of it.

November 19th.

Rained last night. We put up our rubbers for shelter. Drew
one-half ration of meal last night. Weather still continues cloudy.
A load of beef heads was drawn into camp last night and the men

eagerly secured them, although they smelled so strong that they
would have turned our stomachs under ordinary circumstances.
Soup was made of them. Rice, bean soup, biscuits, pies and corn
dodgers were made and sold on Market Street at exorbitant
prices. Alex sold his watch for twenty dollars in greenbacks and
so we still had a little money to use in case of emergencies.
Tommy Houston now bunks with us.

November 20th.

Cloudy and chilly. All the sick have been removed. Just
before dark this evening, very unexpectedly to me, Rollin's name
and mine were called, with orders to get ready to march immediately. Roll afterward told me how it happened. There had been
a special call for two hundred fifty men to fill out the one thousand. Rollin saw the lieutenant, and he, recognizing him as a
member of our fraternity, succeeded in getting his name on and
vouched for me. He also tried to get Milton on. The lieutenant
could not do it, but told Rollin that in less than one week all
would leave and be exchanged, and so, under these circumstances,
we parted in good spirits with our comrades. Milton followed us
down to the bridge and stood until our names were called and we
passed out. A sergeant Reed's name of our company was called and
he was not there to answer to it. Milton was strongly tempted to
answer to it and pass out with us, but fear of detection restrained
him. Besides, he expected to get out soon, anyway. Poor boy!
Better would it have been for him had he acted upon the impulse of
the moment and gone with us! Then he might have been spared the
horrid fate that happened to him! We passed out of the stockade
up to headquarters, where we were paroled. No guard now
dogged our footsteps. We were free. The earth, the air, the
very ground we trod on, seemed to echo our soul's deep gratitude.
Never had the soul-stirring word freedom appeared to us in such
beautiful relief as at this moment. Those of you who have ever
passed weary, miserable days in prison can imagine our emotion
as we shook the dust of prison from our feet and once more trod
the earth, free men. It only wanted our restoration to home and
friends to make our joy complete, save the saddening thought that
our country was still in peril and our comrades still suffering in
prison.

November 21st.

We took the cars the same evening for Savannah. Arrived

there at break of day. It is a splendid looking city on rather low ground. The city troops took us in charge and marched us to the river where we were to embark and proceed to our fleet near Fort Pulaski, at the mouth of the Savannah river. A strong Union sentiment prevailed at Savannah and the Union people would have fed us had they been allowed to. We did not start with any rations, but Rollin and I managed to get hold of an ear of corn and we made this answer for food until we arrived at the fleet. While we were passing through the city, a person dressed in the garb of a federal soldier was seen to quickly take his place in our line. The guard supposing him to be one of us, did not take much notice of it, but it was a Union citizen of Savannah who adopted this method of escaping from the clutches of his enemies. It was raining quite hard all this time and we got drenched to the skin. The day being quite chilly, we suffered not a little. Finally the rebel transport "Beauregard" loosed its moorings, stemmed out into the stream and headed for our fleet. As we passed Ft. Jackson, we noticed how effectually the river was blockaded. It was impossible for a boat to pass the obstructions unless under the guidance of a skillful pilot, acquainted with the channel. About one o'clock P. M. we hove in sight of our fleet. I never saw a sight which awoke more ennobling feelings of pride and devotion in my bosom than when I again beheld our noble ensign floating over our gallant ships which were soon to bear us back again to home and friends. Eyes that had long be strained to catch glimpses of the dear old flag, now grew misty with tears. Yes, soldiers who had faced death time and again with unfailing eye, now wept like children before that flag that had so often guided them on to victory. At three o'clock P. M. we embarked on board one of our ships and passed entirely out of rebel hands. We had been in their power forty-seven days.

November 22d.

Disembarked from the "Star of the South" and embarked on board the "Sedgwick." At four P. M. we weighed anchor and set sail for the Chesapeake Bay. There being a strong wind favoring us, we were soon wafted on the bosom of the broad ocean. When fairly out at sea, the wind increased to a strong gale. The ship rolled and tossed on waves mountain high and we all experienced that very disagreeable feeling of seasickness. Our long fasting and impure food that we had received in rebel prisons and our

overtaxed stomachs which we filled after getting on board our fleet,
made us remarkably fine subjects for seasickness.   Soon there was
not one but what was heaving up "Jonah," and that, with the gale,
made a scene of great confusion.   At times, the boat would give a
sudden lurch on its side and scores of us would be precipitated on
all fours to the other side of the boat.   We did not care much
whether the boat sunk or not, but despite our distress, we could
not repress our laughter at the ludicrousness of our situation.   I
attempted to crawl out on deck and relieve myself.   I went on all
fours, and just as I stuck my head out of doors, a gust of wind
took my hat off.   The next morning when I got out, I found it
filled with the essence of seasickness.   I gave it a toss overboard
and my unlucky hat found a watery bed.

November 23d.

The gale continued to blow all night.   I passed a rough night
of it.   Rollin was also in the same condition.   The ship continued
on in a northerly course.   Toward night the sea became more
calm and we began to recover from our sickness.   Our rations
were furnished us cooked and we got plenty of them.

November 24th.

The morning dawned pleasant.   Passed a comfortable night.
Sea quite calm.   Rounded Cape Hatteras during the night.   The
ship now changed its course to a northwesterly direction.

November 25th.

Smooth sea and fine sailing.   Drew boiled ham for breakfast.
Had a splendid soup for supper, made of onions, tomatoes, boiled
with crackers and ham.   Saw a drove of porpoises following the
ship.   They follow in a regular line extending as far as the eye
can reach.   Entered the Chesapeake about eight o'clock A. M.

November 26th.

The ship anchored about midnight in the harbor of Annapolis.
We disembarked at early dawn and marched to the barracks outside the city.   It seemed pleasant to again to get into God's country
under the protection of the stars and stripes.   Every one seemed
to vie with the others in treating us kindly.   In the evening, we
drew a complete suit of clothing, but before changing we were
required to divest ourselves of every article of prison apparel, go
into a bath room, prepared expressly for us, and thoroughly
cleanse ourselves   We were also obliged to leave our prison
apparel, but we did not care for that.   Our new suit was furnished

us free gratis. Our boys practiced a little deception now, which, under the circumstances, I think was justifiable. Those of our regiment who had not been captured, were now mounted and were bodyguard to General Smith, and as we desired a cavalry suit, we gave in our regiment as mounted infantry. After our change our transformation was complete. We looked like a different set of beings. I do not consider Annapolis a very nice looking city. The State house stands in the center on quite a rise of ground and all the principal streets center there, but the city will ever be noted for its historic associations. The building still remains in which General Washington resigned his commission to the Continental Congress as commander-in-chief of the American army. The venerable oak tree still stands under which he planned the siege of Yorktown which resulted in the capture of the English under Lord Cornwallis. I cannot look on these relics of ''the time that tried men's souls'' without feeling a deeper reverence for my country, a firmer resolve to consecrate my feeble energies to retain inviolate those precious boons of liberty and union which they bequeathed to us.

Sunday, November 27th.

Arose early, after a good night's rest. Ate breakfast and then marched to the parole camp, three miles south of the city. It was a splendid camp, well and tastefully arranged, laid out in regular streets, excellent barracks, warm and well ventilated, with cook houses, etc. The sanitary commission had an office on the ground and it proved a friend to the soldier in time of need. Another boat-load of prisoners came in this morning.

November 28th.

Passed my first night in a parole camp and it proved pleasant and agreeable. Arose early, answered to roll-call and then took breakfast, which consisted of soft bread, boiled bacon or beef and coffee. For dinner, we had bread and bean soup. The sanitary commission has been busy all day distributing needful articles amongst the prisoners, such as thread, paper, envelopes, combs, etc. A large sutler's stand is also on the ground. A large washhouse is near by which contains fifty tubs and other accommodations for washing clothes. The whole camp presents a neat and wholesome appearance, the streets being wide and kept perfectly clean. This camp will accommodate ten thousand soldiers, with good hospitals for the sick. An order was read to us to-day that all paroled prisoners would receive thirty days' furlough and two months' pay as soon as the proper papers could be made out. The glorious news from Sherman fills every heart with joy.

November 29th.

The last of the paroled prisoners have arrived. We were mustered to-day for two months' pay. Received orders to get ready to muster for commutation for rations while prisoners.

November 30th.

Mustered to-day for commutation of rations.

December 1st.

Received two months' pay this afternoon, thirty-six dollars. The officers of this camp labor day and night to get the soldiers' papers straightened out.

December 2d.

Made some purchases at the sutler's stand, including satchel, and foolscap paper stamped with a picture of the parole camp.

December 3d.

To-day's paper reports a hard-fought battle between Gen. Thomas' and Hood's forces. Union troops victorious.

Sunday, December 4th.

My furlough was made out to-day. I am to report to Camp Chase, Columbus, Ohio, at its expiration. Will start for home to-morrow. I have not yet informed my folks of my release from prison. I intend to surprise them and rise up before them like one arisen from the dead.

December 5th.

Will not leave to-day. Am growing somewhat restless.

December 6th.

Left camp at three P. M. Received our transportations and furloughs at Annapolis and embarked for Baltimore at six-fifty P. M. Arrived at the above named place per steamer at ten P. M. No trains will leave to-night. Put up at the Susquehanna House.

December 7th.

Started this morning at ten o'clock via the Harrisburg and Pennsylvania railroad. Harrisburg is a splendid looking place.

December 8th.

Passed through Pittsburgh. Got our vouchers for commutation of rations, while prisoners, cashed here at thirty-one cents per day.

December 9th.

Took the Pittsburgh, Ft. Wayne and Chicago railroad.

December 10th.

Arrived at Chicago at ten A. M. Our pulses glow with a new life to be once more in our own loved land. We here found our names reported in the papers as paroled prisoners and were afraid that our folks had found out that we would soon be at home. Took the twelve o'clock train and arrived at Marengo at three P. M. I saw uncle Almon first, and he had to take the second look before he could make up his mind that it was I. I gave a hurried call at Levi's and uncle Lorenzo's and then in company with uncle Almon, started for Riley. I now learned with deep regret that Manda and Ann had gone to Pennsylvania, and with pleasure that Cinda was married. We had hoped to be home in season to witness that interesting ceremony. It was dusk or deep twilight when uncle Almon drove rapidly up to the house. All were gone except father. He was out doing the chores when I went up and spoke to him. He looked at me as though a vision were passing before him. When the truth flashed upon him, he was nearly overcome. Nivvie was down at Batavia with Libbie. Mother, Rose and Amory were up to uncle Frank's. Being somewhat hungry, I was not long in finding the old, familiar cupboard, and when mother, Rose and Amory returned, they found me coolly devouring the remnant of a chicken pie. When mother saw me, she exclaimed "Oh, my God, here is Lucius!" Rose tried hard to keep from crying and appear unconcerned, but the boo-hoos had to come out. Amory, quiet and dignified as a prince, came forward. Let and Mary, Cinda and Will and Rollin came over the next day. I will pass briefly over my visit home, but soon, very soon, the time came for me to again launch forth on the troubled sea of civil strife.

January 5th, 1865.

The time of my furlough having expired, I bade adieu to kindred and friends and again started for the seat of war. The change from prison life to the magic influence of home operated like a charm upon my physical being and I left with renewed trust in the God of Armies that our country would be preserved from ruin and the blessing of a hallowed peace would soon fold her wings over us.

January 6th.

Arrived at Chicago yesterday. Visited the museum in the forenoon and left for Columbus, via Crestline, at five P. M.

January 7th.

Arrived at Crestline at six o'clock A. M. Waited until afternoon before starting for Columbus. Arrived at the latter place at fifty minutes past two P. M. Reported at headquarters at Camp Chase and found out, much to our surprise, that we had been exchanged and would be sent forward to our command on Monday. This was a keen disappointment to me for I had confidently hoped to be able to visit Manda before I left for the seat of war, but now it was impossible. It was reported that our battalion, or those few that had escaped being prisoners, was doing duty as Gen. Thomas' body-guard. Our barracks here were cold and comfortless and poorly provided with the necessary accommodations for soldiers. The snow lay over one foot deep on the ground.

January 8th.

Passed the day principally in writing letters. The weather is quite cold. Over seven thousand rebel prisoners are confined here and they are well and clothed. We were transferred to Tod barracks this morning and are now awaiting transportation to Nashville.

January 9th.

Left for Cincinnati at nine o'clock last evening. Arrived there at four A. M. next day.

January 10th.

We marched to Kelton barracks to await further orders. This is a dirty and disagreeable place. The lower story is used as a prison in which to keep bounty jumpers and deserters. The upper story is used to receive recruits, convalescents, exchanged soldiers and furloughed men preparatory to sending them to their respective commands. We were kept in close confinement on account of so many trying to get away, and to the disgrace of the government officials, no discrimination was made between men or conditions. According to existing orders, we had no business to be detained and treated in such a manner. In Chicago and other cities in the West, no one pretended to dispute our right to go and come at pleasure while within the limits of our furlough or while we were paroled prisoners.

January 11th.

Stormed hard all day. Barracks cold. Received orders this

morning to be ready to start for New York City at eight o'clock in the evening. This order surprised us much as we were expecting to go to Nashville all the time.

January 12th.

Left Cincinnati at eight A. M. Arrived at Columbus at four A. M. Changed cars and left for Cleveland. Arrived at the latter place at eleven A. M. on the same day.

January 13th.

Took dinner at the Soldiers' Home where everything was nice and comfortable, and then took a stroll about the city. Started for Buffalo at three P. M. via Erie and Dunkirk, but failing to make connections with eastern bound trains, a special train was ordered for soldiers at the latter place. We took the New York and Erie railroad here. Stopped at a small place in central New York and our squad had a nice time on a mill pond near by, where the village gentry was out enjoying a fine skate. On the same train were hundreds of recruits, but they were not permitted to step off the cars. We, being old soldiers and in a gang by ourselves, did just as we pleased. A Lieutenant was in charge of us, but he knew that he could trust us.

January 14th.

Arrived at New York City at four A. M. Went to a Soldiers' Home and got our breakfast and after awhile reported to head-quarters. In the afternoon of the same day, we went over on Governor's Island to Ft. Columbus and Castle Williams with the promise that we would be immediately forwarded to our command. Had we known the treatment we were to receive there, we never would have gone over. The island itself is beautiful. Fort Columbus is situated in its center and mounts seventy guns of heavy caliber. Castle Williams, to which place we were assigned, is situated on the extreme west side of the island. It is an old structure of solid masonry, three stories high. It was commenced in 1807 and completed in 1811. It is built in a circle and access is gained to the different stories by means of winding stairs built in a turret. The entrance is secured by a large gate. The lower story is used principally as a store house and in case of necessity, twenty-five or thirty guns can be mounted in it. The second and third stories are divided into apartments connected with each other by arches large enough to move a heavy gun through. In each apartment is a heavy siege gun. I believe that the Castle mounted seventy-four guns. We were assigned quarters in the second story already crowded almost to suffocation. The upper story was used for rough cases, such as bounty jumpers and deserters. For the first few days, we were allowed the liberty of the island, but a murder was committed one night and some of the soldiers were suspected and all were confined within the Castle after that.

January 15th.

In our apartment were recruits, exchanged prisoners, furloughed men and rebel prisoners. The latter received the same rations and in every respect were treated with as much consideration as ourselves. It was very hard for us to submit to all the indignities heaped upon us here. Andersonville was still fresh in our minds and here were rebel prisoners put on an equality with us, though God knows our fare was an insult even to a prisoner.

January 16th.

Very cold and windy. Heard to-day from the rest of my comrades in rebel prisons by an escaped prisoner belonging to Company D of our regiment. We learned with deep regret that they were suffering horribly, even worse than at Andersonville. Instead of being paroled and sent home as they had been led to believe, they were sent to Florida and were kept moving from place to place, almost naked and nearly starved.

January 17th.

Weather still continues cold. To-day's paper announced the death of the Hon. Edward Everett, the ripest scholar, greatest orator, and one of the best men in the nation.

January 18th.

The electric wires have heralded the glorious news of the capture of Fort Fisher, twenty-five hundred men and seventy pieces of artillery.

January 19th.

Very pleasant. Weather moderating. The soldiers of the Potomac army left this morning. Blair's visit to Richmond as an ambassador for peace has proved to be a canard.

January 20th.

Notning of any interest transpiring. Weather still quite cold.

January 21st.

Had my satchel and everything in it stolen last night. A thorough search proved futile to restore the property or apprehend the thief. I feel the loss more from the fact that my valuables and

keepsakes were in it, such as photographs. The wretch that would
commit such a theft is hardly fit to live.

January 22d.

Nothing of any interest transpiring.

January 23d.

Rained all day. Yesterday came the inhuman order to keep
us confined within the Castle, not even letting us go below. Our
quarters now would shame a hog pen. The treatment of good
soldiers here by those who should be their friends has no parallel
that I know of in American history. Confined within these loathsome walls are one thousand brave men, who on many bloody
battle-fields have attested their devotion to their country by shed-
ding their blood, or suffering in rebel prison pens. Is this a crime
for which we merit this outrageous treatment? Can this be a
nation's gratitude? The patience of the soldiers is taxed to the
utmost. It needs but a spark to ignite a flame which will sweep
over this Castle and cover it with human gore. We get only one-
fourth rations and those of the poorest quality. We have every
reason to believe that the government officials on this island draw
us full rations, but appropriate the greater part to fill up their
purses. We have our pork raw, and as a consequence many have
the dysentery. Our rooms are damp and filthy. The dirt is the
accumuluation of years and a hoe and spade will not remove it. We
have a coal stove for each room, and the only place the smoke has
for egress is through the port holes which are barely large enough
for the cannon to protrude. The only light we get is through
these holes. As a consequence, the air becomes fetid and unwhole-
some. The walls are damp and chilly. Disease is fast laying its
icy chill on many a sufferer. We have borne up all along in hopes
that every day would be our last on the island, but now for-
bearance ceased to be a virtue. We determined to apply for redress.

January 24th.

Our condition seems to be growing worse. Weather quite cool
again.

January 25th.

A petition has been sent to Gen. Sherman, setting forth our
grievances and asking for relief, which we have confidence will
follow as soon as it reaches him. A copy of the petition was also
sent to the New York *Herald* for publication. The language of

the petition animadverted in the strongest terms upon the conduct of the government officials upon the island.

                                                        January 26th.

Very cold to-day.   Yesterday a wife came to see her husband who was confined in the Castle with us.   She was denied the privilege of seeing him.   She could only approach as far as the gate. In his frenzy the outraged husband threw himself over the banister and broke his leg.

                                                        January 27th.

Last evening witnessed the perpetration of an outrageous act which came well nigh creating a scene of great confusion and danger. It was no less than an order for a portion of the soldiers to vacate their rooms and go out in the cold so as to give room to one hundred and fifty rebel prisoners who had arrived that evening.   We protested, refused to obey the order and dared them to do their worst.   Afterwards the order was rescinded and quiet was restored.

                                                        January 28th.

Nothing unusual transpiring.

                                                        January 29th.

Do not feel very well to-day.

                                                        January 30th.

Weather still continues cold.   Harbor full of ice.   The signs of the times indicate peace not far distant.

                                                        January 31st.

We were relieved from our long and unpleasant confinement this morning.   Our petition had the desired effect.   Two thousand of Sherman's men embarked on board the Blackstone and at three P. M. set sail for Hilton Head, South Carolina.

                                                        February 1st.

Pleasant and cold.   Smooth sailing.

                                                        February 2d.

Cold.   Rough sea.   A good many seasick.

                                                        February 3d.

Weather warmer.   Stormed last night.   Had a violent gale. Boat rocked terribly but gallantly outrode the storm.   Experienced some seasickness, but not very bad.

                                                        February 4th.

Arrived at Hilton Head last evening.   Are lying here awaiting further orders.   The town, as far as can be seen from the boat, seems to be a small place of four or five thousand inhabitants.

February 5th.

Left Hilton Head for Pocotaligo Landing. Arrived in the afternoon. Some of the 15th boys left this morning to guard a provision train to the front. The corps is forty miles from here and on the move. They had a severe fight on the 31st. Charged the rebels through a swamp, water waist deep, and drove them from their fortifications. Some of our wounded were drowned while crossing the stream.

February 6th.

Divided off into squads of eighty men in each. I have charge of one mess. We are the only troops here except a small garrison of Foster's men. Gen. Hatch's command is at Pocotaligo Station, six miles from here.

February 7th.

We have been organized into a camp here. A Captain of the 60th Illinois is in command. It is a general supposition that Sherman will open a new base and we will have to take the boat to join him by the way of Hilton Head or Beaufort. We have no arms yet, and it is useless to attempt to join Sherman from here by land except with a well-organized force of several thousand troops. We are very impatient to join our command.

February 8th.

Rained all night and the weather is still unsettled. One hundred and twenty-five wounded men from our division came in to-day and were sent to Hilton Head. It is reported that the rebels made a dash into Savannah and captured eight hundred prisoners. Our force is augmenting daily by new recruits, exchanged prisoners, convalescents and furloughed men. There are now several thousand here. We are enjoying rich feasts now on oysters. We can gather them on the beach when the tide is out. There are several large beds of them near by.

February 9th.

Cold. Moved camp one mile to-day.

February 10th.

Cold and cloudy. The men belonging to the different corps were organized into companies to-day, my squad belonging to Company G, 17th army corps. Six hundred more soldiers arrived to-day. One thousand more are expected this evening. Heard to-day that Sherman had taken Branchville, South Carolina, and was marching on Columbia, the capital of the State. Yesterday the quartermaster of this post was shot by guerrillas while out a short distance from camp. Six of our men have been found hung and their bodies were outraged and mutilated in the most shameful manner. The country is swarming with guerrillas and cut-throats.

February 11th.

Pleasant and warm. One thousand more soldiers came in last night. There are now four thousand soldiers here awaiting orders to join Sherman.

February 12th.

Warm and pleasant. The 15th and 17th corps have gone into camp together, Lieut.-Col. Henry commanding.

February 13th.

There is a rumor that peace is established. Moved camp this morning. Each division of each corps has been organized into companies.

February 14th.

Rainy and cold. Drew three days' rations to-day. We are very poorly organized and some did not draw.

February 15th.

Cloudy and warm. Afternoon pleasant. Drew arms and accoutrements to-day. Are ordered to be ready to march in the morning.

February 16th.

Morning murky and damp. Afternoon pleasant. Had a difficulty with the Captain and orderly sergeant of our company on account of rations. They attempted to cheat my mess, boys of the 15th Illinois, out of two days' rations because the orderly did not wake me up when he issued them. It was two o'clock in the morning when they were issued. I sat up until twelve o'clock waiting for them and then retired, supposing of course, that he would wake me up when he issued them, but he did not. A stranger answered for my mess and lugged off the rations and he could not be found. As soon as I found out how matters stood, I applied to the orderly for my rations and told him that I held him responsible, but I could not make anything out of him, so I applied to the Lieutenant and he said he could do nothing about it. I told them I thought I could find a way to make them do something. So I went up to Col. Henry's quarters and stated the case. He sent down for the Lieutenant and orderly to come up there. Sharp words followed, which finally ended in Col. Henry ordering the Lieutenant to furnish my mess with rations from the rest of the Company's rations. The Lieutenant and orderly had a spite against the 15th boys because we knew our rights and maintained them and we stuck together when any difficulty arose. After this occurrence they changed their tactics and treated us very well. We soon became his favorite men. After that things went on smoothly. We marched at daylight. Arrived in camp near Pocotaligo at noon. Had a difficult march. The roads were very muddy and we had to carry all our camp equipage, such as kettles, frying pans, etc., on our backs. It is a poor country. We relieved a battalion of colored troops stationed here. We found very comfortable quarters already prepared. There is a prospect of our remaining here some time.

February 16th.

It is quite warm and pleasant to-day.

February 17th.

Very pleasant and warm. Am on guard to-day for the first time since my capture.

February 18th.

Pleasant. Am not feeling very well. Have a severe cold. Washed a shirt and pair of drawers this morning.

We are out of rations but expect to draw this evening or to-morrow. We are almost shut out from communication with the outside world. I have not seen a daily paper in a long time.

February 19th.

Pleasant. Had company inspection this morning. Wrote several letters to-day. There is a report that Charleston is taken.

February 20th.

Cloudy and prospect of rain. Had company drill to-day.

February 21st.

Clear and pleasant. Am on picket to-day.

February 22d.

It is the anniversary of Washington's birthday. May it be crowned by a glorious victory of loyalty over treason. Heard this morning of the fall of Charleston. We are within hearing of the heavy guns of the blockading fleet of Charleston which is about sixty miles distant. We are now camped in the immediate vicinity of a country made hallowed and historic by the deeds of the daring Swamp Fox, the gallant Marion, and his men of revolutionary fame. An old revolutionary fort is only a short distance from us. I was poisoned last night on picket by drinking swamp water filled with pine boughs. Was very sick all night but am feeling considerably better to-day.

February 23d.

Rainy. Am still unwell. Have a severe headache. Saw a paper of the 15th inst. Read no news but what I had already heard.

February 24th.

Rainy day. Am still unwell. Drew five days' rations.

February 25th.

Weather foggy and misty. Wrote to Rose to-day. Am still troubled with a cold and headache.

Sunday, February 26th.

Weather changeable. My cold is about the same. Have been reading "Noble Deeds of American Women" nearly all day. During the past week I have read Washington's Life by Sims and "Vestiges of Creation." Time passes wearily, there being nothing of an exciting nature going on around us. The presence of a squad of guerrillas occasionally affords us life for a moment.

February 27th.

Pleasant and warm. Am on picket to-day. Drew clothing this morning. A scouting party sent out yesterday and returned without seeing any armed rebel.

February 28th.

Very rainy. Rained hard all night. Had no shelter and got completely wet through. Rained all day. Mustered for pay.

March 2d

Weather still unsettled. Had a regular army muster to-day. More of the battalion have reported at Blair's Landing. The Colonel, Lieutenant-Colonel, Major and Adjutant are at Hilton Head.

March 3d.

Pleasant. Quite warm. Not doing much to-day.

March 4th.

Cloudy and some rain. Received New York papers yesterday of the 24th of February. It was a rich treat to us. We had been four weeks without seeing any papers from the North. We were rejoiced to learn that the camp rumors about the military situation were correct. Charleston and Wilmington had fallen,

and the dear old flag once more floats over Sumter, in ruins though
it be. Sherman's campaign through Georgia to the sea, and
through the Carolinas into Virginia, is proving to be one continual
series of brilliant successes, on a scale so magnificent that history
scarcely furnishes a parallel.   I doubt not that ere the Northern
flowers bloom, Richmond, through the agency of Sherman and his
veterans, will follow in the train of Charleston.   Such successes
cannot fail to bring soon a permanent and enduring peace.   Had
company drill to-day.   There are a good many recruits in the
company, and they make rather awkward work.   I drill the company occasionally.

March 5th.

Pleasant.   Report that Richmond is taken.   Had inspection
to-day.   Had a long and interesting conversation with Lieutenant
Gillis, a brother of the craft.   Wrote to Manda Mackey and
Lucinda to-day.

March 6th.

Am on picket to-day.   My post is on the main road leading to
Pocotaligo, and contrabands are coming in by the score.   Two
mounted darkies came in on splendid animals, and reported a small
force of rebels out about three miles.   I did not care so much
about the rebs as I did the horses, so I sent them to headquarters,
under guard, and they soon came back minus the horses.   Next
came along a big strapping negro and a good-looking mulatto
girl, and as they asked for protection I sent them on to headquarters.
There was a little domestic squabble connected with this couple.
It appeared that the mulatto was still a maiden lady, and she had
induced her more sable companion to run off with her.   Soon after
the wife and outraged mother, with an infant in her arms, came
rushing up, seeking her false lord.   I could not resist her pleading,
so I sent her on after them.   There was fire in her eyes which
showed the spirit that burned within.   I tried to test her affection
for her false lord by representing how he had misused her and
how false he had been, but it had no effect.   She was determined
to pursue him.   The Colonel sent her on after them.   They had a
few moments before started for the landing, and the Colonel told
her to take a good cudgel and give her man a good pounding
when she found him.   The laws of South Carolina do not tolerate
marriage amongst her colored population, but allow them to live
together like beasts.   Next came along a large squad of darkies

with their wives and children. Then came three negro braves who had captured rebels and their guns, and wanted to act as pilots to conduct a party out to capture a band of rebels hidden in a swamp over twenty miles out. Over twenty darkies and refugees came in to-day.

March 7th.

Cloudy and cool. Came off picket this morning. Was up all night. Took a short nap this morning. Got up and washed a shirt and read two poems, "Orlando" and one "Doctor Dwights." Twenty-five men from Company D have gone out on a scout.

March 8th.

Unpleasant. Rained hard all day. Have scarcely been out of the tent. Cooked a dish of beans and have just got the dishes washed.

March 9th.

Foggy and occasional gusts of rain. A swelling has broken in my head. It was that which caused my almost constant headache.

March 10th.

Rained very hard all night and nearly all the forenoon. I drilled the company this afternoon.

March 11th.

Am on picket to-day and stationed on the main road and have a corporal and seven men with me. I am in charge of the post. Have marching orders the first of next week.

March 12th.

Very pleasant. Cold night. Had quite a frost. Read a book entitled "Heir of ———."

March 13th.

Pleasant and warm. Went on battalion drill for the first time in over a year. Wrote to Nivvie this afternoon.

March 14th.

Went on a scout last night with the company. Took a squad of men and went ahead as advance guard. Started at eleven P. M. and got back at half past four A. M. Traveled eighteen miles without meeting an armed rebel. Three hundred re-inforcements arrived during the night from Blair's Landing but went back in the morning. An attack was expected.

March 15th.

Rainy. Were ordered to fall in line as quickly as possible this forenoon to repel an attack, but it was only a silly scare. We stacked arms and returned to our quarters with accoutrements. A negro came in and reported a large body of rebels at McPherson-ville, three miles from here. A company has been sent out to reconnoiter. Returned and reported no enemy in sight.

March 16th.

Rainy weather. Very disagreeable. One year ago to-day our regiment started for home on a veteran furlough.

March 17th.

Pleasant and warm. Peach trees are in bloom. Nature begins to look spring-like.

March 20th.

Pleasant and quite warm. Gen. Prince and staff inspected our quarters to-day and reviewed us. Gen. Prince commands pro-visional division detachments of Sherman's army at Blair's Landing, numbering eight thousand men. Have been at work to-day remodeling and enlarging our quarters. Went on battalion drill this afternoon. Wrote a long letter to Lester yesterday. Have seen a paper of the 14th. News cheering. Major-Generals Cox and Scofield repulsed the rebels in a hard fight at Kinston, North Carolina. Major-General Sheridan has made another splendid and successful raid in central Virginia, destroying railroad bridges, capturing a large amount of rebel stores and fourteen pieces of artillery.

March 21st.

Rainy. Rollin caught a mess of fine fish to-day.

March 22d.

The morning dawned bright and beautiful. Washed a pair of pants, drawers and shirt. Everything quiet. Nothing of any note transpiring.

March 23d.

Pleasant. Cool and invigorating air. Our company was ordered out on a scout this morning. Started at seven o'clock. Went out into the country fifteen miles. Got back to camp at seven P. M., having traveled thirty miles in twelve hours and making two hours' stop. The result of our scout was the capture of one Johnnie Reb, and twelve bales of cotton which were found secreted in a swamp. A negro piloted us to the spot. We secured any amount of forage. Scores of contrabands with their wives and children came in with us. We had a train nearly a mile long.

1865]	198

March 24th.

Pleasant and cool invigorating air. We get fresh sea breezes. Wrote a letter home this afternoon.

March 25th.

Pleasant. Am on picket to-day. Had a nice mess of fresh fish for breakfast and dinner. Six of my mess went fishing yesterday and caught one hundred pounds.

March 26th.

Fine day. Rebels were seen hanging around the lines yesterday. Scouting parties were sent out but failed to bring them to an engagement. Feel rather dull to-day on account of not sleeping any last night. Inspection at five P. M.

March 27th.

Pleasant. Cool night. Drew four days' rations to-day. Had company drill this afternoon.

March 28th.

Cold rain from the north-east. Saw a Savannah paper of the 21st inst. Contained no further news except an account of the death of the rebel Gen. Whitney at Governer's Island, New York City. He was commander of the troops which surrendered to Gen. Terry at Wilmington, North Carolina.

March 29th.

Morning and forenoon rainy. Afternoon changeable. Bought a Savannah paper of the 24th. It contained no news of interest. The same mournful howl still goes up from the rebel press as regards their desperate situation, and the waning fortunes of the confederacy. At the request of Jeff Davis, Bishop ———— has issued a proclamation calling on the clergy and laity to observe a day appointed for humiliation and prayer (over the sins of the con-thieveracy).

March 30th.

Rained all night and all the morning. Afternoon changeable. Saw a paper of the 26th containing late news from Sherman. That able General had formed a junction with Scofield and Terry and whipped the enemy badly at Goldsboro, North Carolina. Sherman was at last accounts doing well and was likely to succeed in giving the rebels another whipping soon.

March 31st.

Am on picket to-day. Have charge of three posts. The day is fine. Drew five days' rations. Admitted six rebel deserters through our lines. Sent them to headquarters under guard. A Major of the 15th corps commands the detachment now.

Sunday, April 1st.

April with its balmy breezes and refreshing showers is now with us. This morn is as bright and beautiful as was ever gilded by the golden rays of the rising sun. Went on battalion drill this afternoon. Have been reading "The Rattlesnake or Rebel Privateer" and "Ella Cameron," also a story entitled —— —— and the "Pine Tree Town," a story of the South. Wrote to mother to-day and told our folks to direct to me as follows:—Company D, Provisional Division Sherman's Army, 2d Detachment, 17th Army Corps, in care of Colonel Henry.

April 2d.

Day splendid. Inspection at forty-five minutes past five P. M.

April 3d.

Very pleasant. Went on company drill from ten o'clock to half past eleven A. M. Battalion drill from two to four P. M.

April 4th.

Arose early. Washed a shirt. Went on company drill this morning, battalion drill in the afternoon. Colonel Henry drilled the battalion. Made a poor appearance.

April 5th.

Morning very warm. Appearance of rain. Went on picket this morning; afternoon rainy. Late papers report another big fight between Sherman and Bragg in which the latter was defeated.

April 6th.

Very warm. Up all night. The gnats and mosquitoes nearly ate me up. The gnats are the worst. They crawl through our garments and bury themselves in our skin, their bites creating a red blotch. It is poisonous. Went on company drill this afternoon. To-day is the anniversary of the Battle of Shiloh. Have seen northern papers of the 30th ult.

April 7th.

Cloudy. Weather changeable. Occasional showers. Detachment of 15th corps has come back to Pocotaligo. The whole command expect to march to Beaufort soon and take transportation to Morehead City, North Carolina, and from there join Sherman's army at Goldsboro where it is resting and recruiting preparatory to farther work. All troops have left Blair's Landing. We met at Col. Henry's headquarters last night for the benefit of lectures by Brother Tomlinson, Col. Henry, his adjutant and several officers of the detachment being present. We expect to meet again to-night. We will rejoice when we leave this sickly place. It has been one continual series of harassing alarms resulting in forced marches by night and day, in rain or shine. Some frightened darkies would come in nearly every day and report a large body of the enemy out a little way, and notwithstanding our repeated efforts to find them, Col. Henry still put confidence in their stories, and a contraband rushing in was sure to be a signal for a scout. One night a darkey came in and reported a squad of guerrillas within two miles of camp. We seized the darkey and took him as a guide, determined to punish him if he brought a false report. We went out a couple of miles and came in sight of what we supposed to be a rebel camp as seen by the camp fires. I was sent forward with a squad of men to reconnoiter. I approached pretty close to the camp. Everything seemed quiet. The officer in command determined to surprise and capture the whole force, so he divided his men and charged at two different places. I kept on with my squad and was first to reach the camp, when lo and behold, it was a camp of darkies. Please imagine our chagrin and wrath at the darkey who gave the alarm, but when we looked around for him, he was nowhere to be seen. We searched camp for him, but could not find him. Knowing his fate if he was caught, he made good use of his legs. It appeared that several of our boys had been out foraging and when they were returning, this darkey took them to be rebels, and being scared nearly to death, he did not stop until he reached our camp. There was a band of guerrillas around, but none that we needed to fear, with proper caution.

April 8th.

Received orders to pack up and be ready to move. There was a mutiny in the detachment of the 15th corps to-day occasioned by Col. Henry arresting and tying up hand and foot a soldier belonging to said corps for disobeying orders by firing off his gun without leave. A squad of twenty men marched up to headquarters and the sergeant in command boldly walked up to Col. Henry and demanded the prisoner's release. The result was that the fellow was immediately arrested. Col. Henry then went to the door and ordered the others to stack arms which they refused to do. Col. Henry then drew his revolver and told them he would shoot every

one unless they obeyed. So the twenty men were cowed by the
determined manner of the Colonel. They were all immediately
arrested. The detachment was in a blaze of excitement and soon
over four hundred armed men were at Col. Henry's headquarters,
bent on releasing the prisoners. Col. Henry sent orders for the
detachment of the 17th corps to arm themselves and prepare to
enforce his order. We obeyed the order but mentally resolved
that we would never shed the blood of our brother soldiers. A
better feeling began to prevail now. Col. Henry released all except
the ringleader. He had his trial and was sentenced to be shot. I
never learned whether the sentence was carried into effect.

Sunday, April 9th.

Marched at precisely nine o'clock this morning. The boys are
all jubilant at leaving this sickly and disagreeable place and at the
prospect of soon joining our comrades. During the forenoon we
heard a salute of one hundred guns fired and many were the conjectures as to what it was for. When we arrived at Gardners'
Corners, the first telegraph station, we learned that Richmond was
taken. We stopped at this place and got dinner. It now commenced raining, and rained continually until we arrived at Port
Royal ferry, fourteen miles from Pocotaligo. We camped here
for the night.

April 10th.

Early this morning we went on board the ferry and were taken
to the ocean steamer "Alhambra" in the harbor at Hilton Head.
Lieutenant-Colonel Gilman was on board waiting for us. It did us
good to see a familiar face of the old 15th regiment. We lay over
here one day. Drew three days' rations.

April 11th.

Sailed last night at eleven P. M. Beautiful weather and smooth
sailing; nevertheless I was seasick, which was owing to the poor
state my stomach was in by living in the sickly camp of Pocotaligo
so long. We passed Charleston harbor during the day and on the
same evening arrived at the mouth of Cape Fear river where we
now lie. On each side of us are two huge forts, garrisoned by
federal soldiers. Fort Fisher is in sight but five miles farther up
the river. We have learned by official information that Richmond
is captured with twelve thousand prisoners and five hundred pieces
of artillery.

13

April 12th.

Lay at anchor until one o'clock P. M. and then went on board the General Meigs. We soon passed Fort Wilmington, the scene of the great battle which resulted so gloriously on the side of the Union. We had a splendid view of the fort as we passed it. On the other side of the river is Fort Jackson which the rebels blew up by connecting a telegraph wire with a torpedo. We also passed old revolutionary forts and buildings whose dingy walls have a hallowed remembrance in the hearts of all true patriots.

April 13th.

Arrived at Wilmington at ten P. M. We had considerable difficulty in evading the obstructions in the river which the rebels had placed there. Landed early this morning. Marched two miles south of the city and went into camp. A detachment of the 17th army corps was here. The 15th had gone on to join Sherman. I do not like the looks of Wilmington very well. A good many of the houses were built hundreds of years ago and are now moss-grown and gray, but its historic associations still cluster around my memory and they are sacred because connected with revolutionary times. The city in time of peace contained fifteen or twenty thousand inhabitants. We will probably remain here until we set out to join the main army. We are much better situated here than we were at Pocotaligo. It is healthy and a much more pleasant country.

April 14th.

To-day brings us the glorious news that Gen. Lee has surrendered his entire army to Gen. Grant, and we expect to hear soon that Gen. Johnson has followed suit to Gen. Sherman. One hundred guns were fired at this place to-day in honor of the victory. Also one hundred guns in commemoration of again raising the same old flag which was hauled down from Fort Sumter by armed traitors. The salute will be fired by the same guns that commemorated its fall. Henry Ward Beecher delivers the address on this interesting occasion.

April 15th.

Very windy. Received orders this afternoon to be ready to march at daylight to-morrow. Wrote two letters home to-day and expressed my overcoat.

April 16th.

We did not move to-day owing to the fact that the bridges

across the river broke down, and we could not get our rations in time.

April 17th.

Moved at six o'clock this morning. Marched eighteen miles and camped for the night. Went on picket to-night.

April 18th.

Marched at half past five A. M. Went twenty-two miles and went into camp. Rained nearly all night.

April 19th.

Marched at six A. M. Weather very hot. Was nearly overcome by the heat to-day. Marched sixteen miles. Drew two days' rations. Am feeling pretty well this evening.

April 20th.

Marched at half past five A. M. Commenced raining early. Rained hard nearly all day. About two P. M. an order came from Gen. Sherman announcing a cessation of hostilities, and a strong hope of being able to lead us to our homes soon in peace, with our country undivided. The order was received with joy by all the soldiers. Comments are useless on such an occasion, but the joyous tears spoke more eloquently than language. Yet the past could not be forgotten, or the long list of numberless dead, now sleeping in unknown and undistinguished graves on the hillsides and in the vales of the South.

April 21st.

Marched at half past five. The news came to-day that President Lincoln, Secretary Seward and son have been assassinated, resulting in the President's death and severely wounding the others. An now, while the nation is rejoicing with unspeakable joy at its deliverance, it is suddenly plunged into the deepest sorrow by the most brutal murder of its loved chief. We are continually passing paroled men from Lee's army on their way to their homes, or to where their homes were. Many found blackened ruins instead, and kindred and friends gone, they knew not whither. Oh, how much misery treason and rebellion have brought upon our land! Camped on the river three miles from Goldsboro. Col. Hall is here with seven hundred recruits for the 14th Regiment, and Col. Rogers is at Raleigh with seven hundred for the 15th. The old organization is to be resumed. All the veterans are justly indignant at this usurpation of their right and their honor and reputation. Here are seven fully organized companies of new recruits who never saw a gun fired in earnest, and they are to step in and succeed to the name and fame of the old 15th.   Men whom the big bounty and the poor show for fighting have brought into the field are placed over veteran soldiers, scarred with battle marks received in defense of their country. We made the march from Wilmington to Goldsboro in five days, distance one hundred miles.   The first two days' march out from Wilmington, the country was high, sandy and barren.   After that we came into the pine regions where nothing but one interminable forest of pitch pine met our view.   From these trees, tar, turpentine and rosin are made.   The trees are chiseled in grooves, the grooves terminating in a trough cut in at the foot of the tree to receive the pitch.   This is the chief staple of produce in this country.   The pitch is put through a distilling process and converted into turpentine. the thickest part into tar and the dregs into rosin.

April 22d.

Marched at seven A. M. toward Goldsboro and turned off on the Raleigh road.   Went into camp at nine A. M. to draw rations. To-day I received the startling and sorrowful intelligence that Milton had escaped from prison, been home, returned to the army and been captured by a band of rebel cavalry while out foraging and brutally murdered in company with four of his comrades. One escaped and brought the news to camp.   In consequence of this intelligence, my spirits are much depressed to-day.   I have a faint hope that the information is incorrect.   I will soon know. The 17th corps train is in from the front.   Saw some of the 15th boys.   They start back this evening.   Quite a number of our boys went back with them, Rollin amongst the number.   We are ordered to be ready to march at six o'clock in the morning.

April 23d.

Marched at half past five A. M.   Was on advance guard. Marched eighteen miles and went into camp.

April 24th.

Marched at half past five o'clock.   Marched twenty-six miles and camped within ten miles of Raleigh.   We expect to reach our proper command to-morrow.   The matter of peace is not satisfactorily arranged yet according to accounts.

April 25th.

Marched at seven A. M.   Arrived at Raleigh at twelve M.   The corps moved from Raleigh at eight o'clock A. M. in pursuit of Johnson. Hostilities were resumed to-day at seven A. M. We rested awhile at Raleigh and then set out to join the corps, which we overtook twelve miles from Raleigh. Then each soldier reported to his proper command. I am now with the mounted squad but have not yet got a horse. I found here about fifty of my old comrades of the 14th and 15th veteran battalion and several boys whom I had left in prison.

April 26th.

To-day Gen. Johnson surrendered his entire army to Gen. Sherman, and thus the last armed foe of any consequence this side of the Mississippi river has surrendered. We consider the Rebellion virtually at an end, and peace, sweet peace, will now fold her wings over us, and joyful shouts and anthems will ring out over all our land, welcoming back to home and friends, our country's preservers.

April 27th.

Marched back to Raleigh. Expressed Milton's things home. Saw George Lowe. The 15th and 17th corps here turned over their ordnance stores preparatory to marching.

April 28th.

Stayed in camp all day. The seven companies of recruits for the 15th Illinois came in to-day.

April 29th.

On our homeward march. Moved at eight A. M. Am on provost guard. Camped on the east side of Neuse river, twelve miles from Raleigh. Wrote four letters to-day.

April 30th.

Did not move to-day. The consolidation of the veteran battalion, 14th and 15th Illinois Volunteers has been effectually broken up, but we are to remain as we are during the march. We will muster this afternoon as on detached service as provost guard at division headquarters. The mounted squad remains as before. There is not the least desire on our part to affiliate with the recruits of the 15th.

May 1st.

Marched at seven A. M. Moved fifteen miles and went into camp.

May 2d.

Marched at six o'clock. Went eighteen miles and camped for

the night. Passed Forest Dale yesterday. It was a splendid looking place. A college is situated here. Drew clothing to-night. Country broken and barren.

May 3d.

Marched at five A. M. Passed Henderson and Clarksville Junction at ten A. M. We are now resting near the latter place. Marched five miles farther and halted for dinner. Warrenton is one mile on our right. Marched five miles farther and camped for the night. Am on provost guard to-night.

May 4th.

Marched at seven A. M. Marched fifteen miles and went into camp. Are waiting for pontoons to be laid to cross the Roanoke River. Went to corps headquarters. Found one letter there for me from Rose and Callie. A scouting party from the 1st brigade found ten pieces of artillery and a large amount of ammunition secreted in the woods.

May 5th.

Marched at three A. M. Crossed Roanoke River at five A. M. Crossed the state line from North Carolina into Virginia at six A. M. Marched twelve miles farther and halted for the men to make coffee, and so we took our first lunch in the State of Virginia. After dinner, moved twelve miles farther and went into camp. It is now forty-five miles to Petersburg. We expect to make the march in two days. Do not feel well to-night.

May 6th.

Marched at five A. M. Moved ten miles and stopped for dinner. I rode with Tom Venard a short distance this morn-ing in second brigade headquarters ambulance. Am still unwell. After dinner marched eleven miles and camped for the night. For the past two days we have passed through a splendid country, high and rolling, good soil, splendid groves and beautiful planta-tions and country seats. The picture which is now spread out before me fully equals what I have read concerning the Old Dominion.

May 7th.

Marched at five A. M. Moved twelve miles and halted for rest and refreshments. After dinner moved to within two miles of Petersburg and went into camp. For the past day we have been on the tramping and fighting ground of the Potomac army. All along the road is strewed evidence of severe fighting. Our

present camping ground is dotted as far as the eye can reach with
spots where was camped the vast Army of the Potomac, the brave
but unfortunate army which has fought so bravely, suffered so
much and accomplished so little. From the Potomac across the
Rappahannock to beyond the James River, their bodies lie slum-
bering in an unbroken sleep, never more to waken to active life,
but the cause for which they sacrificed their lives will live and
grow, until its splendor eclipses the whole world. The Army of
the Potomac left for Washington on the 3d. We expect to start
for Richmond to-morrow. I am on provost guard to-night at
division headquarters, where Gen. Grant's headquarters were just
before he left. I procured a good supper at the establishment,
consisting of boiled victuals, my favorite dish. The New York
Herald of the 5th gives an interesting account of the conspirators
engaged in the assassination of President Lincoln, Secretary Seward
and son, Jefferson Davis and other prominent Southern men being
implicated in the plot. Also an account of the grand success of
our army at Selma and Montgomery, Alabama, and at Macon,
Columbus and West Point, Georgia; also of the surrender of Jeff
Thompson and his army. It also gives an account of the Fenian
movement both in Ireland and America. Its effect on the British
government, the emigration scheme to Mexico, to enforce the
Monroe Doctrine; the death of the assassinator Booth; the demand
made upon the Canadian government for the delivering up of
Booth's accomplices, and the final obsequies of the late lamented
President, with much more interesting news.

May 8th.

Marched at seven A. M., the 4th division taking the lead.
Marched through Petersburg and four miles beyond. Went into
camp at eleven A. M. Petersburg is a city of some twenty thousand
inhabitants. A great many prominent officers of Lee's army were
there and saw us pass through.

May 9th.

Marched at three A. M., 4th division again being in the lead.
To-day we passed a part of Gen. Custer's division of cavalry of
Sheridan's command. They are a gay set of fellows and have
undaunted confidence in their commander and fairly worship
"Phil" as he is familiarly termed. They are distinguished by a
red necktie which is uniformly worn throughout the division. At
nine A. M. we camped on the plains on the south side of James

river before Richmond and adjacent to Hamburg. From our camp we have a good view of Richmond.

May 10th.

Visited Richmond to-day. Went through Libby Prison and inspected every room accessible to visitors. Went to Castle Thunder, also to the State Capitol used during the Rebellion as capitol of the confederacy. The latter is situated in Washington Square. A splendid equestrian statue of Washington is on the capitol ground, mounted on a marble pedestal representing him in his military attire. The index finger pointing to the south as if giving orders. Richmond is a splendid looking city. Saw Gen. Lee to-day. Also visited Jeff Davis' and Lee's city residences.

May 12th.

Rained hard all day. Marched at four P. M. minus our breakfasts. We are completely soaked, also our blankets and luggage.

I saw Fitz-Hugh Lee to-day. The 4th division again led the column. Marched ten miles north of Richmond and went into camp.

May 13th.

Marched at ten A. M. 4th division in the rear. Marched ten miles and went into camp at Hanover Court House. Was left as safeguard to-day at one of the F. F. V.'s of the most aristocratic kind. They lived in princely style in a splendid mansion. At the present time, they felt rather sober and little inclined to converse. Perhaps the Yankee vandals or "northern mud-sills" as we are termed, who at this time are passing, have something to do with their silence.

May 14th.

Was ordered to march at seven A. M. but the bridge across the Pamunky river failed and we did not move until two P. M. The roads are very bad. Marched ten miles and went into camp. In passing the defenses of Richmond, I confess that I saw nothing that seemed very formidable, but what could have been easily overcome if military movements were properly directed, but perhaps on the other part of the line the works are stronger. Passed near the battle-ground of the Wilderness and Spottsylvania Court House. We are treading the ground now that the army of the Potomac has marched over time and again, sometimes in victory and sometimes in defeat.

May 15th.

Marched at six A. M. Passed Polecat river and halted for refreshments and rest, fourteen miles from our starting point. After dinner, marched six miles farther and went into camp. We are now within twelve miles of Fredericksburg,

May 16th.

Marched at four A. M. Passed through Fredericksburg and crossed the Rappahannock about noon. The town showed evidence of severe fighting, nearly all the houses being perforated with bullets, shells or cannon balls. The country around the city is very hilly. On the north side of the river the country is more open, and for several miles scarcely any woods are to be seen, the land rolling and soil sandy. Saw the spot where the cabin stood where once lived the immortal Washington. It is nearly opposite the city of Fredericksburg. Marched twenty miles to-day. Will get to Alexandria in three days more if we have good luck.

May 17th.

Started at four A. M. Performed a long and wearisome march to-day, making twenty-two miles. The weather is excessively hot.

May 18th.

Marched at half past four A. M. Forded Wolf Creek at nine A. M. and camped two miles on the other side. The country is very mountainous and hilly through which we passed to-day. Marched fifteen miles.

May 19th.

Marched at eight A. M., 4th division being in the rear. Was on rear guard last night. Rained hard until eleven P. M. Marched fifteen miles to-day and camped within two and one-half miles of Alexandria.

May 20th.

Went to the city to-day. The streets were crowded with soldiers from both armies. There was a disposition amongst some to blackguard each other. Alexandria is a city of ten thousand inhabitants and business is very lively, consequent upon so large an army being there. There are over two hundred thousand troops camped in and around it. The old battalion received orders to-day to report to their respective regiments. The battalion is under command of Lieut. Gardner and the 14th under command of Capt. Gellispie. The horses and everything else belonging to the quartermaster department have been turned over to him.

Sunday, May 21st.

Moved camp over to the regiment. Rained hard nearly all day. Received a letter from Let and Mary to-day.

May 22d.

The weather still continues rainy.

May 23d.

Cleared off pleasant during the night. Moved camp to-day to the south side of the Potomac in full view of the city of Washington. The capital towers up majestically above all the other buildings. We can see the White House, War Department, Washington Monument, and Smithsonian Institute. To-day the army of the Potomac was reviewed by Grant, Meade, President, Secretary of War and other high government officials. The army was dressed in its gayest suit. The soldiers appeared splendid, showing the effects of good discipline and good living. Their step was elastic and guided by a strict military gait, quite different from the free, abandon step of Sherman's army. To-morrow Sherman's army appears upon the stage. Thousands of visitors from all parts of the United States are flocking to the Capital to witness these grand reviews, the largest and most brilliant ever known. The interest is enhanced greatly from the fact that the two rival armies are just fresh from the victorious fields where for four years they have fought the foul monster treason, and put down with the valor of their arms one of the greatest rebellions ever known. The nation feels justly proud of them, and particularly on this occasion, with their work so well done, and as they are about to disband and return to their homes, a filial feeling of devotion is manifested toward them.

May 24th.

The eventful 24th of May dawned bright and beautiful. The heart of every veteran in Sherman's army beat high in anticipation of the events of the day. We could not doubt our success. The eye of our matchless leader was upon us. The same brave spirit that had led us from the mountains in Tennessee to the sea, sweeping from his path the foe who had confidently hoped to ruin us. Our banners decked with the glory of many victories, we had reason to feel proud. We determined to show to the Lieutenant-General, who himself had led us on many bloody battlefields to victory, that we had not degenerated while under the guidance of another leader; we would show to our chief magistrate, and to our friends who had come to witness our performance, that we could, when occasion required, make as good a military display as the far-famed Army of the Potomac. Our regiments of recruits were divided off into companies of twenty files each, and veterans placed in each company as right and left guide. The remainder of the veterans did not join us. They were too proud to mingle on this occasion with men who had never smelled gunpowder. We only went at the request of our Colonel to act as guides, so as to make the regiment appear as well as possible. Rollin and I were right and left guide to one company. Early in the morning the army commenced crossing Long Bridge and moved toward the Capitol ground, the 14th and 20th Corps in advance. By ten A. M. we were all massed on the grounds south of the Capitol, and prepared to march in review. At the command to move, seventy-five thousand men in column, with bands playing, drums beating, and colors flying, in exact order and time to the music, marched down Pennsylvania Avenue, saluting our President and commanders as we passed the reviewing stand. For six long hours the steady tramp, tramp, tramp of Sherman's heroes echoed along Pennsylvania Avenue. The shouts of the multitude rent the air. Garlands of flowers were strewed in our pathway, and blessings showered upon us. Though our attire was not as gay as the Potomac Army, yet we excelled them in appearance. We wore the hard, bronzed visage of war incident upon a march of one thousand miles, fighting day after day, bridging rivers, corduroying swamps that before were deemed impassible. I do not wish to detract from the just merits of the Potomac Army, but the press and public bear me out in saying that Sherman's army bore off the palm. We marched five miles north and went into camp. This is to be our camp while we remain here. We expect that steps will soon be taken to procure our discharges. Our camp is situated on a high ridge of ground in a good shady place, with good springs near, and plenty of wood. I should judge it to be a healthy camp.

May 25th.

Went to the city to-day to get some government vouchers cashed. Was again disappointed.

May 26th.

Rainy. Wrote a letter home to-day and one to Ann. Received three letters last evening.

May 27th.

Rainy.   Am on guard to-day.

May 30th.

Warm and pleasant.   Went to Washington to-day and visited the Capitol.   My admiration was raised to the highest pitch at viewing its beauty, vastness, strength and splendor.   The architecture of the building is sublime, while the ancient relics of our country demand our reverence as much as the fine works of art excite our admiration.   The Senate Chamber and House of Representatives are perfectly magnificent.   I cannot do them justice to attempt to give a description of them, so I will not try. The most sacred relic I saw was the original Declaration of Independence with the original signatures attached.   The marble statue of Tecumseh represented in the agonies of death is splendid. Statues of our most illustrious men adorn the picture gallery and splendid paintings are on the walls.   I next visited the Patent Office where equal admiration enchained me.   Here are laid up in the archives of the nation many ancient relics of our country.   Here Washington's personal and military effects are deposited consisting of coat, vest, pants, hat, shoes, sword, cane, mess-chest and kit consisting of four iron plates, knives and forks and camp stool, which at the present day, an officer of our army would consider unfit for use, tent, tent-poles and pins, bed and curtains, worked by his wife, saddle, secretary and numerous other articles, all in a perfect state of preservation, all of which possess a sacred charm and interest for me.   Here is Franklin's original printing press and the coat that Jackson wore at the battle of New Orleans; the military suit worn by Gen. Paez, successor of Simon Bolivar in the command of the army of liberation in South America; a set of chinaware, and a saddle presented by the Tycoon of Japan to President Buchanan, etc., etc.; a model of all patents ever issued at the Patent Office is here with the inventors' names on them.   I next visited the Treasury and War Department and White House, each of which was full of interest to a stranger.   I passed one of the most delightful days I ever experienced.   It needs a week's time to visit these places and see everything of interest.   I shall visit them now as often as opportunity will permit while I remain at Washington.   I intend to visit the Smithsonian Institute and Mt. Vernon next.   The talk is now that we will be sent to Louisville soon and from there to our respective States to be mustered out.

May 31st.

A portion of the 15th corps left this morning on the Baltimore & Ohio Railroad for Parkersburg, Virginia. From thence they will go by water to Louisville.

June 1st.

Very warm and pleasant. It is fast day. Soldiers are once more allowed to visit the city.

June 3d.

Visited the Smithsonian Institute. Was much interested in what I saw. Got my vouchers cashed. Most of the 15th corps have left.

June 4th.

Very warm. Same unbroken quiet as of yesterday.

June 5th.

Little cooler. Prospects of rain.

June 6th.

Colonel Rogers received a commission as Brevet-Brigadier-General to-day.

June 7th.

Expect to start this afternoon for Louisville. I have enjoyed myself well while here. It is a beautiful country and a splendid climate. It has given me a good chance to view the Nation's Capitol which I have so long desired to see, and the thought that we will soon be home, with our work successfully performed, is a joy too deep for words.

June 8th.

En route to Parkersburg, Virginia, by way of the Baltimore & Ohio Railroad, and then by steamer to Louisville. We are making slow time. I am with the baggage train. It is a very difficult road. It winds over and around mountains, passes over abysses hundreds of feet deep, and anon running through the mountain in tunnels from one-fourth to one mile long, and strange to say, Sherman's whole army was transported over this road in a little over one week's time, without any serious accident occurring.

June 9th.

Made good time last night, but slow time this morning. Passed through Harper's Ferry last evening, the scene of so many thrilling events. We are now in western Virginia, the scene of McClellan's early campaign. The country is very mountainous, rocky and barren. We are now at Piedmont. We take another road here.

June 10th.

Arrived at Parkersburg at four P. M., and immediately embarked on transport "G. R. Gilman."

June 11th.

Weather cloudy and misty. We are progressing finely.

June 12th.

Passed Cincinnati last night and Marietta about noon. The scenery on the banks of the river is beautiful. Passed Murrell's Cave to-day, a place which the notorious highway robber and cut-throat used as a rendezvous for his gang and stolen property. We arrived at Louisville at nine A. M., and immediately proceeded to camp six miles southwest of the city. Louisville is a very nice looking city. The country around it is rich and pleasant. Our camp is poorly selected, but we expect to move it soon.

June 13th.

Received letters from Manda and Mary to-day.

June 14th.

Received a letter from Cinda, and wrote to Manda and Mary to-day.

June 15th.

Very warm. Moved camp twelve miles. We are now camped four miles southeast of the city. We are now under marching orders for St. Louis, but for what purpose we do not know, only our brigade is under marching orders.

June 16th.

I am on safe-guard, guarding a man's property who owns a large vineyard and garden. His berries are ripe now, and we have all that we wish. I have six guards with me. The proprietor invited me into his family to board with him while I remain, an invitation which I gladly accepted. Wrote to Cinda, Manda and Uncle Charles to-day.

June 17th.

Very warm. There is no prospect of our moving this week.

June 18th.

Very warm. Worked a short time in the harvest field for recreation. Secured a fine sample of wheat to send to father for seed.

June 20th.

Was paid off this evening. Received three hundred sixty-nine dollars. Invested two hundred and fifty in government seven-thirty bonds and expressed them to Lester.

June 21st.

Marched at five A. M. Took the transport "Camilla" for St. Louis. Are just shoving off from shore and slowly dropping down stream. This sudden move still remains a mystery to us. Some think we are going to be mustered out. Some think that we are going to some distant post to do garrison duty. We veterans cannot believe that the government will be guilty of so great an injustice as still keeping us in the service after we have so faithfully performed our part of the contract.

June 22d.

Arrived at Cairo.

June 25th.

At St. Louis. Our astonishment and anger knew no bounds when we found out that we were to be sent to the frontier to fight Indians. Our brigade commander, Gen. Stolbrand, was the author of this outrage. The recruits had no reason to complain as they were bound to service one year if their services were required, but we had fulfilled our part with the government to the very letter. Symptoms of mutiny began to manifest itself. A large number of the veterans took French leave, determined not to go. To quiet the tumult, orders were issued to grant furloughs—twenty per cent. of all enlisted men, but about ninety per cent. were given to the veterans. I obtained a furlough without the asking, and it came very acceptable just at this time, for the day before I received a letter from Manda announcing her betrothal to one Albert Sheldon, with an urgent appeal for me to visit them if possible. In a somewhat desponding mood, I sent word that it would be impossible, as we were ordered off on distant service, but the very next day I received a furlough and could reach Pennsylvania nearly as soon as the letter.

June 27th.

Started for Pennsylvania this morning. The regiment also starts for Leavenworth City, Kansas, to-day. Arrived at Springfield and found most of my comrades, whom I had left at the rebel prison at Millen, there waiting for their pay, they having already been discharged.

June 28th.

Started for Titusville on the Atlantic and Great Western railway. Made connection with the Terre Haute and Indiana railroad and then took the Chicago, Pittsburgh and Fort Wayne road, then the Northern Indiana and Southern Michigan for Erie, then the Pennsylvania and Erie for Corry; from there I took the Oil Creek railroad for Titusville, at which place I arrived on the 29th. Uncle Henry had gone to New York City and I did not get a chance to see him.

July 1st.

I went up to Brevoort to-day. Found Manda washing. Went up to her and spoke before she saw me. The surprise was perfect and she laughed and cried by turns. Ann also acted a little childish. Uncle Norm and aunt Nell had gone East on a visit. Myron and Minnie were at Brevoort. Was very glad to see them. Like the appearance of Minnie very much. It looked hard to see Myron with only one arm, but with his qualifications and the use of his right arm, he can earn a competency with his pen. After the first emotions had somewhat subsided, Amanda brought forward Albert and presented him to me. I was prepared to like him and my impressions concerning him were good.

July 4th.

I have enjoyed myself well here, but I cannot pass this day at all in consonance with my feelings. Albert, Manda, Ann and I went up to what is called the "Big Rock."

July 12th.

Amanda has concluded to go home with me. She did not intend to go until September and Albert was coming up in October, and they were to be married in November on Manda's birthday.

July 13th.

We left to-day for home. Left Brevoort yesterday and came up to Titusville.

July 14th.

Arrived at home, where a joyful welcome awaited us.

July 16th.

On arriving at home I found that Rollin had got his and my descriptive list sent by Captain Garder with the privilege of using them to get mustered out if we can.

July 27th.

We went to Springfield to see if we could not procure our discharge, but did not succeed. I went to Colonel Oaks, chief mustering officer for the State, and presented my descriptive list, but my furlough ordered me to report back to the regiment and he could do nothing for us. I then went to Adjutant-General Hayne and he told me to go to the commandant of the post and if I could induce him to give me an order for a discharge, I would be all right, but he would not do it, so I had no other resource left but to go back to the regiment or return home. I chose the latter alternative, and in company with five of my comrades, I returned on the evening train. I helped father do his harvesting and then Rollin and I started for the regiment. From Chicago, we took the Chicago, Burlington and Quincy road. I passed over some as fine country as I ever saw. On arriving at Quincy, we took the Hannibal and St. Joseph railroad and arrived at St. Joseph the next day. We then took the cars for western Missouri and from there the steamer for Leavenworth City, Kansas, where we arrived at eleven A. M. We found that the regiment had been gone several weeks. We went down near the Fort and camped with the rest of our comrades who had returned before us. We got fresh accessions to our ranks every day and soon we had a larger number here in camp than were on the march. Leavenworth is a city of some eighteen thousand inhabitants. Its growth surpasses that of any other city in the West. Five years ago it was nothing but a village. Large trains of wagons are leaving daily, loaded with government stores and provisions for distant posts on the plains. Leavenworth at the present time is infested with a desperate gang of thieves and murderers. One day three dead soldiers were found between our camp and town, and they were so bold as to attempt to murder one of our boys in sight of camp, but he happened to have his revolver with him and he turned upon his assailants, wounded one and the other took "leg bail." After this, when we went outside of the camp far, it was in squads. We now learned that the regiment had received orders to return to be mustered out. They went within fifteen miles of Fort Kearney. Arrived back at Fort Leavenworth about the 1st of September, and preparations were immediately made to muster us out. I assisted in making out our company's rolls. I had now been promoted to 3d sergeant. We were mustered out about the middle of the month and the next day started for Springfield for our pay and final discharge. Our progress over the Hannibal and St. Joseph railroad was very

14

tedious and slow.   There was hardly a mile of the track but what
had been disturbed by guerrillas during the war and it was not yet
repaired.   We had one smash-up which gave me a sore head and
a great many others bruised noses.   The road passes through the
best part of Missouri.   On arriving at Quincy, we took the Chicago, Burlington and Quincy road for Springfield.   A person
could not help but notice the contrast between the thrift and
culture of the soil in Illinois and Missouri.   Every time that I
pass through the state, my heart glows with renewed pride that I
am a citizen of the State of Illinois.

                                                September 30th.
     The next morning we arrived at Camp Butler and went into
camp in the woods near by.   We found several regiments here
waiting to be discharged.   It was nearly two weeks before our
papers were made out.   On the 30th of September we received
our final pay and discharge.   I had worn the livery of Uncle Sam
for four years, five months and twenty-seven days.   I have tried to do
my whole duty in sustaining the integrity of our nation.   I have
the proud satisfaction of knowing that my labor has not been
in vain, and thousands who have fought in the same cause and
endured hardships in common have at last found their full recom-
pense in a Union restored and a re-union with home and friends.
To the fallen who have yielded up their lives on the altar of their
country, it will ever hold them unshrined in its brightest glory.

     Our work has been effectually done, and if we prove wise and do
not let mad passion and hate engendered by the war rule the mind,
I can see nothing to prevent a perfect and speedy reconciliation, and
our flag and the authority of our government will be honored and
respected all over our land, and both North and South may learn
lessons of wisdom by the folly of the past, and hand in hand, with
all bitter feelings and animosities obliterated, march forward to
their destiny, to the very acme of civilization, freedom and
power.   I am proud to know that my feeble efforts helped con-
tribute to this glorious end, and now, after strife and bloodshed
has ceased and sweet peace once more broods over our land, it is
with a thankful heart and intense joy that I lay aside the honorable
title of *Soldier* and once more enjoy the proud title of an *American
Citizen*, a subject of the best and truest government on God's
earth.   Before leaving for home, in company with several of my
comrades, I paid a parting visit to the tomb of Lincoln at Oak

Ridge Cemetery. We passed within the inclosure and registered our names besides hundreds of thousands of others who had been there before us. We then went to the grated opening of the sepulchre and took one last lingering look at the narrow resting place where sleeps all that is mortal of Lincoln, whose noble heart and mind had guided us through all the dark and bloody years of our Nation's struggle for existence. Lincoln's tomb will ever be the shrine to which patriots will resort as homage to the man who *preserved* our Nation, as Washington's now is as its *founder*. We took the evening train for Chicago where we arrived the next morning at five o'clock. We took the nine o'clock train for Marengo and arrived there at twelve M. and were once more welcomed home by kind and true friends to enjoy again the sweets of civil life.

Now, kind friends, I will close this imperfect sketch of my observations and experience while in the service of my country, hoping that you will overlook all deficiencies and imperfections, of which I am conscious that there are many. I have relied a great deal on my memory for guidance and as a consequence, I have omitted many things which might be interesting and put in some things that are not interesting, but such as it is, I submit it to you, and when I shall have fulfilled my allotted part in life and shall have passed to a better stage of existence, may the descendants of the family to which I belong, who may chance to read these lines, remember that in all the years of my life, there was no time to which I could refer with so pleasing a recollection of duty performed as when I raised my hand to help snatch our nation from the whirlpool of secession and ruin in which it was struggling for existence, and to help purge it from the foul stain of human slavery. I ask no prouder monument to my memory than that of having my name inscribed amongst my country's defenders and may that Power that rules the universe and guides the affairs of nations and of men, still continue His protecting care over us all and guide our Nation to the highest pinnacle of greatness and glory.

SERGEANT L. W. BARBER,

Company D, 15th Illinois Veteran Volunteer Infantry.

ROSTER

OF THE 15TH ILLINOIS VOLUNTEER INFANTRY.

Colonel Geo. C. Rogers.—Promoted Brevet Brigadier-General, May, 1865; vice Thos. J. Turner, resigned November 2d, 1862.

Lieutenant-Colonel James Raney.—Vice Geo. C. Rogers, promoted, vice Lieutenant-Colonel E. F. W. Ellis, killed at Battle of Shiloh.

Major Adam Nase.—Resigned July 7, 1863; vice James Raney, promoted; vice William R. Goddard, killed at Battle of Shiloh, April 6, 1862.

Adjutant Geo. Q. Allen.—Vice Charles F. Barber, resigned June 2d, 1863; vice C. C. Clark, transferred to staff.

Surgeon Wm. J. McKim.

Assistant Surgeon —— Buck.

Chaplain B. F. Rogers.

OFFICERS OF COMPANY "D."

Captain Harley Wayne.—Killed at Battle of Shiloh.

Captain Fred A. Smith.—Mustered out June 18, 1864.

1st Lieutenant Frank S. Curtis.—Resigned September 9, 1861.

1st Lieutenant John Waldock.—Mustered out June 18, 1864.

2d Lieutenant Fred A. Smith.—Promoted to 1st Lieutenant, September 16, 1861; wounded at the Battle of Shiloh, April 6, 1861; pro moted Captain April 7, 1862.

2d Lieutenant Michael Schoonmaker.—Mustered out June 18, 1864.

MUSTER ROLL

OF COMPANY "D" NON-COMMISSIONED OFFICERS.

1st Sergeant Peter I. Labaugh.—Promoted 2d Lieutenant, September 16, 1861; resigned April 18, 1862.

2d Sergeant John Waldock.—Promoted 1st Sergeant, September 16, 1861; promoted 2d Lieutenant, April 7, 1862; promoted 1st Lieutenant September 3d, 1862.

3d Sergeant Michael Schoonmaker.—Wounded at Battle of Shiloh; promoted 1st Sergeant April 7, 1862; promoted 2d Lieutenant September 3, 1863.

4th Sergeant Aaron C. Perry.—Transferred to Invalid Corps, September 15th, 1860.

5th Sergeant Ira R. Curtis.—Discharged August 31st, 1861.

CORPORALS.

1st, Calvin H. Shapley.—Promoted Sergeant, September 16th, 1861; reduced to ranks, November 9th, 1861; promoted 2nd Lieutenant April 16th, 1862; resigned September 3d, 1862.

2d, Alonzo V. Howe.—Promoted Sergeant September 16th, 1861; promoted 1st Sergeant December 17th, 1862; captured soon after; exchanged and returned to duty; mustered out June 18th, 1864.

3d, Jacob D. Lansing.—Discharged April 18th, 1862.

4th, George C. Oakes.— Promoted Sergeant November 9th, 1861; promoted 1st Sergeant September 3d, 1862; discharged December 17th, 1862.

5th, John C. Thompson.—Promoted Sergeant April 7th, 1862.

6th, Robert K. Andrews.—Discharged August 23d, 1861.

7th, Charles W. Onthank.—Promoted Sergeant September 18th, 1862; discharged June 18th, 1864.

8th, Eugene A. Wells.—Died of wounds received at Battle of Shiloh.

MUSICIANS.

George A. Clark, Fifer.—Discharged July 28th, 1862.

Nathaniel F. Andrews, Drummer.—Died November 8th, 1862.

PRIVATES, MUSTERED IN MAY 24TH, 1861.

Allen, Morris H.—Discharged July 30th, for wounds received at Battle of Shiloh.

Arnold, Robert F.—Deserted January 15th, 1862.

Avery, Francis W.—Deserted June 18th, 1861.

Bremen, James.—Deserted June 24th, 1861.

Barber, Lucius W.—Appointed Corporal September 18th, 1862; Re-enlisted January 1st, 1864; promoted Sergeant; taken prisoner October 4th, 1864, at Ackworth, Georgia; taken to Andersonville Prison; paroled November 20th, 1864; exchanged January, 1865; Discharged September 16th, 1865.

Barber, Elon G.—Discharged August 31st, 1861.

Barber, James R.—Died September 18th, 1861.

Barnes, Ezra.—Discharged January 18th, 1862.

Babcock, Sidney S.—Died August 19th, 1861.

Bigelow, Marlin.—Discharged June 18th, 1864.

Bliss, John D.— Wounded at battle of Shiloh; discharged December 17th, 1862.

Burst, John W.—Discharged August 13th, 1861.

Burroughs, John B.—Discharged June 18th, 1864.

Barnes, Alden.—Died February 22d, 1862.

Calkins, Ebenezer D. Jr.—Mustered out June 18th, 1864.

Clark, Alva M.—Mustered out June 18th, 1864.

Conley, Christopher.—Discharged May 3d, 1862.

Crosby, James H.—Discharged August 12th, 1861.

Crumb, George H.—Deserted August 18th, 1862.

Cassidy, Patrick.—Re-enlisted December 25th, 1863; deserted May 1st, 1864.

Cronan, John D.—Deserted August 7th, 1862.

Countryman, Darius.—Re-enlisted December 17th, 1863; captured at Marietta, Georgia, September 18th, 1864. Held as prisoner until the close of the war.

Cooper, Samuel.—Discharged October 23d, 1862, for wounds received at Battle of Shiloh.

Dimmick, George.—Discharged January 27th, 1862.

Dimon, Moses.—Re-enlisted December 17th, 1863; taken prisoner at Ackworth, Georgia, October 4th, 1864; held as prisoner during the war.

Dean, Alfred.—Wounded at Shiloh, April 6th, 1862; mustered out June 18th, 1864.

Delany, Patrick.—Died at hospital; record not kept.

Delany, William.—Transferred to gunboat service February 11th, 1862.

Eaton, John C.—Reported dead, but supposed to be still living.

Eagan, James.—Wounded at Battle of Hatchie, October 4th, 1862; mustered out June 18th, 1864.

Ellis, Samuel.—Recruit; discharged January 16th, 1862.

Fox, William S.—Died at Lafayette, Tennessee, January 24th, 1863.

Gray, Thomas T.—Wounded at Shiloh, April 6th; mustered out June 18th, 1864.

Gould, Edward G.—Discharged December 13th, 1862, for wounds received at the Battle of Shiloh.

Handy, Philo.—Appointed Corporal; promoted Sergeant September 18th, 1862; discharged May 1st, 1863, for wounds received at Hatchie.

Hardy, Thompson.—Killed at Shiloh.

Haskins, Orville T.—Deserted August 18th, 1862.

Hotchkiss, Charles E.—Died June 19th, 1862, from wounds received at Shiloh.

Hotchkiss, Walford M.—Taken prisoner at Ackworth, Georgia, October 4th, 1864; held as prisoner during the war.

Holgate, Amos.—Mustered out June 18th, 1864.

Huntington, George W.—Re-enlisted December 17th, 1863; mustered out September 30th, 1865.

Huntington, Harvey C.—Discharged August 13th, 1861.

Huston, Thomas E.—Re-enlisted December 17th, 1863; taken prisoner at Ackworth, Georgia, September 26th, 1864; held as prisoner during the war.

Hiner, Emery.—Mustered out June 18th, 1864.

Harrison, Edward A.—Transferred to N. C. S. as Quartermaster-Sergeant November 11th, 1862; mustered out May 24th, 1864.

Hancock, William.—Died December 8th, 1862.

Ham, Henry.—Re-enlisted December 27th, 1863; taken prisoner at Ackworth, Georgia, October 4th, 1864; held as prisoner during the war.

Johnson, Joseph.—Recruit; mustered out September, 1864.

King, Oscar W.—Recruit; re-enlisted December 25th, 1863.

Killen, Alexander.—Recruit; re-enlisted December 25th, 1863; appointed Corporal September 18th, 1862; taken prisoner at Ackworth, Georgia, October 4th; held as prisoner during the war.

Langlis, Francis.—Discharged January 16th, 1862.

Loomis, Frank S.—Appointed Corporal September 16th, 1861; discharged July 8th, 1862.

Lincoln, Albert.—Discharged February 5th, 1862.

Lillibrige, Henry F.—Died December 31st, 1861.

Maude, Charles.—Discharged July 28th, 1862.

McDonald, Daniel J.—Mustered out June 18th, 1864.

Meyers, William H. H.—Discharged November 22d, 1862.

Mallory, Rollin.—Appointed Corporal September 18th, 1862; re-enlisted December 17th, 1863; taken prisoner at Ackworth, Georgia, October 4th, 1864; sent to Andersonville; paroled November 20th; exchanged January 1st, 1865; returned to duty; promoted Sergeant; discharged September 16th, 1865.

Mallory, William B.—Appointed Corporal April 23d, 1862; promoted Sergeant May 1st, 1863; Mustered out June 18th, 1864.

Mackey, Milton.—Recruit; re-enlisted December 17th, 1863; taken prisoner at Ackworth, Georgia, October 4th, 1864; escaped in December by running the gauntlet of the rebel guard; traveled through a trackless forest one hundred miles; reached our lines in Florida; came home; returned to duty; captured again by guerrillas, near Raleigh, North Carolina, and brutally murdered.

Mitchell, Charles W.—Recruit; re-enlisted December 17th, 1863; mustered out September 16th, 1865.

Nealon, P. R.—Appointed Corporal April 23d, 1862; promoted Sergeant September 15th, 1863; re-enlisted December 17th, 1863; taken prisoner at Ackworth, Georgia, October 4th, 1864; held as prisoner during the war.

Oakes, Horace.—Discharged February 13th, 1863.

O'Donald, William.—Deserted June 14th, 1861.

Pelton, Addison G.—Died December 6th, 1861.

Page, William.—Discharged April 1st, 1862.

Parker, William.—Discharged February 5th, 1862.

Pettit, George W.—Died April 1st, 1861.

Pettit, Joseph.—Mustered out June 18th, 1864.

Pettingill, George S.—Mustered out June 18th, 1864.

Pierce, Charlie G.—Discharged August 13th, 1861.

Porter, Dennis.—Discharged August 13th, 1861.

Parker, Joel B.—Discharged August 13th, 1862, for wounds received at the Battle of Shiloh.

Page, Franklin.—Discharged November 23d, 1862.

Robinson, Charles R.—Discharged August 11th, 1861.

Russell, Michael.—Deserted June 14th, 1861.

Stockwell, William H.—Recruit; discharged September 22d, 1864.

Shapley, N. F.—Discharged, August 9th, 1862, for wounds received at the Battle of Shiloh.

Smalldridge, Thomas G.—Re-enlisted December 23d, 1863; mustered out September 16th, 1865.

Spencer, Leroy.—Transferred to brass band; mustered out April, 1862.

Smith, Simon.—Re-enlisted December 17th, 1863; mustered out September 16th, 1865.

Stewart, Clark.—Appointed Corporal September 16th, 1861; promoted Sergeant, September 18th, 1862; discharged October 21st, 1862.

Stephens, Marshall.—Appointed Corporal October 26th, 1862; discharged October 26th, 1862, for wounds received at the Battle of Shiloh.

Stephens, Henry E.—Mustered out June 18th, 1864.

Stevens, John F.—Deserted 1861.

Spicer, John M.—Killed at the Battle of Shiloh, April 6th, 1862.

St. John, Thomas H.—Wounded at Siege of Corinth; mustered out June 18th, 1864.

Stull, Marenas P.—Discharged February 3d, 1862.

Smith, Richard W.—Mustered out June 18th, 1864.

Slocum, Myron J.—Recruit; re-enlisted December 17th, 1863; mustered out September 30th, 1865.

Shearer, Egbert R.—Discharged December 3d, 1862, for wounds received at Battle of Shiloh.

Thompson, Harrison.—Mustered out June 18th, 1864.

Thompson, Lewis.—Recruit; discharged July 28th, 1862.

Tourle, Thomas.—Died October 14th, 1861.

Timmony, James D.—Mustered out June 18th, 1864.

Thomson, Milo A.—Mustered out June 18th, 1864.

Trumble, Albert E.—Recruit; re-enlisted; taken prisoner at Ackworth, Georgia, October 4th, 1864; held as prisoner during the war.

Underwood, Charles A.—Wounded at Shiloh; appointed Corporal September 28th, 1861; re-enlisted; mustered out September 16th, 1865.

Underwood, Richard J.—Mustered out June 18th, 1864.

Underwood, William H.—Mustered out June 18th, 1864.

Venerd, Charles.—Mustered out June 18th, 1864.

Venard, Thomas.—Re-enlisted December 17th, 1863; taken prisoner at Ackworth, Georgia, October 4th, 1864; taken to Andersonville; was paroled November 20th; exchanged January 1st, and returned to duty; discharged September 30th, 1865.

Virtrees, John W.—Re-enlisted; mustered out September 30th, 1865.

Welch, William.—Deserted September 27th, 1861.

Walden, Delenzo A.—Recruit; discharged July 28, 1862.

Williams Robert M.—Mustered out June 18th, 1864.

TABLE OF DISTANCES

1861.

Miles.

June	18, Freeport. ....to	Alton.................... By	rail ..	250
July	19, Alton.............. "	St. Charles, Mo .... "	water	25
July	29, St. Charles......... "	Mexico, Mo.............. "	rail ..	80
Aug.	1, Mexico (R. Wing).. "	Fulton, Mo.............. "	foot..	25
Aug.	1, Mexico (L. Wing).. "	Hannibal, Mo........ .... "	foot..	80
Aug.	8, Fulton............. "	St. Auburt, Mo. .... "	foot..	35
Aug.	10, Hannibal(L.Wing). "	Jefferson Barracks....... "	water	150
Aug.	10, St. Aubert(R.Wing) "	Jefferson Barracks....... "	water	125
Aug.	13, Jefferson Barracks. "	St. Louis................. "	water	12
Aug.	13, St. Louis.......... "	Rolla, Mo................ "	rail ..	110
Sept.	30, Rolla.............. "	Gasconade River, Mo.... "	foot..	13
Sept.	30, Gasconade River... "	Rolla.................... "	foot..	13
Oct.	4, Rolla .... "	Tipton, Mo.............. "	rail ..	200
Oct.	21, Tipton............ "	Springfield, Mo.......... "	foot..	150
Nov.	5, Springfield......... "	Tipton, Mo.............. "	foot..	150
Nov.	27, Tipton .... "	Syracuse, Mo............ "	foot..	6
Nov.	27, Syracuse........... "	Tipton .... "	foot..	6
Dec.	8, Tipton............ "	Otterville, Mo .... "	foot..	18
Dec.	15, Otterville.......... "	Sedalia, Mo.............. "	foot..	25
Dec.	25, Sedalia............ "	Otterville, Mo............ "	foot..	25
1862.				
Feb.	7, Otterville.......... "	Jefferson City, Mo....... "	foot..	50
Feb.	12, Jefferson City...... "	St. Louis................. "	rail ..	100
Feb.	16, St. Louis........... "	Ft. Donelson, Tenn...... "	water	400
March	5, Ft. Donelson....... "	Ft. Henry, Tenn......... "	foot..	15
March	6, Ft. Henry......... "	Savanna, Tenn.......... "	water	110
March	17, Savanna........... "	Pittsburgh Ldg, Tenn ... "	water	20
April	20, Pittsburgh Land'g. "	Corinth, Miss............ "	foot..	20
June	2, Corinth .... "	Grand Junction, Tenn... "	foot..	45
June	16, Grand Junction... "	Holly Springs, Miss...... "	foot..	30
June	18, Holly Springs..... "	Grand Junction, Tenn... "	foot..	30
June	25, Grand Junction... "	Lagrange, Tenn......... "	foot..	5
June	30, Lagrange...... ... "	Coldwater, Miss.......... "	foot..	18
July	6, Coldwater.......... "	Lagrange, Tenn.......... "	foot..	18
July	17, Lagrange........... "	Memphis, Tenn.......... "	foot..	50
	Reconnoissance			24
Sept.	6, Memphis.. .... "	Bolivar, Tenn............ "	foot..	88
Sept.	15, Bolivar............ "	Dunlap Sp'gs (and return) "	foot..	10
Oct.	4, Bolivar............ "	Hatchie River.......... . "	foot..	30
Oct.	7, Hatchie River...... "	Bolivar .... "	foot..	30

Nov.	3, Bolivar............ to	Lagrange ....By	foot..	22
Nov.	7, Reconnoissance....			10
Nov.	28, Lagrange.......... "	Lumpkins Mills, Miss.... "	foot..	32
1863.				
	Lumpkins Mills..... "	Springdale............... "	foot..	30
Jan.	13, Springdale......... "	Lagrange, Tenn.......... "	foot..	62
Jan.	20, Lagrange.......... "	Lafayette, Tenn......... "	foot..	20
	Lafayette.......... "	Moscow and counter-		
		marching back and		
		forth.................... "	foot..	60
Jan.	29, Lafayette.......... "	Stockade .... "	foot..	3
	Reconnoissance.....			20
March	11, Stockade.......... "	Memphis................. "	foot..	28
May	13, Memphis.......... "	Youngs Point, La........ "	water	400
May	18, Youngs Point...... "	Grand Gulf, Miss .... "	water	60
May	20, Grand Gulf........ "	Chickasaw Landing, Miss. "	water	85
May	21, Chickasaw Landing "	Haines Bluff, Miss....... "	foot..	12
May	24, Haines Bluff....... "	Waterton, Miss.......... "	foot..	20
July	5, Waterton.......... "	Jackson, Miss............ "	foot..	50
July	20, Jackson .... "	Vicksburg, Miss .... "	foot..	50
Aug.	12, Vicksburg .... "	Natchez, Miss............ "	water	125
Aug.	13, Natchez .... "	Kingston, Miss .... "	foot...	20
Aug.	20, Kingston .... "	Natchez, Miss .... "	foot..	20
Sept.	1, Natchez .... "	Harrisburg, La .... "	foot..	60
		Returned		60
Oct.	Natchez .... "	Vicksburg, Miss.......... By water	125
	Vicksburg .... "	Camp Cowan, Miss....... " water	12
1864.				
Feb.	2, Camp Cowan....... "	Meridian, Miss........... " water	200
Feb.	20, Meridian .... "	Camp Cowan, Miss....... " water	200
	Camp Cowan ...... "	Cairo, Ill................. " water	700
	Cairo .... "	Clifton, Tenn .... " water	300
	Clifton............. "	Huntsville, Ala .... " foot..	250
	(Non-veterans)..... "	Springfield, Ill........... " rail..	700
June	1, 14th and 15th regiments consolidated and known as the 14th			
	and 15th Veteran Battalion.			
May	26, Huntsville.........to	Decatur, Ala ....By foot..	35
June	10, Decatur .... "	Rome, Ga................ " foot..	150
June	16, Rome............. "	Kingston, Ga............ " foot..	18
	Kingston .... "	Allatoona, Ga............ " foot..	20
June	20, Allatoona .... "	Etowah Bridge, Ga ..... " foot..	20
		Returned .... " foot..	20
July	8, Allatoona.......... "	Marietta, Ga............ " foot..	20
	Marietta........... "	Roswell, Ga............. " foot..	20
		Returned .... " foot..	20
July	10, Scout..... .... "			28
July	12, Scout.... .... "			30
July	18, Marietta.......... "	Ackworth, Ga............ " foot..	12
July	19, ... "	Returned		12
July	25, Scout............. ...			40

Aug.	25, Marietta.......... to	Dalton, Ga...............	By rail ..	80
	Scout.............. "		" foot..	40
Aug.	31, Dalton............ "	Ackworth, Ga............	" rail ..	63
Sept. to				
Oct.	4, Scouts............ "			150
Oct.	5, Ackworth... ...... "	Marietta, Ga............	" foot..	12
Oct.	8, Marietta .... "	Dalton, Ga..............	" foot..	80
Oct.	10, Dalton .... "	Atlanta, Ga.......... ...	" foot..	100
Nov.	Atlanta........... "	Savannah, Ga...........	" foot..	300
1865.				
Feb.	Savannah.......... "	Raleigh, N. C............	" foot..	400
May	Raleigh............ "	Washington, D. C........	" foot..	400
June	Washington........ "	Louisville, Ky..........	" rail ..	500
July	1, Louisville.......... "	St. Louis, Mo......... . "	water	500
	St. Louis........... "	Ft. Leavenworth, Kan... "	water	400
	Ft. Leavenworth.... "	Ft. Kearney, Neb........ "	foot..	300
		Returned............		300
Sept.	Leavenworth....... "	Springfield, Ill.......... "	rail ..	500

Grand total................................... 10,897

LETTER FROM THE 15TH REG'T ILL. VOL.

MEMPHIS, Tennessee, March 20th, 1863.

Respected Parent: Your kind letter, bearing date of March 1st, was received last evening. The sad news that it contained, regarding the death of Alsera, had been anticipated by me. I have expected the letters which I received from home for the past two weeks would contain an account of her decease. From what had been written, in regard to her sufferings, I had inferred that she could not remain with us much longer. Although, in a measure, prepared to receive the sad intelligence, and knowing it to be far better for her to be relieved from suffering than to drag out weary days and nights in misery and pain, which she bore with commendable fortitude, patience and resignation, I cannot forbear to express that the event we have so long anticipated cast a deeper shade of sorrow over my heart than has existed there since my own dear angel sister bid adieu to earthly things and took up her abode with angels. And now, as imagination faintly glimmers to me the beauties of that angel home, I see Alzina with outstretched arms and joyful smiles, welcome Alsera from her long period of suffering and pain to the love, holy light and affection of her spirit home, surrounded by a multitude of kindred friends who have preceded her to that world of light and joy. To her, the reality of those beauties has been realized.

"—— Oh, how happy, sweet, will that meeting be
When over the river, that peaceful river, the angel of death shall carry me!"

Thus the last one of that family has passed away, but I trust, only to bloom in a brighter clime where separation and death are unknown, and as the angels are gathering us all, one by one, into that spirit-land where dwell our departed friends, we begin to realize that this is not our permanent home and that we, too, will soon lay aside the clay tenement and join in an unbroken circle the friends of our earlier years. In conclusion, I will add, let us all endeavor to live as pure and blameless a life as she has lived. Let us emulate her virtues and press forward on the journey of life, gain-ing victory after victory of goodness over evil, truth over error, conquering even the sting of death itself and finally triumph in a glorious immortality.

In your last letter you spoke of our National difficulties and spoke of a remedy. It is my lot to differ with you slightly and what I shall write in reference to the matter will emanate from a pure motive and a desire to vindicate the truth. You also spoke of a letter that I had written home that accused the copperheads of trying to break up this Government, which caused some to rejoice. I do not remember of accusing the copperheads of any such thing. If I did, I did not express what I intended to, but I will say this much, I do believe that if they could carry out their designs, it would result in the dismemberment of our Union. I say this without accusing them of being traitors or stigmatizing them as tories. From what you wrote, I would infer that some of my friends think that I have changed my political belief or opinion in regard to the manner in which this War is conducted. Now, I do not claim to have changed my opinion in the least. Those persons who wage such a suicidal, venomous and destructive war against the administration, I claim do not represent the time-honored principles of the Democratic party. If they would devote the time and talents they use in denouncing and endeavoring to weaken the power of the administration, to the purpose of helping us save our country from ruin and destruction, I would call them Democrats, and unite with them heart and hand. The motto of the Democratic party under the leadership of that noble, firm old patriot, Jackson, was "The Federal Union it must and shall be preserved," and that motto still finds a responsive echo in the heart of every true Democrat. Now, how is this Union to be preserved? Is it by fighting and waging a suicidal war against the administration and our rulers, while nearly one-half of the Union is openly arrayed against the other in deadly conflict, seeking to destroy the government by force of arms, and now, while it is reeling and tottering on the verge of destruction, bleeding at every pore? Again I ask, is finding fault with the administration and bitterly denouncing the measures it has taken to crush this Rebellion, thereby weakening its power and efficiency, when every true lover of his country should sustain him in this trying hour —is this going to save us? Can any sane man believe it? What, then, is going to save us? What has been the secret of the success of the rebels thus far? It is a unity of purpose and action. You hear no caviling amongst them about this measure or that. Their motto is: "We will triumph. We will establish our independence, even if we have to pull down the bulwarks of Liberty and plant our banner of Treason over the ruins of the mightiest republic that ever existed," and they act in harmony and concert, and with a valor worthy of a better cause. So we, too, if we would not have Star of Liberty set, and our glorious Republic and her institutions prove a failure, must act in concert and harmony, and heart and hand sustain our executive, help save our country and the glorious old Stars and Stripes, the flag our fathers bore, and under which they achieved, our liberties from dishonor and shame.

Now, what good has this determined opposition to the administration done? No one can tell. But it has done incalculable injury. It gives hope and encouragement to the traitors. They see that we are falling fast by our own hands. They believe that the stab in the back which the President is receiving will crush us and proclaim their independence. They rely more to-day upon dissensions and divisions in the North for the success of their cause, than they do upon any victory they hope to obtain over us by force of arms. Are the people blind to this fact? If not, why, oh! why will they persist in so fatal a policy, while our country is nearly in its death agonies, reeling and tottering from centre to circumference? Is there no blood of our Revolutionary sires coursing through their veins? Have they so soon forgotten the blessings of civil liberty and republican institutions for which they fought, as to be dead to all sense of shame? No! No! I cannot believe it! I will yet have faith in the American people that they will preserve to us and our posterity the blessings bequeathed to us by our Revolutionary fathers. It is a mystery to me why these peace and compromise men will persist in their course, when the South spurns with contempt and scorn the olive branch they would hold out to them. I should think that even those yile traitors who propose to unite the great Northwest with the slave oligarchy would shrink back aghast at the terms the learned judge of Mississippi has seen fit to offer us, i. e., if we will purge ourselves of all Union sentiment, pride for our flag, they might let us in. Magnanimous, indeed! If there is a traitor base enough to accept these terms, he is unworthy even the vile name of traitor. He would be a fit companion for his Satanic Majesty. I will not question the motives of these copperheads, until their acts belie their words, but I claim the right to criticise their views and what their principles will lead to if carried out. Now, I reverence and respect the Constitution as much as any one. It is indeed the foundation on which rests our liberties and the nucleus around which has gathered all our glory, greatness and prosperity, and for this reason I am the more anxious that it shall be preserved, therefore, I am with the President in his efforts to save it and against those who are seeking its overthrow. The Constitution was made for the Nation and if after following it and exhausting all the resources it contains to crush the Rebellion and then fail, and if a slight deviation in one or two places from that sacred instrument will save it, I say, "For heaven's sake, save the Nation. Then you will have the Constitution preserved to you also." The President saw that slave labor was one of the main dependencies for support. It would cripple their power and the Nation is now awaiting the issue. It is not for us to determine whether the means he uses to crush this Rebellion are constitutional or not. There is a proper tribunal to refer such cases to. I am not here to find fault with such measures. My duty is plain and clear. The laws are being violated and the country trampled under foot. The civil authorities have proved unequal to the task of restoring order, hence the necessity of calling on military aid and each soldier has taken an oath to obey all legal orders of his superiors and support the President of the United States. That oath I cannot break, neither can I countenance the acts of those who are constantly throwing stumbling blocks in the way of the President. The President is just as much bound by his oath as I am by mine and until he violates his oath to support the Constitution and a court of impeachment finds him guilty, let us support him. Without the aid of the people he can do nothing and we are lost. Shall it be said that Americans have proved recreant to their trust? Shall it be said that we have permitted our Nation to fall, to go back to the darkness of midnight, to become a by-word, a stench in the nostrils of haughty monarchs and crowned heads? My God forbid! I want to look forward to the future of America with brighter hopes and brighter visions than ever before, and when this Rebellion is crushed, I shall begin to look for the realization of my wishes. Perhaps I ought to stop here, but I will make one more remark. I would be pleased if the President would change his policy in some respects. I do not agree with him in all his measures, still, I consider it my duty to support him. It will not do to let our passions and prejudices run in so fearful a crisis as this. You need not feel alarmed about my leaving the Democratic party. When our country is saved, there will be time enough to talk about that. Until that time arrives, party strife and party feelings adieu. A higher and a nobler aim beckons me onward and you cannot mingle in the strife. When quiet and order again returns and we be permitted to return home, if we have any wrongs to redress, we can do it peaceably at the ballot box. Then we can with safety pass our judgment on the wisdom of the President in his course during the Rebellion. I suppose, to sum it all up, we do not differ much, but I, being in the army, see some things in a different light from you. I have to deal with traitors face to face. I have talked with them and know their feelings. Our greatest fault is being too lenient with them. I am wearied with writing and will close.

The boys are all well and in good spirits. Probably we will remain here some time.

Your affectionate son,

L. W. BARBER,
Company D, 15th Regiment Illinois Volunteers.

Obituary.

Died.—In Riley, Illinois, March 12th, 1872, of consumption, Lucius W. Barber, aged 32 years and 9 months.

Deceased was a very worthy, exemplary young man, much beloved by his friends and acquaintances. When the Rebellion broke out he was one of the first to enroll his name amongst his country's defenders and, with others of his comrades, joined Company D, 15th Illinois Infantry, and shared in the fortunes of the 15th during their full term of service. Was taken prisoner during the War and lodged in Andersonville Prison, where from exposure and maltreatment, he received the seed of a disease which finally terminated his life. He returned home, at the close of the war, shattered in health, yet hopeful that a change of climate and proper treatment might work a cure, but it seemed that no earthly power could stay the inroads of the disease which had taken such sure hold upon him. Gradually his system sank under it, yet, he was always hopeful and cheerful. As his days were drawing to a close he disposed of all his keepsakes and mementoes to his friends, made all the necessary arrangements for his funeral services and then calmly and patiently awaited death. He retained the full use of all his mental faculties until a short time before his death, when he became unconscious and soon expired, without a struggle or a groan. Thus has passed away a very worthy young man, another victim of the horrible cruelties practiced at Andersonville. Kind friends laid his body carefully and tenderly away in the family burying ground on the old homestead, by the side of two sisters who had preceded him to the spirit-land. Faithful friend and brother, fare thee well!

Library of Congress Cataloguing in Publication Data

Barber, Lucius W., 1839-1872.
Army memoirs of Lucius W. Barber, Company "D,"
15th Illinois Volunteer Infantry.
(Collector's library of the Civil War)
Reprint. Originally published: Chicago: J.M.W. Jones
Stationery and Print. Co., 1894.
1. Barber, Lucius W., 1839-1872.
2. United States—History—Civil War, 1861-1865—Personal narratives.
3. United States. Army. Illinois Infantry Regiment, 15th (1861-1865)—Biography.
4. Soldiers—Illinois—Biography.
5. United States—History—Civil War, 1861-1865—Regimental histories.
I. Title. II. Series.
E505.5 15th.B37 1984   973.7'81   83-24236
ISBN 0-8094-4459-3 (library)
ISBN 0-8094-4458-5 (retail)
Printed in the United States of America

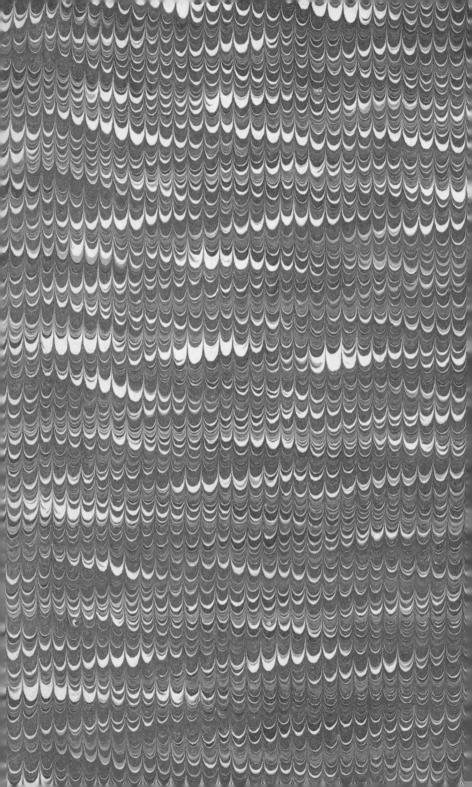